TRIUMPH OR TRAGEDY?

To John and Pauline Richard

TRIUMPH OR TRAGEDY?

Rhodesia to Zimbabwe

by

Miles Hudson

Miles Hudson

HAMISH HAMILTON LONDON

British Library Cataloguing in Publication Data

Hudson, Miles
  Triumph or tragedy.
  1. Zimbabwe – History
  I. Title
  968.91   DT962.5

  ISBN 0–241–10571–4

Printed and bound in Great Britain by
REDWOOD BURN LIMITED
Trowbridge & Esher

To Mercedes

CONTENTS

ACKNOWLEDGMENTS

This book is the result of an association with Rhodesia which started in 1965 when, to my horror, I was put in charge of Rhodesian affairs in the Conservative Research Department four days after the Unilateral Declaration of Independence. Since then I have had a constant and, at times, very close interest in Rhodesian affairs in a number of official and unofficial capacities.

I have listed most of my written sources in the Bibliography but I would like to mention the books by Robert Blake, Claire Palley and Martin Meredith as being particularly helpful.

As regards other sources, I have been lucky enough either to work with or to meet and talk to very many of those involved in one capacity or another and it would be impossible to list them all: in any case many of them would not wish to be mentioned in connection with this book for various reasons. I will, therefore, have to be content with a generalised statement of gratitude to all those who have helped me and particularly to those who have read through and commented on the various drafts. I must, however, mention Viscount Boyd of Merton whose boundless energy and enthusiasm have been a constant source of inspiration. Similarly I must thank Lord Home of the Hirsel for putting up with me as his political secretary for three years and for his constant kindness over a long period. The responsibility for everything in this book is entirely mine and no unpublished official documents have been used.

I would also like to record my special thanks to Vikki Tate who has coped magnificently in typing and retyping my drafts in spite of my wholly illegible handwriting.

Anyone writing about the country now known as Zimbabwe

will have difficulties about nomenclature. I have described the two major groups of tribes by the names 'Ndebele' and 'Shona', and the territories in which they live as 'Matabeleland' and 'Mashonaland'. As regards the country itself, its name has changed as often as has its Constitution. It has been called, successively, 'Southern Zambesia', 'Southern Rhodesia', 'Rhodesia', 'Zimbabwe/Rhodesia' and 'Zimbabwe'. I have contented myself with the name 'Rhodesia' up to the elections of 1980, except where one of the other names is necessary for clarity.

INTRODUCTION

The recent history of Rhodesia embodies many of the age-old problems which have bedevilled mankind since Adam. How can a direct conflict of interest be reconciled without consequent misery and bloodshed? Where does morality lie when both sides genuinely believe themselves to be right and indeed when both sides have perfectly tenable arguments to that effect? Can two or more groups of individuals possibly live together in peace and harmony when their whole approach to life is totally different? Can a conflict be confined to the protagonists themselves or will outside interests distort the issue until it becomes almost unrecognisable?

These and other problems have been plain to see in Rhodesia. The response of politicians was, on the whole, muddled and inconsistent. There was a constant series of miscalculations by almost everybody concerned. Many mistakes were made, in retrospect often palpable and gross. The whites in Rhodesia were obtuse and blinkered. The blacks were disunited to an almost incredible degree and, often, self-seeking. British Governments were vacillating, torn between self-interest and the demands of the situation within Rhodesia itself. Black African countries to the North were strident but largely ineffective. South Africa was hypocritical and indecisive, veering between support for the whites and pressures on them to abdicate power. The Russians and, in the earlier stages, the Chinese stirred the pot. The United States, to a great extent ignorant of the real situation, was largely conditioned by its own internal political pressures. The United Nations, that contradiction in terms, by its constant stream of futile and impossible demands, made itself almost irrelevant.

The result of all this was that a great deal of misery was caused to a very large number of people. Thousands were killed, often dying in prolonged and extreme agony. Hundreds of thousands had to leave their homes for one reason or another. Families were torn apart. Crops were destroyed, schools closed, medical facilities disrupted. Fear was a constant companion to millions of human beings caught in a situation over which they seemed to have no control and for which they, certainly, had no individual responsibility.

It can be argued that these miseries were the necessary birth pangs of progress. Or that evil, by force of arms, triumphed over good – or the reverse. Or that outside influences, for nefarious reasons of their own, ruined what was a prosperous, happy country. Beauty is in the eyes of the beholder. 'Terrorists' or 'freedom fighters' or even that catch-all word 'guerillas' – one's views of events is largely conditioned by background and environment not by an objective assessment of reality.

All that can be said with certainty is that a great deal of misery was caused and that black rule has now come to Zimbabwe. What the outcome will be, we cannot tell. If the past is anything to go by, almost every forecast will be wrong. Lord Home once said to me that the only certainty in politics is that the unexpected will happen, and this has certainly been true in Rhodesia.

But why did events turn out as they did? And could the whole story have taken a different course if political leaders had taken different decisions at various stages and, if so, when?

The temptation is to moralise. But this is a fruitless exercise, leading nowhere. Morality should be an individual, not a group, concept. There is no evidence to the effect that the whites or the blacks or any other group of people are inherently more or less moral than any other group. We are all caught up in the ambience of our contemporaries and, by and large, will have similar attitudes to them. If Mr Smith had been born as Mr Mugabe and vice versa can it seriously be supposed that they would not, both of them, have had the basic attitudes of the other?

An attempt can be made, however, to assess the impact of faulty judgement. Here again, however, it is necessary to be extremely careful in apportioning blame, if that is the right word. To a far greater extent than is commonly realised, political leaders are constrained by circumstances in the decisions they come to. This is particularly so in democracies although the same is true, even if perhaps to a lesser degree, in dictatorships. Willy-nilly, a politician represents a particular, not a universal, view. Indeed in a democracy he is chosen because he does represent that view. If he strays too far from the general approach to affairs which he has espoused, in a democracy he will be kicked out; in a dictatorship he will, eventually, be removed in one way or another. He can edge away from previous positions; he can, occasionally, if he has enough popular esteem, change course on one particular issue provided that he is successful in doing so (Macmillan and de Gaulle are examples), but by and large the constraints of his domestic constituency hem him in. It would have been impossible for Mr Smith to accept the concept of majority rule very much earlier than he did, even if he had wished to. It would have been impossible for Mr Wilson to lift sanctions or for President Kaunda to recognise the Smith regime – and so on. They were all bound inexorably to general lines of action by the very circumstances in which they found themselves: indeed because of their backgrounds they believed that what they were doing was right.

Nevertheless, there are choices which politicians can make even if their options are limited not only by their political circumstances but also, of course, by economic, geographical, military and social factors over which they have, often, little if any control.

The mistakes which politicians, of all complexions, have made in the Rhodesian drama have nearly all been the result of wishful thinking. Mr Smith thought he could perpetuate white rule 'for a thousand years'. Mr Wilson thought that sanctions would work in 'weeks not months'. African leaders thought that rhetoric could replace action – and so on. One could go on almost indefinitely. But, again, it is a prime function of the politician to keep hope alive. To acknowledge impotence is to fail in the eyes of his supporters. Public despair is not an option open to the politician who wishes to retain credibility and to influence events in the future. The boundary between the retention of hope for the future and wishful thinking is narrow; in order to retain coherence and a measure of domestic stability it may well be that wishful thinking, albeit often hypocritical, is necessary.

The real damage is done when a whole policy is based on a total misunderstanding of the situation, when reality is submerged in a dream world of self-delusion or when personal ambition becomes the prime motive of action wholly divorced from the interests of others. The difficulty is, of course, that politicians become convinced by their own rhetoric, necessary to gain and maintain support, but nevertheless rhetoric. In order to explain highly complex situations to the public at large, the politician has to over-simplify and in this process he can well, himself, lose sight of the realities. The demand of the political leader for a brief on one sheet of paper is as dangerous as it is, perhaps, inevitable.

There have been three facts about Rhodesia which should have been basic to any appreciation of the situation at any stage of the recent history of that country. First, black rule was certain to come sooner or later: with a proportion of 1 white to about 25 blacks the whites could not possibly have held on indefinitely. Second, the whites were not going to hand over power without a considerable struggle; and, third, black unity was essential if the transition of power was to be achieved with the minimum of difficulty and bloodshed. No policy could be successful unless it took these three factors fully into account. Almost all politicians concerned with Rhodesia failed fully to appreciate at least one of them.

This book will examine these assumptions. It will try to establish how they arose and why. It will also attempt to answer the question as to whether all the violence has been inevitable or whether politicians, given the circumstances in which they found themselves, could have made decisions which would have lessened or avoided it. To the extent that it will dwell on incidents and personalities of which the writer has personal knowledge, it will lack balance. Finally the book will, of course, have the inevitable and enormous advantage of hindsight, that vastly hypocritical tool of the armchair critic, who in this particular case has often been as totally wrong as has everyone else.

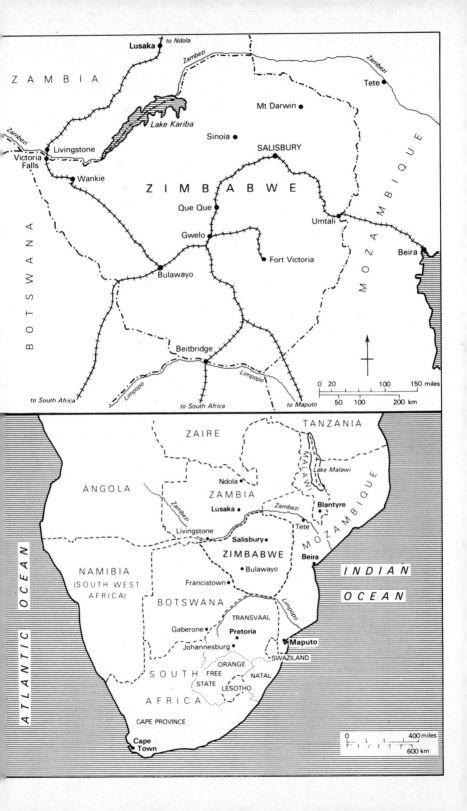

CHAPTER ONE

Early Days

The European carve up of Africa has proved to be a temporary phenomenon – at least north of the Republic of South Africa, and that nation, owing allegiance to no European country, is in a different category. For a brief period in the scale of history Europe gained the prize of considerable mineral wealth in certain areas and an outlet for the questing energies of some of its peoples. The price it has had to pay for these benefits has lain in the difficulties of extricating itself from what, increasingly, became a series of impossible political situations. The deeper the involvement, the more difficult it has been to pull out with dignity and without loss of life.

Until the nineteenth century, Central Africa had been largely bypassed by the growth of civilisation as we know it. That is not to say that there were not elements of real value in the organisation of tribal society before the white man came. In many cases a hierarchical and ordered structure of society was created. But the deep religious insights, the magnificent cultures of Europe and Asia and the technological skills which flourished elsewhere were not in Africa south of the Sahara except to some degree in areas where the Arabs had penetrated in search of slaves and, mainly, Portuguese enterprise had touched the fringes of that vast continent. This was probably due primarily to the almost total absence of communications and to malaria and other, now preventable, diseases.

So it was that, in the nineteenth century, the Europeans, realising that there were rich prizes to be taken without any effective opposition from the indigenous inhabitants and driven on by rivalry of each other, really set about the task of grabbing for themselves what they could. Motives, as always,

1

were mixed. Missionaries played a notable part both in exploration and in trying to bring a civilising presence to communities which they believed to be dominated by fear and ignorance. Unfortunately, in some cases the bible followed the sword, thus totally negating the instructions of the Founder Himself. Apart from the missionaries there were others, too, who genuinely believed that their role was to rescue the Africans from barbarism. But the truth is that self-enrichment, together with the love of adventure for its own sake, were the real spurs to much of what was done. There is nothing particularly or uniquely vicious about this. Africans who castigate the Europeans for seizing their territories should remember that the prime motive in much of the tribal movements in their continent over the centuries was either the seizure of land or cattle or both or escape from a stronger and acquisitive neighbour. The milk of human kindness was not a notable feature of intertribal relations before the Europeans came. Might was right. Enemies were slaughtered, their wives and daughters appropriated and their possessions seized. It may well be that the Europeans to a large extent continued in the same tradition. But there was an element of conscience, albeit often difficult to discern and laced with hypocrisy, in their behaviour and indeed this conscience did play a part, arguably small when compared to the powerful and eventually overwhelming stirrings of African nationalism, in the voluntary relinquishment of much of Africa by the European powers.

But, in retrospect, it was inevitable that the European countries, as indeed had already happened in virtually the whole of the rest of the world, jealous of each other and supremely self-confident, would spill over into an Africa, backward, in many ways ignorant and containing wealth of which the inhabitants had little conception let alone the ability fully to develop.

Whether Africa has benefited in the long run from the temporary dominion of Europe over its territory must be a matter of conjecture. This can be argued both ways. Education, medical facilities, agricultural expertise, the Christian religion, communications – all these and many other benefits have followed. These would certainly not have come so quickly, if at all, without the European invasion. The loss of dignity, tribal culture and the wisdom which comes from continuing responsibility are the balancing features. The difficulty is, of course, that to super-impose one culture on another is a highly dangerous business, particularly when the two are totally different in almost every way. The result could be that the worst of both remains – the acquisitive individual materialism of the European and the inter-tribal slaughter of the African. But the argument is academic. The fact is that Europe did acquire Africa and, given the circumstances, there is nothing anyone could have done to prevent it.

As far as Rhodesia and the surrounding territories were concerned, the European invasion did not really take place until the end of the nineteenth century. The Portuguese, that remarkable race of adventurers, moved into Rhodesia as long ago as 1569 in search of trade and gold. However, they were in the end foiled mainly by the mosquito and, prey to malaria and other difficulties, they had left Rhodesia for all intents and purposes by 1693.

It is interesting, but fruitless, to ponder the connection between science and politics. If quinine had been discovered in the sixteenth century, what would the effect on Rhodesia, and perhaps on Portugal, have been?

The Portuguese had brought the wheel – that most notable of human inventions – with them to Rhodesia. But for reasons shrouded in mystery, even that essential tool of agriculture and communications was lost or forgotten after the Portuguese quit. The tribes in Rhodesia appear to have reverted to their previous life as if the Portuguese had never descended upon them. We have little information as to what happened in Rhodesia for more than a century after that.

In the early decades of the nineteenth century two events occurred, the repercussions of which are still with us, which were to condition the future of Rhodesia. The British acquired the Cape in order to protect the route to India and, clashing with the Dutch, who had been there before them, forced that tenacious race to push up to the north, a process which led eventually to the Boer War and a continued and continuing struggle between these two very different peoples which spilled over into Rhodesia. With more immediate impact as far as Rhodesia was concerned, Shaka, a Zulu Chief, brave, ruthless and militarily efficient, became master of northern Natal. Such was Shaka's despotic cruelty that two sub-tribes of the

3

Zulu people were impelled to escape his wrath. The first, in 1821, was the Ndwandwe people led by their chief Zwangendaba who crossed the Limpopo and eventually finished up west of what is now known as Lake Malawi. The second were the Ndebele people under Mzilikazi who, fleeing the wrath of Shaka and picking up other tribesmen en route, established a separate kingdom near what is now known as Pretoria. After moving further west to avoid Zulu reprisals they were, however, defeated by the Boers and they crossed the Limpopo in 1837, establishing their capital near what is now known as Bulawayo. Once there, they were joined by some of the Shona speaking tribesmen of the area who became absorbed in the Ndebele tradition. There were, and are, therefore, three species of Ndebele in descending order of status: the original Zulu people who had left under Mzilikazi, known as the Abe zansi; those who had been picked up on the way, known as the Abe nhla, and those who were recruited on arrival, known as the Amaholi. Although the edges have been blurred, this hierarchy still exists and plays an important part in the politics of the country.

The Ndebele were a warrior race, proud and distinct, with a language and character of their own. In those days they lived under a rigid military discipline with chiefs, or Indunas, responsible to the king whose power was absolute. They lived mainly by raiding their unfortunate neighbours and this was to continue until the white man prevented it. The original inhabitants of the country were largely of Bantu stock who had, many centuries previously, come down from the north. They were a mixture of a number of different tribes with different traditions and customs but were able to communicate with each other since they spoke the same, Shona, language, albeit with different dialects. They, too, had a proud history, although the absence of a written language has vastly complicated the task of historians. It is believed that at least two powerful Empires were created. The first, the Empire of Mwene we Mutapa, is thought to be responsible for the stone structures of which the Great Zimbabwe ruins are the most famous. This Empire appears eventually to have been superseded by the Rozwi Dynasty which in its turn was damaged by Zwangendaba on his way to Lake Malawi and finally destroyed by Mzilikazi. Over the centuries the Shona speaking

4

tribes had established a primitive but effective agriculture. Gold was mined and traded. Pottery was made. Cloth was woven. Ivory and soapstone were carved. But they were basically a pastoral people, and were no match for the disciplined but cruel excesses of the Ndebele.

It is impossible to understand recent Rhodesian history unless the basic division between the Ndebele and the Shona is grasped. The Ndebele are accustomed, and react easily, to firm control. The Shona, on the other hand, are far more diffuse and their leaders will normally enunciate a consensus rather than dictate a policy. The contrast between Nkomo (Ndebele)[1] and Muzorewa (Shona) was a very good example of this as was the difference between the ZIPRA (Nkomo's) Army – disciplined and cohesive – and the ZANLA (Mugabe's) Army – a relatively undisciplined body.[2] Mugabe, a Shona, found control of his party a difficult business. At the time of writing, it remains to be seen whether he will be able to overcome the many centrifugal pressures to which he will undoubtedly be prone.

When Mzilikazi died in 1868 he was, after a struggle, succeeded in 1870 by one of his sons – Lobengula, a powerful and resourceful leader. He continued the practice of constant raids into the neighbouring Mashonaland. In some cases these raids were plain aggressive forays; in others they were a punishment for failure to acknowledge the Ndebele sway which was gradually extending far from Bulawayo.

Here we come to one of the arguments which has divided historians of this period. As we shall see, one of the *post facto* justifications of the seizure of Rhodesia by the whites lay in the concessions granted by Lobengula. The question at issue was the size of the territory over which that monarch could reasonably be said to have the power to give concessions. The Shona argument was that Lobengula had no right to give concessions over any of their land since he had no title to it. It was clearly to the white advantage, however, to take the view that Lobengula's suzerainty was very considerable. A further white justification for their subsequent actions was that, by taking Mashonaland, they protected the Shona from Ndebele attack. There was truth in this but, again, the extent to which Ndebele attacks reached into Mashonaland had a direct bearing on the amount of relief to the Shona which white occupation brought.

5

Clearly it was to the white advantage to argue that the Ndebele were terrorising the whole, or a very considerable part, of Mashonaland. The truth probably lay somewhere between the two extremes.

Gold had been re-discovered by the Europeans in 1867 (the Portuguese invasion three centuries earlier had been largely prompted by the lure of that metal), and as soon as he came to the throne Lobengula found himself surrounded by white concession hunters and traders, trying to persuade him to give them special and exclusive rights of all kinds. Missionaries were also attempting to sell their spiritual wares and indeed Robert Moffat, Livingstone's father-in-law, had been allowed by Mzilikazi to set up a mission station at Inyati in 1859. The Portuguese, too, were again trying to extend their influence inland from the coast. It was, therefore, a confused scene on to which burst that remarkable phenomenon Cecil Rhodes. Born in 1853, the son of a vicar, Rhodes was sent to South Africa in 1870 for health reasons. After three years, during which time he amassed considerable wealth at the diamond mines in Kimberley, he returned to the University of Oxford. Commuting between South Africa and Oxford, he eventually graduated in 1881 by which time he was a millionaire and a member of the Cape Parliament. There can have been few, if any, undergraduates like him at Oxford or indeed at any University. He was unique. One wonders, in passing, what he must have been like to teach.

Rhodes had the vision of a British corridor right through the centre of Africa from the Cape to Cairo. He was intensely patriotic and believed profoundly in the mission of the British race and the great benefits which Britain could bring to Africa, and indeed elsewhere. It is difficult in these days of comparative mediocrity and disillusionment to understand the fervour with which many young Englishmen (or Scots for that matter) were gripped when they saw the boundless opportunities for personal and national aggrandisement in Africa. Proud, tough, vastly self-confident and independent in spirit they were able to overcome enormous difficulties in a relentless advance over ever-widening horizons. At once ruthless, romantic, single-minded and bursting with restless energy, Rhodes epitomised the questing, albeit self-seeking, spirit of adventure which brought Britain its vast Empire. He was determined that it was to be the British, not the Boers, the Portuguese, the Germans, the Belgians or anyone else who would dominate Central Africa.

The story of Lobengula's various concessions and their precise validity is complex and overcast with intrigue, double-dealing, lies, evasions, treachery and hypocrisy by almost everyone concerned. In 1887 he signed a treaty of friendship with Grobler, an emissary of the Boer leader Kruger. In 1888, apparently totally ignoring this agreement, he signed a treaty with John Moffat, an emissary of Rhodes, whereby he agreed not to give away any of his territories without the consent of the British High Commissioner in South Africa. A few months later he signed a concession with Rudd, a partner of Rhodes's, giving 'complete and exclusive charge over all metals and minerals situated and contained in my kingdom, principalities and dominions together with full powers to do all things that they may deem necessary to win and procure the same.' He also undertook 'to grant no concessions of land or mining rights without the grantee's consent and concurrence.' Although he signed a separate document certifying that the treaty had been properly explained to him before affixing his seal he appeared later to repudiate it, but even this is not absolutely clear in this confusing affair. He certainly did not take delivery of part of the *quid pro quo* of an armed steam boat for use on the Zambezi. Furthermore, as mentioned above, the extent of his 'kingdom, principalities and dominions' was in great doubt. The only thing that is certain is that the concession concerned only mineral rights, not the grant of land.

The equivocal attitude of the British Government towards the acquisition of territory, which had for long been a feature of the spread of British influence and power, was exemplified in its attitude towards all this. On the one hand it was obsessed by the need to keep the Cape firmly in its own hands as a safeguard of the route to India in spite of the opening of the Suez Canal in 1869. Furthermore, if Central Africa was to be carved up, the British Government was determined that as much as possible should accrue to Britain as opposed to Portugal or any other European power. On the other hand it did not wish to be burdened with financial responsibility for ventures which might or might not turn out to be successful. On top of this, the Victorian conscience was a powerful factor in the whole

7

British attitude towards 'the natives'. Without the burden of instant communication or indeed, in many cases, any communication at all, there was no question of mass involvement in events far from the experience or knowledge of a people interested, as always, largely in its own affairs. But, nevertheless, it was a part of the whole ethic which pervaded Britain at the time that the British Empire was not only a glorious extension of the self-evident virtues of the British race but was also to the benefit of those who were conquered. This could hardly be so if 'the natives' were misused. It was important, therefore, to the British Government that some residual powers were kept to prevent gross and unfair exploitation of the Africans. In these general attitudes, Britain can, indeed, be found guilty of hypocrisy, but it is only too easy to judge a bygone age by the standards of the present.

It can well be argued, indeed it is probably true, that the British Government's attitude at the end of the nineteenth century led straight to the traumas of the 1960s and 1970s in Rhodesia. Britain was not prepared then, or at any subsequent moment until Lord Soames' descent on an astonished people in 1979, to take full responsibility for that territory; neither was she ready to wash her hands of the whole affair. Hence the continuing dichotomy, the responsibility without power, which has been a central difficulty to successive British Governments. None of this, of course, was apparent to those who had responsibility in Britain at the time. Constrained by the circumstances and general attitudes in which they lived, they sought to balance advantage with conscience within the inevitable limitations of their contemporary vision, as best they could.

Rhodes solved the dilemma in which the British Government found itself by applying for a Charter for a Company to develop 'North and South Zambesia' – the name by which he called the territories which were subsequently to bear his name. After a number of difficulties, including a journey to England by two of Lobengula's Indunas to see Queen Victoria, had been surmounted and much manoeuvring between rival claimants, some of whom were paid off out of Rhodes's vast fortune, his very considerable powers of persuasion and skilful handling of the personalities involved were successful and the Charter was granted in 1889.

The Charter delineated no northern frontier to the operations of the Company. On the other hand its operation depended on the concessions it had obtained from local chiefs or those it would be able to extract in the future. However, the Company was authorised – 'To acquire by any concession agreement grant or treaty, all or any rights interests authorities jurisdictions and powers of any kind or nature whatever, including powers necessary for the purposes of government, and the preservation of public order in or for the protection of territories, lands, or property, comprised or referred to in the concessions and agreements made as aforesaid or affecting other territories, lands, or property in Africa, or the inhabitants thereof, and to hold, use and exercise such territories, lands, property, rights, interests, authorities, jurisdictions and powers respectively for the purposes of the Company and on the terms of this Our Charter.' This legal gobbledygook must have been almost totally mystifying to Lobengula, even when explained to him. The Charter was to run for twenty-five years, but could be renewed at ten-year intervals thereafter.[3]

Rhodes's next task was to give substance to the opportunities he had thus acquired. Although providing the driving force behind the whole venture, he did not himself go to the territory until much later. He planned to send a column north, bypassing Ndebele territory, to establish a base deep in Mashonaland. The organisation of the column was entrusted to Johnson, a twenty-three-year-old adventurer with a murky past. The legendary Selous, a Rider Haggard prototype, who already knew the country well and who had been paid £2000 by Rhodes not to publish articles to the effect that Eastern Mashonaland was not under Lobengula's suzerainty, was to guide the column, which eventually consisted of 196 pioneers. They had a military escort of 500. Each pioneer was to be given fifteen gold claims and 3000 acres of land, the latter in direct contravention of any of the concessions which had been obtained whether or not they covered the area in question. The pioneers were in theory chosen in an attempt to provide a fair cross-section of the frontier society of the time with people of British extraction predominating. Whether this was successful or not depends, like so much of this story, on the eye of the beholder.

It is easy to scoff at the venture: indeed to ridicule it as a collection of self-seeking adventurers intent on seizing land which did not belong to them in order to find easy wealth. But this would be to belie the real spirit of adventure which motivated many of those who took part, the risks involved, and their questing defiance of the unknown. Certainly to take part in this historic venture was no easy option. Like those Americans who were the first to travel to the moon, their journey was fraught with danger and what they would find on arrival was far from clear.

In any event, on 12 September 1890, they arrived at what is now known as Salisbury, named after the brooding and powerful British Prime Minister of the time, and from this event came the British occupation of Rhodesia.

Deep African resentment at the white occupation of what they considered to be their century has been a factor in all the subsequent history of Rhodesia. As we shall see, it was expressed very quickly in three rebellions. It then appeared to subside for some considerable time until resurfacing in extreme form recently. Indeed there were long periods when the status quo seemed to be accepted by the African population. No doubt there were many Africans who found great advantage in the material improvements which followed white rule and in the structure of law and ordered government which, after a time, was imposed on the whole country. But African nationalism was certain to become a dominant factor in the life of the country sooner or later, particularly since the whites continued to see themselves as different (as indeed they were) and superior to their fellow inhabitants. There could be no question of equality between black and white Rhodesia in 1890. The whites were indeed superior in a whole range of material aspects and this belief in the innate superiority of the whites remained deep in the majority of white minds throughout the tragic story. The moral issue – if indeed it is possible to consider it in this context – is much less clear. The right of conquest was at that time accepted as a part of existence in Africa as elsewhere. It is only comparatively recently that acceptance of the sword as the ultimate arbiter has really become unfashionable. Why should a white tribe not have the same rights as anyone else in Africa? The fact that they came from another continent is, in a sense, irrelevant. How long do you have to be in one continent before you have the same rights as others? The real spur to discontent lay in the fact that the new dominant tribe was so totally different in almost every human attribute, clothed in a skin the colour of which permanently set it apart, and determined to remain permanently separate and superior.

The question of whether Rhodes's pioneers had any legal rights at all, or to what extent the concessions justified them in their activities is, and was, really almost irrelevant. The issue here was not so much between white and black as between the various contestants for the spoils. The Europeans had by and large accepted the existence of concessions as evidence of national rights to extend their domination.[4] A piece of paper sealed by an African chief gave substance to the claim of one European (and in this one must include the Boer) nation as against another of a 'sphere of influence' over a particular area of territory. The Chancelleries of Europe argued among themselves about the legalities while their citizens on the spot vied with each other to obtain often *post facto* justification for what they intended to do anyway. In the event Rhodes was highly, although not totally, successful. He obtained the whole of what was later to become Northern and Southern Rhodesia[5] but failed in Katanga and Mozambique. Nyasaland was secured for Britain, but not directly by Rhodes, although he did have considerable influence on Sir Harry Johnston who was primarily responsible for British sway over that territory.

The pioneers had a very difficult time at first and barely survived the first rainy season. They did not find much gold and the Eldorado they had hoped for must have seemed to be a mirage, particularly as in the early stages there were no white women (apart from a few missionaries' wives and some Dominican Sisters) and, surprisingly, all alcohol was banned. However, after a time things began to improve and their numbers rapidly increased (there were 5000 Europeans in Southern Rhodesia by 1896). A *modus vivendi* of a kind with a frontier was established with the Ndebele. The pioneers required a considerable amount of Shona labour, and there was no one to ask questions as to exactly how this labour was procured or recompensed.

In May 1891 Southern Zambesia [*sic*] became a British Protectorate by Order in Council (in practice this Order referred

11

only to Mashonaland). In October 1891, in an attempt to curb the activities of the Company, Lobengula granted a concession to a German – Lippert – giving him the right to make grants of land to Europeans in both Matabeleland and Mashonaland. But Rhodes bought the concession off Lippert. By this subterfuge, therefore, the occupation of land by the pioneers and their successors was given some legal validity.

However, relations with the Ndebele were becoming increasingly uneasy. The Ndebele way of life, still largely consisting of raids against their neighbours, could hardly be reconciled with the Company's tenure of Mashonaland and its need for a stable source of Shona labour. After one particular, and confused, incident in 1893, war broke out in which the Ndebele were heavily and quickly defeated, largely because they were no match for the well-armed British in the set piece battles to which the Ndebele were addicted. Bulawayo was captured and Lobengula retreated to the north. In the pursuit a small British patrol of thirty-three men – the Shangani patrol – was cut off and annihilated, thus becoming part of the heroic folklore of white Rhodesia which endured until at least 1980.

Lobengula died shortly afterwards. There were no difficulties about concessions in the case of Matabeleland which was secured by 'right of conquest'. But, again, for mainly financial reasons, Britain deliberately decided against direct administration and the Company's rule was extended over virtually the whole of what is now known as Zimbabwe under the Matabeleland Order in Council of July 1894.

The whites now set about the task of exploiting their success. They seized a high proportion of the Ndebele cattle and parcelled out large areas of land. Although the Company was entrusted with the administration of the country, it was a commercial undertaking concerned primarily with commercial profit, not good government. The Ndebele had been defeated in a war and Mashonaland had, apparently peacefully, been occupied. The welfare of the Africans was certainly not of great importance to those who found themselves in power and many things were done which would have horrified Victorian Britain, if known.

To add to the miseries of the Africans, the land was afflicted by drought, locusts and rinderpest. The Ndebele became desperate. After a series of misunderstandings, Dr Jameson,

Rhodes's principal lieutenant, led his ill-fated raid into the Transvaal against the Boers and when the whites were at their weakest the Ndebele rose again (in March 1896). When this war was at its height the Shona, too, rebelled. The settlers were taken completely by surprise by both rebellions, particularly the latter.

One of the recurring factors in the Rhodesian situation has been over-optimistic white intelligence about the real feelings of the Africans. In 1896 the settlers thought that the Ndebele were crushed and would not mount a second rebellion and that the Shona were actually grateful to them for protection against the Ndebele. They were wrong on both counts.

However, after a series of appalling massacres of isolated white communities – reminiscent of many incidents in the 1970s – the whites recovered their poise. With the aid of Imperial troops – the last time Britain had an actual military presence in Rhodesia until 1979 – the tide was turned. Rhodes, showing great personal bravery, talked the Ndebele Indunas into surrender at a famous meeting in the Matopos Hills. The Shona were also defeated after an often ruthless and savage war. The whites had, however, suffered a severe shock. They had lost 372 dead and 129 were wounded, no less than 10 per cent of the entire population. The high proportion of dead to wounded showed the severity of the fighting. But white control of the entire country was now total and in October 1897 the first train steamed into Bulawayo, the line from the Indian Ocean to Umtali being finished in 1898 with an extension to Salisbury in 1899 and the Bulawayo/Salisbury link being completed in 1902, the year that Rhodes died.

White administration of the country during the early days after the arrival of the pioneers cannot be defended in terms of present-day morality. A hut tax of ten shillings – a considerable sum of money to the Africans – was imposed in 1894 in order to force the Africans to seek European employment. Cattle were seized when payment could not be made. Rents were charged for Africans who lived on land which Europeans had appropriated, although in many cases the new owners were absentee landlords. Repressive measures of many kinds, including in some cases forced labour, were instituted. The Ndebele, who had parleyed with Rhodes in the Matopos Hills, had agreed to surrender on the understanding that they would

13

be able to return home in peace, but when they got there they discovered that their land had been seized. The reserves allocated for them were barren and waterless. To the Shona, land was sacred because it contained the graves of their ancestors. It was held in trust by their chiefs but it could not be wholly alienated. To do so was sacrilege. The European concept of land ownership was contrary to their whole way of life and there was bitter resentment. The three wars fought, albeit hopeless from the start largely because of superior European fire power, became part of the heroic folklore of the Africans, like the Shangani patrol to the Europeans. The Europeans may have thought that the 'native question' had been settled once and for all. Not so to the Africans. For instance, Muzorewa, in his final election appeal to the nation in 1980, referred with much emotion to the exploits of his fellow countrymen in 1896 in their heroic resistance to the foreign invasion.

The British authorities were uneasily aware of what was happening, but did little about it. Their physical control was very limited, and they did not wish to alienate the whole of white South Africa at a time when they were facing grave problems of a totally different nature there.

Nevertheless it was clearly necessary to pay far more attention to the African situation in Rhodesia and in 1901 Milton, an efficient, humane and far-seeing man, was appointed Administrator, quickly bringing some order to the almost anarchic situation.

There were, however, two aspects of the administration at that time which were to have far-reaching implications later. First, the natives were governed by an entirely separate administration from that which regulated white affairs. Milton eventually wore two hats – head of the Civil Service and Secretary for Native Affairs; and, second, virtually all officials were recruited not from Britain but either from the existing settler community or from the Cape. Both these facets of Rhodesian life were, in the main, to continue right through the whole story: the whites were seen as a totally separate entity from the blacks, and the links between Rhodesia and Britain were far more tenuous than was the case in other British colonies in Africa where officials were recruited from and responsible to Britain. Many of the native commissioners did indeed have the welfare of the Africans very much at heart, but in the last resort they were themselves not independent agents of Whitehall but a part of the settler community, with the advantages and disadvantages of that fact.

The settler community in Rhodesia began to increase fast. From about 5000 in 1896, it rose to 12,000 in 1904, 14,000 in 1907 and 24,000 in 1911. It was the size of the settler community which was to set Rhodesia apart from all other British Colonies in Africa north of the Zambezi and was to contribute to the vital fact that Britain never exercised direct control over it. Furthermore the settlers came almost exclusively from the south, not straight from Britain. They were already independent in spirit and were not going to be dictated to from Whitehall.

It is not always realised that in the early stages of European power in Rhodesia, there was comparatively little European farming. In 1904, out of a white population of 12,000, there were only 545 farmers. The Africans were able to profit from this situation. They had the additional European market to supply, those that lived near the railway were able to use it to transport their produce and the Shona were at last relieved from the prospect of Ndebele raids. A number of foreign workers came to Rhodesia to work on the European mines and they too required food. There was indeed an era of prosperity for many Africans which lasted until about 1908 when, as an act of policy, European farming was promoted by an Estates Department, a Land Bank and other measures which brought about a rapid and considerable increase in both company and individual European farming. It was this switch of emphasis from mining to agriculture with the ever-increasing demand for European land which eventually gave rise to the Land Apportionment Act – the core of that later African resentment which was to fuel the fires of radical nationalism.

The process of establishing an ordered system of government with settler representation began in 1898 with an Order in Council setting up a Legislative Council of ten consisting of the Administrator, an Imperial representative (the Resident Commissioner), five appointees of the Company and four unofficial members elected on a franchise restricted by property and literacy qualifications.[6] There was no actual colour bar but very few Africans in fact qualified. This general principle was to continue until 1969, when voters' rolls were for the first time segregated on grounds of colour. The whites can indeed claim that colour did not play a part in the legislative process during the whole of the period from 1898 to 1969. Equally the blacks can claim that this was a hypocritical façade erected to cover the obvious fact that they were in practice excluded from power by virtue of the franchise qualifications. Both arguments are true. On the one hand the whites never approached the situation of South Africa where colour was a definitive bar to political power of any kind in the areas of that country which really mattered and where the blacks were officially regarded as a different species. On the other hand, by manipulating the franchise qualifications, by erecting a wholly different and vastly inferior system of black education and by excluding Africans from much of the process whereby wealth could be acquired, the whites could retain power in their own hands.

In any event, there was no question of any black control back in 1898. There was, however, continuing pressure for more power for the settlers. The composition of the Legislative Council was changed to bring unofficial parity in 1904 and an elected unofficial majority in 1907. This did not, in practice, mean a great deal because all financial propositions had to be advanced by the Administrator and, in theory at least, the Colonial Office retained wide powers. After the Jameson Raid of 1895 the Colonial Office did use its powers to a considerable extent, particularly in relation to native affairs, although intervention diminished after 1907.

As the number of settlers increased it became clear that a decision would have to be taken about who would control the country – there was increasing friction between the Company and the settlers. The Charter was due to expire in 1914 (unless renewed) and the possibility of association with the Colonies south of the Limpopo was widely canvassed. This came to a head in 1908 but it received little support at that time because of the fear that Southern Rhodesia, as the territory was now called, would be swamped in the far larger entity to the South. The basic British decision was taken in 1911. It was decided that Southern Rhodesia would be given 'Responsible Government' and that it should preferably be incorporated in the Union of South Africa. This solution would, it was hoped, avoid the twin evils of a continuing British financial responsibility and eventual clashes between the settlers and the British Government. Opinion in Southern Rhodesia at that time was, however, still against joining the Union. The matter was, therefore, deferred and Company rule was to be maintained until an overall settlement could be obtained. The 1914 war diverted attention from all constitutional progress and the Charter was extended until 1924.

After the war, in which the white settlers played a notable part, the discussion was resumed with increasing urgency. The argument became polarised between the options of union with South Africa or 'Responsible Government' under which 'Southern Rhodesia' would become a British colony with a large measure of self-government. Those favouring union with South Africa were the South African Government under Smuts, the Colonial Office (distrusting the settlers), the Company (which would have obtained very good terms from the South Africans) and much of the establishment in Southern Rhodesia (though not the Legislative Council). The bulk of the population, robustly independent and well led by Coghlan, their leader in the Legislative Council, under the slogan 'Rhodesia for the Rhodesians, Rhodesia for the Empire', voted at a referendum in 1922 for 'Responsible Government' by 8774 votes to 5989. The European population was 35,000 out of which 20,000 were on the register. There were 900,000 Africans with 60 on the register.

It is interesting that the division of opinion in 1922 was very similar to that at the time of UDI, forty-three years later. On one side were the big business community and the intellectual establishment – pro-union with South Africa and anti-UDI. On the other were the farmers, small businessmen and artisans – pro-'Responsible Government' and pro-UDI. The analogy should not be pressed too far, but in both cases the artisans and small businessmen were afraid of being swamped (in 1922 by the South Africans and in 1965 by the blacks) and the farmers were determined to retain independence, but large-scale business saw financial difficulties if the more radical solution was taken. However, one of the factors responsible for the outcome in 1922 but not in 1965 was a deep anti-Afrikaner feeling and a burning desire to remain British. The Africans were not consulted in either case.

The decision by the British Government to offer 'Responsible Government' and the acceptance of that offer by the settlers was the key to the whole subsequent history of Rhodesia. Effective power in the country was placed firmly in the hands of the settlers.[7] It was certain that they would not relinquish it without a considerable struggle. But at the same time Britain retained the ultimate responsibility – a fact which led to very considerable British embarrassment later. Britain had similar problems in South Africa in some ways but, for a variety of reasons, responsibility was relinquished much earlier when that country obtained virtual independence as the Union of South Africa by the South Africa Act of 1909: its sovereign independence was assured by the British Statute of Westminster of 1931. In the whole of her Colonial Empire it was only in Rhodesia that Britain became directly involved with the rising tide of nationalism in a situation where she had no physical power on the ground to insist on radical change to take account of a totally different environment.

The classic definition of the British attitude to any clash of interest between the settlers and the natives in a British Colony was laid down in the Devonshire Declaration of 1923 in which the British Government recorded 'their considered opinion that the interests of the African natives must be paramount; and if and when these interests and the interests of the immigrant races should conflict, the former should prevail... His Majesty's Government regard themselves as exercising a trust on behalf of the African population'. But the decision to grant 'Responsible Government', whether within the Union of South Africa or not, had been taken back in 1911 and, as a result, Britain did not have effective power to implement that doctrine in Southern Rhodesia.

Could a far-seeing statesman in Britain in 1922 have foreseen the difficulties which were to stem from the granting of 'Responsible Government' and, if he had, could he, in the ambience of the time, have taken the necessary action? The answers must almost certainly be 'No'. The situation in 1922 had evolved, step by step, from the initial decision to grant a Charter in 1889 and not to take direct responsibility for the territory. Once that decision had been taken, and the numbers of the settlers increased so dramatically, it would have been virtually impossible for the British Government to initiate direct colonial rule, particularly when the general thrust of British policy was to avoid financial commitments wherever possible. And, in any case, although there may have been some misgivings in the Colonial Office, the general impression was that 'the natives' in Southern Rhodesia were well looked after. It was not in the minds of anyone that those same 'natives' would before long demand power for themselves, let alone actually achieve it. (Indeed even after 1945 people were persuaded to emigrate to Rhodesia from Britain without any kind of warning that the future of white control of that country was at risk.) African nationalism barely existed, if at all. Very few Africans had been educated in the Western sense of that ambiguous word. Belief in the continuing glory of the British Empire was still deep in the consciousness of the British people. It was to remain so until well after the 1939–45 war.

The conclusion must be that, given the circumstances, the decisions taken were largely inevitable and that an eventual clash between whites and blacks in Rhodesia together with the British involvement in that tragic event was inevitable, too. The details of how that clash would occur, the severity of it and the precise form of the final dénouement are, of course, another matter. But, given the general course of events described, it is impossible to see any other result but eventual tragedy, both for the blacks who were certain at the least to suffer great indignity and the whites who were certain in the long run to lose much, if not all, of what, with great courage and tenacity, they had created.

There was much hypocrisy about white attitudes, then and later. They may have brought with them European skills which undoubtedly brought much material advancement to many Africans. But the harsh fact, not to be gainsaid, is that they did seize the country from the Africans who, certainly, did not acquiesce in that process either in 1890 or at any time later. There was, also, much African hypocrisy. Life for the Africans before the Europeans came was certainly far from the idyllic haven of content described by some African writers. Although there were many positive features of the African way of life, material and social, which have been consistently underestimated by many whites in Southern Africa, for many people their existence was indeed nasty, brutish and short. Had the Europeans not arrived on the scene there is no reason to suppose that change would have come quickly, if at all.

Tribal antagonisms led to much human misery before the white tribe arrived. And it looks as if that Achilles heel of African Nationalism will continue to plague the continent in general and the new Zimbabwe in particular for decades, if not centuries, to come.

CHAPTER TWO

Responsible Government to UDI, 1923–65

There is some confusion about the constitutional position of Southern Rhodesia after 1923. The claim that the country was fully self-governing since that date, sometimes advanced in support of the Unilateral Declaration of Independence, is simply not true. The powers of the Southern Rhodesian Government were far more restricted than is commonly supposed. For instance Britain could legislate for Southern Rhodesia by Act or Order in Council, she could disallow Bills discriminating against Africans, the Governor had in theory very considerable powers and, above all, native affairs were the responsibility of the High Commissioner who was in fact the Governor General of South Africa (this control was much diminished after 1937 when the Southern Rhodesian Government obtained control over its own native administration albeit still with certain safeguards). As far as Bills by the Legislative Assembly were concerned, it became the practice for discussions to take place with the British Government before Bills were put forward. A number of Bills were amended and, in some cases, withdrawn because of British opposition. Britain did, therefore, exert a considerable restraining influence over Southern Rhodesia. A convention grew up under which Britain would not legislate without the consent of the Southern Rhodesian Government. This was not formalised as such until 1961 but it was only broken once, inadvertently, in 1946 when Britain bound Southern Rhodesia to the Bretton Woods Agreement without any prior consultation.

It can well be argued that Britain ought to have intervened to a far greater extent than she in fact did. But in the atmosphere of the time the policies of the Southern Rhodesian Government were not seen as racially oppressive to any marked degree. Furthermore there was clearly a limit to interference in the affairs of a country which had 'Responsible Government' however ambiguous that phrase might have been.

A further factor, stemming from the decision to grant 'Responsible Government', was that Southern Rhodesia was put under the Dominions Office (later to be known as the Commonwealth Relations Office) set up in 1925, rather than the Colonial Office. The function of the Dominions Office was to deal with territories which were fully self-governing. It did not supervise the legislation they passed in their own Parliaments and did not, elsewhere, have the task of protecting the natives. Given the line of responsibility, it was, therefore, probably inevitable that Britain did not exercise her restrictive power as much as she would have done had Rhodesian affairs been dealt with by the Colonial Office. And this tendency became even more pronounced in 1930 when the two offices, previously under one Secretary of State, were given separate Ministers.

At the first election (in 1924), Coghlan, who had led the movement towards 'Responsible Government' and against union with South Africa, was highly successful, his new Rhodesian Party being returned with 26 out of 30 seats. There were four Independents and the Labour Party, which was for the next few decades to represent a wholly reactionary approach to race relations, was annihilated.

At this time, too, appeared the first glimmerings of African Nationalism since the cataclysmic military defeats at the end of the nineteenth century. Before the 1923 Constitution was granted, Nyamanda, the eldest son of Lobengula, had attempted to achieve some kind of Ndebele home rule in Matabeleland. He failed. And in 1923 a Rhodesia Bantu Voters' Association was formed in order to get as many Africans as possible on to the voters' electoral roll. It failed too.

Shortly after the accession to power of Coghlan's administration there occurred an event which was to set the pattern for 'native' policy in Rhodesia right up until the advent of Bishop Muzorewa's Government in 1979. After considerable pressures from the Rhodesians the British Secretary of State for the

Colonies agreed to the setting up of a Land Commission under Sir William Morris Carter to investigate whether separate areas should be designated for exclusive African and European occupation and whether special native purchase areas should be permitted. It reported in 1926. There had been no particular African pressure for such a Commission and it must be accepted that the spur to its creation was white, not black.

It is important to understand that the Native Reserves, as they were then called (they later became Tribal Trust Lands) already existed and did not come under the Land Apportionment Act (until 1941) which was derived from the Morris Carter Report. The Native Reserves had been created as long ago as 1894 under the Matabeleland Order in Council of that year. These were, however, only in Matabeleland and were not only on extremely poor land but were clearly totally inadequate in area. By 1902 they had increased to 20 million acres (20 per cent of the total area of Rhodesia). The rest of the land still unsold was open to purchase by anyone of any race.

However, the Morris Carter Report advocated a total change of policy. The Native Reserves were to be left as they were (by this stage 21.1 million acres). Of the remainder, 49.1 million acres were to be open to purchase by either race and 7.5 million acres were for African purchase only (a total African area with the Reserves of 29 million acres). The rest of Rhodesia comprised forest and game reserves. The European s had all the towns and the best agricultural land. For the first time the principle of racial segregation was clearly established.

Coghlan was succeeded on his death by Moffat in 1927 and the Land Apportionment Act was eventually passed in 1930, coming into effect in 1931.

It is difficult to be certain as to the motives behind the Report which was to have such profound repercussions. The white argument, then and throughout the Rhodesian saga, was that the Africans needed protection from the whites. If some allocation of this kind had not been made, it was said, the Africans would have been unable to progress because the whites would have been at their elbow buying up their land and dominating their economies. African traders would have been seen off by their white competitors. African culture would have been submerged by the immensely powerful and dominant Western influence. There was indeed much truth to this –

and some Africans welcomed the general idea of Land Apportionment. But there were a number of snags. First, the actual
division of land was not only wildly unfair in terms of the proportions given to Africans and Europeans, but Africans were
to be excluded, as far as the ownership of property was concerned, from all the main centres of Rhodesian economic life.
As with the policy of separate development in South Africa,
given the, arguable, premise that multi-racialism would not
work, there could be an argument for segregation if indeed this
was really intended. But, of course, the Africans were needed
to provide all the lower echelons of society in the white areas.
In effect, segregation discriminated against those blacks who
lived and worked in white areas.

The fact was that the white farmers bitterly resented Africans buying land in their midst. Since 1894 it had been laid
down by law that 'a native may acquire, hold, encumber and
dispose of land on the same conditions as a person who is not a
native' and this had been enshrined in the Constitution
granted in 1923 (Article 43). Very few Africans had in practice
bought farms in European areas, and at least half of those who
did had come from South Africa. But the possibility was there
and European farmers (by then nearly 25 per cent of white
income earners) were violently opposed to any African ownership of land in areas they considered to be their monopoly.

Whatever the motives behind the Land Apportionment Act
may have been – and there is no doubt that many Europeans,
including both Coghlan and Moffat, saw it primarily in terms
of safeguarding the Africans from white domination and it was
only later that the whites believed it to be their prime protection against what they saw as the black hordes – the result in
the long run was that it became the prime focus of African
Nationalist discontent.

It is interesting that this vital piece of legislation was not
opposed by Lord Passfield (Sidney Webb) who was the
Dominion Secretary in Ramsay MacDonald's Labour
Government. Certainly if blame is to be attached to Britain for
acquiescing in this radical measure – and support by the
British Government was essential – the Labour Party cannot
be absolved.

One of the results of the Land Apportionment Act was that
many Africans had to move from land they had occupied for

generations. In practice it became impossible to carry this out to the letter and although there were very many cases of individual hardship the full implementation of the Act was not completed.

In 1933 came another example of the anti-establishment drive to the political right which, except for the immediate post 1939–45 war era, was a continuing and consistent feature of white Rhodesian politics. Dr Huggins (in fact himself an establishment figure) left the Rhodesian Party and became leader of the Reform Party which had a clear and unequivocal policy of separate development, known as the policy of the Twin Pyramids. He won the election and remained in power for twenty years. At that time his party stood for the protection of the white artisan class against black competition, territorial segregation and the exclusion of 'native voters' from the common roll. He won the election with sixteen seats to the Rhodesian Party's nine and the Labour Party's five.

This was to be one of the occasions when the Rhodesian claim to have been fully self-governing since 1923 is not borne out by the facts. Britain prevented the enactment of legislation to take Africans off the common roll. But the white artisans were in practice protected by a measure known as the Industrial Conciliation Act. Huggins came under criticism from within his own party and formed a new United Party with elements of both the Rhodesian and Reform parties. He triumphed again in the election of 1934, winning twenty-four out of the thirty seats.

Huggins was to dominate Rhodesian politics as Prime Minister of the territory and then of the Federation from his advent to power in 1933 until his retirement in 1956 – a very considerable, and indeed at the time (under the Crown) unique, span of office. A man of high intelligence, considerable charm and great ability, he towered over his contemporaries in Rhodesia and was not in the least overshadowed when he attended Commonwealth Prime Ministers' Conferences.[8] Pragmatic in his approach to race relations and aware of African aspirations as they developed, his political skills were of enormous value to his country during a very difficult period. If anyone could have steered Rhodesia through the 1960s and 1970s so as to avoid confrontation (he was opposed to UDI when it came) he might have done so. It was a tragedy that there was no one of his calibre to replace him.

One of the features of political life in Rhodesia throughout its comparatively short existence was a constant desire to change its consitutional status, probably because the economic and political situation within the country and in those of its neighbours was constantly changing and because its relationship with Britain throughout remained somewhat equivocal. In the late 1920s and the 1930s pressures began to build up within both Southern and Northern Rhodesia for an amalgamation of the two territories. This was partly because of the discovery which had led to the exploitation of Northern Rhodesia's vast copper reserves. It was said that the white Southern Rhodesians wished to get their hands on this new asset and there may well be some truth in that. But there was also the very rational argument that it was folly to persist with two British territories, adjacent but totally separate, just to the north of the great Dominion of South Africa, Afrikaner led and liable to dominate its fledgling neighbours. A union of the two would produce a stronger single entity, more able to resist outside pressures.

The majority of the settlers, both in Northern and Southern Rhodesia were in favour of union of the two territories as was the Dominion Office. The Africans and the Colonial Office were against because they feared that the Southern Rhodesian policies of segregation would be extended to Northern Rhodesia. There was also the question of whether Nyasaland should be included. A Commission under Lord Bledisloe was set up by the British Secretary of State to consider the whole question of closer links between Northern and Southern Rhodesia and Nyasaland. It reported in 1939 to the effect that neither amalgamation nor the main alternative, Federation, were desirable because of the very different native policies of the countries in question. It did however favour some co-ordination of economic policy and this was to lead in 1944 to the establishment by Oliver Stanley, the Colonial Secretary, of a body known as the Central Africa Council.

The advent of war in 1939 pushed all such constitutional questions far into the background. For the second time, the white Rhodesians played a valuable part in Britain's struggle. From the European population, 8500 men and 1500 women were involved (out of a total population of 65,000), a remarkably high percentage. 693 were killed. This sacrifice by the white community on Britain's behalf (although it could well be argued that a defeat of Britain would have led to the disappearance of British Rhodesia) was to be a powerful factor in the great disillusionment with Britain when later it appeared that the mother country was deserting its 'kith and kin' in their desperate struggle with their mortal enemies. Southern Rhodesia also played a most useful part in the war under the Empire Air Training scheme whereby large numbers of airmen were trained in the country. After the conflict many of these were to return to settle. It is, however, sometimes forgotten that 14,000 Africans also took part in the war of whom 126 were killed.

As in Britain, the war brought in its train a swing to the left in Southern Rhodesia and Huggins crushed his right wing opposition, known paradoxically as the Liberal Party, in the election of 1948.

It was not long before the whole question of a closer relationship between Northern and Southern Rhodesia and Nyasaland surfaced again. There were, clearly, enormous difficulties, not least in the fact that the constitutional positions of the three territories were totally different. Southern Rhodesia was a self-governing Crown Colony. Northern Rhodesia was a British Protectorate with an unofficial majority in the Governor's Council. Nyasaland was also a British Protectorate with no electoral representation at all. However, Huggins and Roy Welensky, the leader of the white settlers in Northern Rhodesia, pushed the point hard and eventually the British Labour Government convened a Conference at official level to recommend a scheme. Amalgamation had little support within official circles in Britain but a report advocating Federation was published in 1951 and the Labour Colonial Secretary, James Griffiths, commended it to the House of Commons, although at no stage was the Labour Government formally committed to Federation.

The arguments for Federation were economic and political. Southern Rhodesia, a country of comparative affluence with great possibilities for almost boundless development, needed a larger market for its secondary producers; Northern Rhodesia's economy was almost entirely tied to copper, which had received an enormous boost from the requirements of the war, and diversification was highly desirable. The economies of these two countries, with a number of communication links including transport and power already largely integrated, were complementary. Nyasaland was poor with its economy almost entirely based on agriculture. It badly needed an economic boost. There was, therefore, an obvious economic case for close association of some kind. As in the 1930s, the political arguments in favour were based on the fear that the South African way of life, now firmly rooted in apartheid, would spread northwards, dominating Southern and perhaps even Northern Rhodesia. A strong and self-sufficient Federation would be able to resist such pressures. It was this latter argument which attracted some left wing opinion in Britain.

The counter arguments were based on the fact that racial segregation was now endemic in Southern Rhodesia and any form of union was liable to change the position of the Africans in the other two territories. The vision of a prosperous, multiracial pool of enlightenment in Central Africa with its ripples spreading far and wide was counterbalanced by the possibility of another South Africa appearing under British auspices. The whites of all three territories were in general in favour of the venture, although there was some doubt in Nyasaland and Southern Rhodesia. The blacks were in general against it – vehemently and understandably in Northern Rhodesia and Nyasaland – but there were some in Southern Rhodesia who thought that the scheme had possibilities because the percentage of whites to blacks would be greatly reduced if the two northern territories, with comparatively few whites, were joined to Southern Rhodesia.

After a series of conferences and a change of Government in 1951 in Britain, the Federation eventually came into being in September 1953. One of the two Southern Rhodesian Africans who took part in the preliminary Conference held at Lancaster House in April/May 1952 was Joshua Nkomo. In his closing speech he said that much of his worry about Federation had been dispelled but that it would be difficult to sell Federation to Southern Rhodesian Africans unless there were moves within that territory towards a real partnership between the races. He shifted his position later and came to oppose the whole concept. The vehement opposition from Northern Rhodesian and Nyasaland Africans (the latter under the leadership of Dr Hastings Banda) remained. The Labour Party, except for a small body including Gordon Walker the previous Commonwealth Secretary, voted against the Federation mainly on the grounds that the Africans opposed it.

There were five Governments concerned in the operations of the Federation – the National Assemblies[9] of the three territories each with different Constitutions, the Federal Government and the British Government, the functions of which were variously performed by the Colonial Office and the Commonwealth Relations Office later combined under the Central African Office). The Federal Government was responsible for economic policy, trade, railways, electricity, health, customs and a number of other matters including higher education; the three territorial Governments were responsible for African affairs, including African education under university level, labour, agriculture and many other matters of local importance. In the Federal Legislature there were a number of members elected or nominated to represent the Africans, at least four of whom had to be African.

Huggins took over as Prime Minister of the Federation and was succeeded as Prime Minister of Southern Rhodesia by Garfield Todd, who was to play a very controversial political role thereafter.

The Federation, which started off with such high hopes, was to founder on the rock of African opposition. Was it a mistake ever to have set it up? And, in the long run, did its creation affect the eventual outcome in Rhodesia? Certainly, one of the factors which minimised its chances of success was the choice of Salisbury as capital. A number of other towns, including Livingstone in Northern Rhodesia, had been canvassed as possibilities. Salisbury was clearly the best economic choice, being the centre of finance in the area and with the infrastructure of a capital city largely already in existence. But power and prosperity were, thereby, inexorably drawn to the South and away from the other territories who were thus confirmed in their view that they were junior partners instead of colleagues in a joint venture. It was, in retrospect, a very bad mistake. Furthermore the racial segregation which existed in Salisbury was a grave affront to the dignity of the African leaders from the other two territories. For instance, when the Nyasaland delegation passed through Salisbury on its way to

London for one of the Federation Conferences, its African members had to walk a long way to the lavatories set aside for black and coloured people rather than using the more accessible 'whites only' lavatories. Not surprisingly they arrived in London in a very touchy mood. And when the Federation was set up there were obvious difficulties about where the Africans from Nyasaland and Northern Rhodesia would live in Salisbury.

It has also been argued that the Colonial Office – responsible for affairs in Northern Rhodesia and Nyasaland – was at best half-hearted in its support of the project. The failure of the civil servants on the spot to try to sell it to the Africans in those countries led, it is said, to a generally negative reaction by those who were accustomed to accepting what their District and Provincial Commissioners told them. There is probably much truth in this.

Nevertheless, again in retrospect, it is doubtful if the Federation could have succeeded in the long run. It was a success in economic terms, although that has been overstated, and there were indeed elements of multi-racialism in its structure. It had African Junior Ministers and Africans to play a far more significant role in the Federal Civil Service than they were allowed to do in Southern Rhodesia (although there was criticism that multi-racialism did not go far enough to convince African leaders that they really had a stake in Federal success). The multi-racial University of Salisbury came into being, and the great Kariba Dam scheme was implemented – the latter again to the benefit mainly of Southern as opposed to Northern Rhodesia which had the alternative Kafue River project (implemented much later after UDI). Many whites hoped that the Federation would before long qualify for Independence: indeed this was one of the reasons why they supported it. But if the Federation was ever to become an entity which enjoyed the long-term support of its inhabitants, it was vital that the whites in Southern Rhodesia should be prepared to entrust real power to the blacks. If they were not prepared to do this later in the face of the combined pressures of nearly the whole world, can it seriously be supposed that they would have done so under a Federal structure in which they had control over African affairs in their own territory? And if the Federal Constitution had been drawn up so as to give control

30

over this, to them, vital element of life to the Federal authorities, the whites of Southern Rhodesia would never have accepted it. Constitutional arrangements, however admirable, can only consolidate and codify relationships which already exist or are ripe for development. They cannot change attitudes. It has been a recurrent feature of all British Governments, throughout the Rhodesian affair, to hope, vainly, that often abstruse Constitutional niceties will in some way paper over real and deep conflict.

But there was nothing ignoble about the aim of the British in creating and trying to sustain the Federation. It was indeed a great objective. The British did not see it as a vehicle for increasing white power over the Africans. They saw it as an attempt to bring prosperity and, eventually, multi-racialism to the whole area, an exercise in true partnership between the races. It might conceivably have worked. It was a gamble which failed.

It is doubtful, also, if the Federation in its comparatively short existence had much long-term effect on the eventual outcome in Rhodesia. The essential conflict between black and white for domination would have taken place with or without the Federation. The blacks in Rhodesia would probably have been as ham-fisted, the whites as intransigent, as they respectively turned out to be in any case. The coming tragedy arose from factors which could not be altered by new political arrantements however grandiose.

Garfield Todd was a strange mixture. He was liberal minded in many ways and genuinely hoped that the Federation would evolve in a multi-racial way. But in fact while Prime Minister he achieved little in the way of breaking down segregation which had by now become almost total in Rhodesian life and, according to Lord Home, he refused to have an African in his Cabinet. On the other hand, he was extremely tough when it came to law and order. Among other actions, for instance, he proclaimed a State of Emergency when there was a coal strike at Wankie in 1954 and called out the troops. He gained popularity in right wing circles as a result of this action although in fact the troops were not used. His general sentiments were, however, directed towards the advancement of the Africans, whom he saw as eventual equals of the Europeans, although the time scale to him was inexact and remote. He argued strongly for a common roll in the Federal Parliament and in 1956 set up a Commission under Sir Robert Tredgold, the Federal Chief Justice, to examine the franchise in the Southern Rhodesian Parliament. It recommended further liberalisation as far as the Africans were concerned. Todd supported these recommendations. There was some uneasiness in the United Rhodesia Party, which Todd led, about his general line of policy. There were also personality clashes. The outcome of all this was eventually the resignation of Todd and the succession of Sir Edgar Whitehead which was confirmed in the election of July 1958.

The ousting of Todd is often cited as evidence of a continuing white refusal to contemplate any move towards a more liberal attitude to the Africans, a precursor of the various shifts to the political right which occurred later. There is probably some truth in this, but Todd's political fall was far more concerned with the dictatorial manner in which he conducted cabinet affairs. Originally a missionary (from New Zealand), he was a brilliant speaker in public (one of the comparatively few orators in recent Rhodesian history), but he failed to consult his cabinet colleagues before announcing policies which they might have agreed to after proper discussion, but were not prepared to accept blind. Todd fought hard to retain his position – and indeed ran the country virtually single-handed for a short period – but he could not rally enough support and, after a prolonged struggle, he was defeated.

Whitehead was at that time Minister for the Federation in Washington. He was persuaded to return, partly by Huggins who, although retired, was still a father figure. Whitehead was a most unlikely politician. Very deaf and almost blind, a bachelor and shy with it, he had little appeal to the average white Rhodesian voter. Nor was he a popular figure with the Africans, who were upset about Todd's displacement and who found it difficult to relate to Whitehead's rather withdrawn intellectualism. But he was a man of high intelligence and he saw clearly the abyss which lay in front of his country if more liberal attitudes were not adopted – and quickly. As will be seen later, his eventual rejection by the whites was a tragic and indeed crucial event. This might not have occurred if he had had greater political skills.

32

The following period in Rhodesian affairs was marked by four major themes – increasing difficulties within the Federation, a genuine attempt by Whitehead to liberalise the status of the Africans, and the rise of African Nationalism which in its turn brought more restrictive measures. They were all interconnected.

Huggins (by then Lord Malvern) had resigned as Federal Prime Minister on 1 November 1956 and was succeeded by Welensky, who was to dominate the Federation until its eventual dissolution.

Like Huggins, although totally different from him in background, Welensky was a figure of very considerable stature. With a Polish Jewish father and an Afrikaner mother, he had risen to the top of the political tree by sheer force of personality (he had also been the heavy-weight boxing champion of Rhodesia!). After a tough upbringing in Salisbury (he was the thirteenth child and left school at fourteen) he became a fireman on the Rhodesia Railways where he educated himself by reading on the footplate. He became a leading trades unionist and in 1938 was elected as an unofficial member of the Northern Rhodesian Legislative Council while still a railwayman. His rise continued inexorably, culminating in his position as Prime Minister of the Federation. He was combative but compassionate, efficient yet humane, a leader to his fingertips. It was a tragedy that his very considerable energies and abilities should have been devoted to a cause which was not capable of coming to fruition. He blamed the British Government (notably Macleod and Macmillan) for what he saw as its many mistakes, evasions and deceits. But, whatever truth there may be in these accusations, the Federation could not have survived in the long run against a background of continuing white Southern Rhodesian intransigence.

There was considerable discontent in the African townships outside Salisbury when it was proposed to increase the fares which the Africans had to pay to get to work. The City Youth League, founded by James Chikerema, George Nyandoro and Edson Sithole, organised a boycott of the buses. It also called for 'One Man One Vote', thus for the first time articulating a demand for Black Rule. The less militant African National Congress was operating in Bulawayo with Nkomo as its President. These two organisations were merged in 1957 as the

33

Southern Rhodesian African National Congress (SRANC) with Nkomo as its President, Chikerema as Vice-President and Nyandoro as the Secretary General. There was considerable unrest in Nyasaland and Northern Rhodesia which spilled over into Southern Rhodesia and the security situation throughout the Federation became extremely grave. The result was the arrest of Kaunda and Banda, and in February 1959 Whitehad declared a State of Emergency, banned the SRANC and arrested no less than 500 Congress leaders, Nkomo avoiding this because he was abroad at the time.

A Commission under Lord Devlin was set up to investigate the riots in Nyasaland. Its report, published in July, did not castigate the authorities for the action they had taken in the circumstances but it talked about the existence of a 'police state' in Nyasaland. It was becoming apparent that the whole future of the Federation must be in question and Macmillan, who was shortly to make the tour of Africa in which he talked about the 'wind of change', set up a Commission under Lord Monckton to advise on the future of the Federation and to prepare for the review conference which was due in 1960. Welensky was highly suspicious of the establishment of the Commission. He was eventually persuaded to accept it with the utmost reluctance. He was vehement in his opposition to its findings.

In January 1960, a new African party – the National Democratic Party (NDP) – was founded to take the place of the banned SRANC and this was followed by even more serious riots in Salisbury, Bulawayo and elsewhere in which a number of Africans were killed. This led to even more stringent, indeed drastic, security measures including the Law and Order Maintenance Act and the Emergency Powers Act of 1960.

The Monckton Report was published in October 1960. It made a number of recommendations about the franchise, the distribution of functions between the Federal and Territorial Governments, the colour bar in Southern Rhodesia and other matters but it also – undoubtedly exceeding its terms of reference[10] – said that the British Government should declare its intention to allow secession after a stated time, if it was asked for. It was this, more than any other single act, which led to the break-up of the Federation. There was an uproar at the time, but Monckton was doing no more than bringing reality to notice. It has been argued that if the British Government had ignored the references to secession in the report and had acted on its positive recommendations the Federation might have been saved. But, by the time the report was published, African opinion was solidly against the whole concept and the undoubted improvements which Monckton had suggested could only have been temporary palliatives: they would not have satisfied the Africans who, sooner or later, would have brought about dissolution.

It was clear that something had to be done about the Constitution in Southern Rhodesia. The differences between the Constitutional structure in that territory and that of the other two territories which were also under review was too great and there was great pressure from the Southern Rhodesian Government to be rid of the reserve powers which Britain still retained. Duncan Sandys, the powerful, stern and incisive Commonwealth Secretary, convened a Conference in Salisbury attended by all the political parties in Rhodesia including the NDP representatives – Nkomo and Ndabaningi Sithole. With great skill and considerable determination, he obtained agreement. In return for surrender of most of the reserve powers held by Britain, the franchise was greatly extended, a Declaration of Rights was made which was justiciable in the courts with an appeal to the Judicial Committee of the Privy Council, and a Constitutional Council was set up which could bring instances of unfair treatment of the Africans to the notice of the Legislative Assembly. Some clauses of the Constitution were specially entrenched and could only be amended either with the approval of the British Government or if agreement was obtained in four separate referenda of the four races – British, African, Coloured and Asian. There were accusations of double-dealing when the exact form of the residual reserve powers appeared in the Bill and these were later cited as one of the reasons for the Unilateral Declaration of Independence (UDI), but the convention whereby Britain would not legislate for Southern Rhodesia on matters within the competence of the Southern Rhodesian Legislative Assembly without the agreement of the Southern Rhodesian Government was maintained, and indeed for the first time officially recognised. There were to be 65 members of the Assembly, 50 elected on an 'A' roll with comparatively high property and educational qualifications required, and 15 on a 'B' roll where the qualification was lower, thus including many more Africans. There were provisions for cross-voting between the two rolls which opened up considerable possibilities for African political influence.

Having agreed to the Constitution, Nkomo and Sithole came under heavy attack from the Nationalists within and outside Rhodesia and soon repudiated it. For diametrically opposite reasons Ian Smith, in protest, resigned from the UFP, the party of Whitehead and Welensky. A referendum among white voters was held in Southern Rhodesia and the Constitution was approved by a majority of 2 to 1.

The NDP opposition to the 1961 Constitution resulted in a wave of violence, which permeated the entire country, urban and rural. This led to the banning of the party on 10 December 1961 and, again, many African Nationalist leaders were arrested. For the second time, Nkomo happened to be abroad.

The banning of the NDP did not deter the Nationalists and almost immediately yet another party, the Zimbabwe African People's Union (ZAPU), was formed with Nkomo as President and Ndabaningi Sithole as Chairman.

The 1961 Constitution was a massive achievement. For the first time, it opened the possibility, indeed the eventual certainty, of African power. The Declaration of Rights put Rhodesia firmly in the Western tradition of tolerance, equality and respect for the individual. The Constitution opened the path towards real African political participation in the future of the country. But it had defects from the point of view of both sides. For the whites, it did not give a firm promise of independence. As far as the African Nationalists were concerned it certainly did not offer one-man-one-vote and the time scale of majority rule was inexact and comparatively remote (although the estimate of about fifteen years, made by Whitehead, came to have a general currency). Furthermore, it did not deal with the hated Land Apportionment Act which, as an existing law, was not affected by the Declaration of Rights.

Whitehead, meanwhile, had been continuing with his policy of African advancement. He vastly improved African education, albeit still on a totally different scale to that enjoyed by Europeans. He removed racial discrimination in wage awards. He opened up the higher grades of the civil service to Africans.

He did away with racial discrimination at post office counters, municipal swimming baths and in the sale of alcohol. He repealed the discriminatory Immorality Act. And above all he started the process of review and possible abolition of the Land Apportionment Act.

In 1957 Todd had set up the Plewman Commission to consider the African situation in urban areas. It proposed freehold tenure for Africans in the towns and the abolition of the pass system. Whitehead temporised on this report and set up the Quinton Commission, the second report of which in August 1960 advocated the total abolition of the Land Apportionment Act together with the opening up of the Native Reserves. The report was unanimous in spite of the fact that two of its members came from the right wing Dominion Party from which they subsequently resigned. At its Conference in 1961 Whitehead's party, the UFP, agreed that the Land Apportionment Act should be abolished.

We now come to what was, perhaps, the most crucial turning-point in the whole of recent Rhodesian history – the 1962 election. This, rather than UDI or indeed any other event, perhaps even including the 1980 election, was the decisive point in deciding whether Rhodesia was to evolve in peace or turn to civil war with all the consequences of that tragic happening.

The Africans had to decide whether, by taking part in the electoral process, they were going to make an attempt to move peacefully, albeit slowly, to eventual power within the constraints of the realities of existing white domination or whether they would turn their backs on the possibility of co-operation and move towards violence. The Europeans had to decide whether they would, by voting for Whitehead's party, allow Africans to participate on equal terms with themselves and abolish some of the more indefensible aspects of racial discrimination or whether they would turn irrevocably away from any real attempt at partnership with the Africans. In the event the African Nationalist Party (ZAPU), under Nkomo, followed the logic of their opposition to the 1961 Constitution and called for a boycott of the elections; and the election resulted in a narrow defeat of Whitehead's party in favour of the new Rhodesian Front (RF) formed from the remnants of the squabbling right wing Dominion Party, together with other whites who were worried about the current policy of liberalisation, led by Winston Field with Ian Smith as his principle lieutenant. The Rhodesian Front fought the election on the platform of leaving the Land Apportionment Act alone and slowing down the rate of African advancement. As Winston Field put it, their objective was 'to hold on to the control of affairs and not to hand over to people not trained and not versed in the arts of government'. Both parties were in favour of Independence but a Unilateral Declaration was not yet at issue.

The Rhodesian Front won 35 seats and the UFP 29 including 14 African UFP candidates elected on the 'B' roll. There was one Independent. African participation was low – 2200 out of a possible 5500 on the 'A' roll and 10,000 out of 60,000 on the 'B' roll. Whitehead subsequently claimed that if only 500 more Africans had voted on the 'B' roll he would have won because of the cross voting provisions between the 'A' and 'B' rolls.

Effectively, therefore, the African Nationalists ensured the victory of their arch enemies, turning Rhodesia away from a genuine move towards peaceful evolution and towards eventual war. Why did they do this, and did they realise what they were doing?

There were a number of factors which led to their decision to oppose the 1961 Constitution and, then, to bring about a boycott of the 1962 election. First, and probably most important, was the ferment of nationalism to the North. It seemed that Africans either had, or were shortly about to have, total control in virtually the whole of Africa north of the Zambezi. Why should they acquiesce in a slow and, they thought, very doubtful movement towards the freedom which their colleagues were achieving without great difficulty? They were, understandably, impatient. Then there was the lure of personal power. By accepting gradualism, African leaders would have ensured a subordinate role for themselves for some considerable time whereas they saw their colleagues to the North in positions of total domination. There were, of course, moderate Africans who saw the future in terms of constitutional advance but the fear of being dubbed as 'Uncle Tom' was then, as later, a formidable obstacle to partnership. The pendulum of change was swinging and it seemed that the prize

38

would come to those who waited for the swing to reach its ultimate. Furthermore, African Nationalist leaders were hoist on the petard of their own extreme statements. By its very nature a radical movement trying to excite opposition to an establishment tends to extreme rhetoric as its leaders vie with each other in devotion to the cause. There was, too, a genuine distrust of white motives, born of a million slights to African middle class dignity.

There is no reason to suppose that the Nationalist leaders did not grasp the implications of their actions. They undoubtedly understood precisely what they were doing – turning away from co-operation and towards violence. The question is whether, in the circumstances, they could have done anything else. It may have appeared at the time that they had a choice, but in the climate of Nationalism in which they moved, to accept anything short of one-man-one-vote would have been extremely difficult, if not impossible. Nkomo's initial acceptance of the 1961 Constitution was an aberration, which could not have been sustained. And once the Constitution had been repudiated, a Nationalist boycott of the consequent election was inevitable.

Nevertheless, the boycott was particularly unfortunate because African Nationalism at that stage was still a relatively coherent force (indeed the success of the ZAPU campaign against participation in the election gave evidence of its power albeit to a large extent based on violence). It had not yet split – a development which made any agreement immeasurably more difficult later.

Nkomo was the only leader who straddled the whole period of Nationalist ferment. His emergence on to the central stage of the drama stemmed from no less a personage than Sir Winston Churchill who, in 1952, asked Huggins why the Southern Rhodesians had no African representatives to attend the London Conference on the Federation. After a hurried and rather undignified scramble, Nkomo, who had been Secretary of the Railway Workers' Association and was President of the African National Congress, was nominated, together with Jasper Savanhu. It is difficult to be certain as to what the mainspring of Nkomo's political activities has been. Vastly ambitious, proud, touchy and with no deep ideological beliefs he was inordinately fond of the good things of life. On the other

39

hand he was far more intelligent than was commonly supposed, and he did have a genuine feeling for what he believed
to be the appalling indignities his people were suffering and
was able to appeal to African emotions in terms which they
could understand and to which they reacted easily. Shrewd,
tough and endowed with the stuff of charismatic leadership,
for many years he was the one figure with a national as
opposed to a sectional following. He was prepared to undergo
long periods of detention with no apparent light on the
horizon. But he made many mistakes and he appeared to be
indecisive. He always seemed to be in the wrong place –
abroad when he should have been in Rhodesia, and vice versa.
And, as will be seen, he eventually lost his national support,
having to content himself with a largely Ndebele following.

A further factor in the Nationalist attitudes at the time, and
one which was to grow in importance until it eventually
became almost predominant, was the international dimension. As far as Britain was concerned, the Labour Party had
opposed the 1961 Constitution and many of its members had
close associations with the African Nationalist leaders.
Without responsibility from 1951 to 1964 it was inevitable that
Labour sentiments would veer to the left, above all in the colonial field where the issues were apparently simple as seen
from Britain. If the Labour Party had been in power there is
little reason to doubt that it would have been gratified by the
achievement of the 1961 Constitution: in opposition it called
the agreement a 'sell out'. To say this is not to attack the
Labour Party in particular. The imperatives of opposition in
our system of adversary politics leads to such anomalies whatever party is in office. However, just as, later, the Labour
Party in power was to attack the Conservative Opposition for
adding to the intransigence of Smith, so the Labour Party's opposition to the 1961 Constitution must have had some effect on
the overall African Nationalist decision not to go along with
the constitutional settlement.

The United Nations, too, began to play a role in fanning the
flames of intransigence, flames which were eventually to
consume so many people, black and white.

The whites were, therefore, confronted by a situation in
which, as they saw it, their Government was moving fast
towards emancipation of the Africans in virtually every field.

This had, however, only led to increased discontent, violence and a refusal to compromise in any way or, indeed, even to take part in the constitutional process. The Federation was clearly on its way to collapse and Britain was dragging her feet on the question of independence. In retrospect it was likely that the new Rhodesian Front, led by the sensible and down-to-earth Winston Field – far from being a wild man of the right – would defeat the UFP under the rather remote figure of Whitehead, who added fuel to the fire by making some very forthcoming remarks about African advancement in a widely reported speech at the United Nations. In retrospect the only surprise was that the Rhodesian Front did not receive a greater majority and that, if the Africans had participated on even a comparatively modest scale, Whitehead would have won.

In 1962, the two curves on the graph – African Nationalist demands and the voluntary white movement towards liberalisation – came as close as they were ever to come. For probably inevitable reasons, given the circumstances in Rhodesia and abroad, they did not meet. The die was cast.

In June 1962 Nkomo went to the United Nations and succeeded in having a resolution passed in the General Assembly demanding a new Constitution after a Conference in which all races would take part. His return in July 1962 was followed by yet more violence and more repression, including the banning of ZAPU in September 1962. The circle was indeed vicious.

Meanwhile the Federation moved to its end. In May 1962, Macmillan, wearying of the conflict between the Commonwealth Relations and the Colonial Offices, each of which had separate responsibilities towards the constituent parts of the Federation, appointed Rab Butler – that enigmatic but immensely able figure – as Minister in Charge of Central Africa; and in July 1962 Duncan Sandys was given charge of both Colonial and Commonwealth Offices. In December 1962 it was announced that Nyasaland would be permitted to secede. This was followed, in March 1963, by a similar statement with regard to Northern Rhodesia. It was announced that there was to be a Conference at Victoria Falls to divide up the assets.

By now it had become a prime objective of virtually the entire white electorate in Rhodesia to obtain independence and Winston Field saw it as his first and primary task to give effect to this wish. Playing the only card he had, he said that he

41

would not attend the Conference unless he had a prior commitment to independence. But the British Government was not prepared to agree unless there were amendments to the 1961 Constitution, which would give Africans considerably more political power, and sufficient safeguards were secured to ensure that its provisions were not tampered with. The reasons for this stand were summed up by Lord Home, the then Foreign Secretary, in his memoirs – 'Ought the British Government to have faced the Governments of Northern Rhodesia and Nysasaland with the independence of all three parts (of the Federation) or none? It would have been possible, and perhaps in terms of real politics we could have done so with a reasonably clear conscience but hitherto, when handing over power to another Government, we had always done so to a majority; and if there was to be an exception and we were to pass the authority to a minority, we felt that we must take scrupulous care to ensure that the majority would be helped along the road of shared political authority, and eventually of majority rule.'[11]

One of the factors behind the decision taken was undoubtedly the likely Commonwealth reaction had independence been granted. One must remember that in the early 1960s Britain was still in the throes of the conversion of Empire into Commonwealth. This was seen as a great, indeed a unique, experiment in the creation of a viable and multi-racial entity girding the world which would retain, without bitterness, some of the unity which had been imposed by the Imperial power. The transition had already been successfully achieved in much of the erstwhile Empire. Africa was the most important remaining element in the jigsaw. Deliberately to jeopardise the entire structure because of some 200,000 whites in Rhodesia who seemed to be intent on refusing equality to four million or so blacks, must have seemed like an insane gamble. There was also, as there always is, a domestic dimension. The Conservative Government had been in power for twelve or so years. If it was to be re-elected, retention of the middle ground was important. By moving into the territory of the extreme right in British politics, not only would much informed opinion have been thrown straight into the arms of the Labour Party but the loyalty of the left wing of the Conservative Party would have been strained to breaking point, In any case, to grant independence to Rhodesia under the 1961 Constitution without any further ado would have been against the better judgement of Conservative leaders, notably Macmillan, whose perceptions were, as always, based on the longterm sweep of history, not the immediate pressures of the moment.

But how, without giving away what could not be given, to get Winston Field – and Welensky whose presence depended on him – to the Conference which was necessary if the Federation was to be wound up without appalling difficulty? That was the problem. Butler was the man for this. Without apparently actually giving any promise, either in writing or verbally, he persuaded Winston Field to attend and kept him at the Conference in spite of a near-breakdown during its course. The Rhodesian Front subsequently claimed that promises of independence had been given, and indeed one of the justifications of UDI was that the British had acted with perfidy. This has been denied by Butler and, indeed, it seems most unlikely that any such promise would have been given. In any event the Conference was successful and Southern Rhodesia obtained most of what it asked for, including virtually the whole of the Federal armed services, except for the only thing it really wanted – a clear promise of independence. The Federation was dissolved on 31 December 1963.

Before this happened, however, African Nationalist activities in Rhodesia had disintegrated into bitter personal dispute and violence. Winston Field had let many of the Nationalist leaders out of restriction and the executive of the still banned ZAPU was set up in Tanzania. When Nkomo returned to Rhodesia in June 1963 an attempt was made in Tanzania to mount a coup against his leadership. He sent off a telegram sacking Ndabaningi Sithole and Robert Mugabe. In August Sithole formed the rival Zimbabwe African National Union (ZANU). The result was a level of violence in Rhodesia which probably exceeded anything yet seen. Arson and murder became commonplace as the rival parties fought each other. Appalling atrocities were committed and intimidation became widespread in the African areas. The two parties which were to dominate the Nationalist scene in one form or another until 1980 became bitter enemies. The split was not at this stage due to tribal rivalries (although these did exist). The division arose from personality differences and from frustration with

Nkomo's leadership. In the long run this conflict was to preclude Nkomo from power and to make any negotiated settlement vastly more difficult.

In an attempt to revive his fortunes Nkomo formed the People's Caretaker Council (PCC) to take the place of the, banned, ZAPU. But the security situation was such that in 1964 there was a further complete clamp down, and law and order was restored, greatly to the relief of most Rhodesian Africans whose lives had been made a misery. It was to be many years before memories of the chaos and violence which gripped African (not European) areas was to subside. Most ordinary Africans were opposed to Nationalism in the ensuing period because they associated it purely with communal violence and murder. This explained the comparative ease with which the Rhodesian Government was able to deal with Nationalist incursions in the early stages of the war which was to come.

As a result of all this the white backlash was exacerbated still further and the pressure for independence became ever more insistent. It was this issue which was to dominate affairs in Rhodesia until the final break in November 1965.

The history of the tangled negotiations which led to the Unilateral Declaration of Independence (UDI), first with Sir Alec Douglas-Home's Conservative and then with Harold Wilson's Labour Governments have been described in minute detail in White Papers and the memoirs of those who took part. There were three main elements which were to remain constant throughout. First, the British Government would not agree to independence unless there was some movement on the franchise and guarantees that the Constitution would not be tampered with after independence. Secondly, the white Rhodesians were opposed to any effective fetters on their actions after independence. And, lastly, before granting independence the British Government insisted that it should have proof to the effect that the proposed Constitution was acceptable to the people of Rhodesia as a whole. This latter point was put forward by Smith, after he had ousted Winston Field, in discussion with Douglas-Home in an attempt to get round the difficulties. However, his proposed method of measuring African opinion, a gathering (Indaba) of chiefs was not acceptable to the British Government, and this was made absolutely clear.

44

Although the implications were not widely understood at the time, the replacement of Field by Smith in April 1964 was a major turning-point in Rhodesian history. Although the leader of a party (the RF) which drew its support from the right of the political spectrum, Field was essentially a moderate. He had good personal relations with Africans inside and outside his country (notably with Dr Banda). He had called for an appreciation of the likely results of UDI from all his Government departments. With one exception they had said that this course would lead to disaster. Very much an establishment figure himself, he would in any case have reacted against unconstitutional action and this confirmed and strengthened his opposition to any such move. But there were powerful figures within his Government, notably Clifford Dupont, Lord Graham, Desmond Lardner-Burke and Smith himself who were already – even at that stage – determined to go ahead with UDI, come what might, and they brought about Field's replacement by Smith. The question thereafter was not whether UDI would take place, but when and in what circumstances. Unlike Todd, Field did not fight his corner. Had he done so, it is just possible, although unlikely, that he might have been able to stave off defeat. But he was too much of a gentleman to do so, perhaps a sad commentary on the realities of politics.

In October 1964 Welensky attempted a come back in a by-election as leader of a new Rhodesia Party on the platform of opposition to UDI. He was defeated after Smith had, with great tactical skill, cut the ground from under his feet by saying in London that 'a unilateral declaration of independence we have thrown out of the window for the time being.' This was to be the end of any effective liberal opposition in Rhodesia.

The change of Government in Britain in the 1964 election led to no change in the situation of deadlock. Negotiations between the two Governments were conducted on the basis of five principles which had been evolved by Wilson and Arthur Bottomley, the Commonwealth Secretary. They were as follows:

1. The principle and intention of unimpeded progress to majority rule, already enshrined in the 1961 Consti-

tution, would have to be maintained and guaranteed.
2. There would also have to be guarantees against retrogressive amendment of the Constitution.
3. There would have to be immediate improvement in the political status of the African population.
4. There would have to be progress towards ending racial discrimination.
5. The British Government would need to be satisfied that any basic proposed for independence was acceptable to the people of Rhodesia as a whole.

A sixth principle was added by Wilson in 1966 –

6. The need to ensure that, regardless of race, there is no oppression of the majority by the minority or of the minority by the majority.

All six principles were eventually accepted by the Conservative party. Indeed the first five did represent the general lines of policy on which the previous Government had been operating. The sixth principle was accepted later, although it was not a feature of the 1971 negotiations.

In spite of repeated declarations by the British Government to the effect that an Indaba of African chiefs would not satisfy the fifth principle – including a message from Duncan Sandys actually on the day of the election (15 October) – Smith held his Indaba which resulted in a unanimous 'Yes' to independence under the 1961 Constitution and a white referendum produced the same result by 58,000 to 7000 votes.

Wilson had written to a Dr Mutasa during the election campaign stating that 'The Labour Party is totally opposed to granting independence to Southern Rhodesia so long as the Government of that country remains under the control of the white minority'. This was a vast hostage to fortune and, although in practice Wilson departed totally from this commitment, the existence of the letter, which was never formally repudiated, was to be a continuing strain in the relationship between Smith and Wilson.

At a General Election in May 1965 Smith's Party won all fifty white seats. Although UDI was not a direct issue during the campaign it soon became clear that this was a very real possibility. Negotiations became ever more frantic. Wilson flew to Salisbury on 25 October in a last attempt to avert a break. A number of ideas were floated in order to do this, including a Treaty guaranteeing the five principles, a Commonwealth Mission to be headed by Robert Menzies – the Australian Prime Minister, a referendum in Rhodesia, a Royal Commission and a further meeting between Smith and Wilson in Malta. But after a last minute telephone call by Wilson to Smith, UDI was declared on 11 November 1965.

What were the reasons for UDI and could the British Government have averted it? Not long after the event the writer asked six Rhodesian Cabinet Ministers why this action had been taken. A different answer was given in every case. There was a variety of explanations – resolution of the uncertainty which was affecting not only the people of the country but foreign investment, fear of Britain forcing further and unwanted moves to majority rule, exasperation with British double-dealing, the example of chaos to the north (notably the flood of refugees from the Congo in 1962) and a genuine belief that independence under the 1961 Constitution had been promised. In fact many Rhodesian fears were largely a figment of their own imaginations. There was never any question of changes to the 1961 Constitution if Rhodesia wished to continue as she was. The real issue was independence, not British interference with their existing way of life – although RF propaganda was successful in persuading the bulk of white Rhodesian opinion that the British were determined to meddle in their affairs.

The true explanation of UDI was that independence became a test of virility for the majority of the whites in Rhodesia. The fact that Zambia and Malawi, in particular, had obtained their independence and that, unless they were prepared to agree to conditions which to them were impossible, the Rhodesians were to be refused similar treatment, was an insufferable affront to their dignity. Their country had a far higher standard of living for both blacks and whites than did either Zambia or Malawi. They had an extremely efficient and incorruptible civil service and a buoyant economy. As they saw it, apart from a few agitators, their Africans were content, living under a civilised and civilising Government which understood and did its best to cater for the needs of Rhodesian society. They believed that Britain, already after Suez on the wane as a world power, did not begin to appreciate the true situation. 'Free us from the shackles of Britain,' they said, 'and we will really take off. Just leave us alone and we will deal with our own problems in our own way. As long as Britain has the responsibility, world interest will continue to focus on us with the Commonwealth, the OAU, the United Nations and every other ignorant busy-body meddling in our affairs and exciting our Africans to ever greater violence and bitterness.'

This feeling of constraint and imposed restrictions on their freedom of action was widespread. The old-time settlers were proud of their great achievements and failed to see why Britain should have any control whatsoever on their actions. Many of the post-war immigrants had come to Rhodesia precisely to escape from what they believed to be the restrictions of a dull and drab Socialist post-war Britain where opportunities for advancement were meagre and unexciting: they were determined to retain their high standard of living which they saw threatened. There was a genuine grass roots obsession with the idea of independence. There were of course those who saw UDI in a different light, in particular the businessmen and intellectuals in Salisbury. Many people were extremely unhappy about the legal aspects of what was contemplated and Major General Anderson, who commanded the armed services, was retired, thus averting possible revolt. A genuine affection for the Queen was widespread; there was great reluctance to be disloyal to her and this was an additional and very considerable hurdle to be overcome. To deal as far as possible with this difficulty the Declaration of Independence ended with the words 'God Save the Queen'.

But given all these circumstances it was virtually inevitable that a Unilateral Declaration would have been made sooner or later unless Britain was prepared to grant independence herself. Smith was merely the vehicle through which it came. Given that he, too, shared these feelings – and if he had not he would never have been the Rhodesian leader – he played his hand with great skill. His timing was masterly. He allowed the movement for independence to grow until it became irresistible. If he had made his declaration much earlier, there would have been far more internal dissention than there actually was. He secured his flanks with South Africa and Portugal and prepared the country psychologically for the great step. His tactical skills helped greatly in the process, but the strategic decision stemmed from the circumstances of the time – not as a result of one man's determination. Indeed if Smith had refused to go ahead with UDI he would have been replaced by someone else who was prepared to take the plunge, precisely as had happened when he himself replaced Field.

As far as Britain was concerned it would have been totally impossible for Wilson to grant independence on terms less stringent than those proposed by the previous Conservative Government. It is often argued – and indeed the Conservative Party in opposition did argue this – that Wilson's personal handling of the Rhodesians was brusque and tactless, and Bottomley, the Commonwealth Secretary, was certainly not noted for his diplomatic skills. There is much truth in this, and certainly Douglas-Home did appear to the Rhodesians in a far more sympathetic light than did Wilson. But there was no real difference in policy between the two Governments. The same factors would have been at work on the Rhodesian minds with a Conservative as with a Labour Government in Britain. The conflict really was inescapable without a climb down by one side or the other and it is difficult to see how this could have been done by either. Wilson's statements, and those of Bottomley, before UDI to the effect that Britain would not use force must have had some effect on the appreciation of the possible repercussions of UDI made in Salisbury. But even without these unwise remarks, feelings in Rhodesia were so strong that their Government would have had eventually to go ahead trusting that the difficulties, political and logistic, of intervention would inhibit a descent from the skies by their British 'kith and kin'.

However one looks at it, one is drawn to the conclusion that UDI came as the inevitable result of the past histories of Rhodesia and Britain. Given the situation in which Rhodesia and Britain found themselves in 1964 and 1965, different personalities and differences of emphasis during the negotiations might have altered the timing but the eventual dénouement could not have been avoided by either side.

To say this is not of course to argue that UDI was anything but a tragic miscalculation leading eventually to great misery and totally failing to secure its main objective – the avoidance of majority rule. It was not a rational decision, but human

49

beings are in the main governed by the heart and not the head: it is emotion not reason which in the end decides the course of history.

CHAPTER THREE

Reactions to UDI, 1965–70

The immediate impact of UDI was to shift the centre of the storm from Rhodesia to Britain. There was surprisingly little unrest in Rhodesia, The Smith Government was dismissed by Sir Humphrey Gibbs, the Governor, but this could only be in the nature of a gesture. For his part Smith appointed Clifford Dupont in Gibbs' place with the clumsy title of 'Officer Administering the Government',[12] and told Gibbs to leave Government House. Gibbs refused to quit. In spite of some petty measures taken against him, such as cutting off his telephone, Gibbs stuck to his guns and remained in Government House. He was a valiant and steadfast figure who refused to compromise in any way until the result of the Referendum on Republican Status in 1969 (81 per cent in favour) led to his resignation. He was a focus of loyalty for those who refused to accept UDI, but there were not very many who took that view. Sir Hugh Beadle, the Chief Justice, who had been much involved in the hectic negotiations just before UDI, stayed with him for a time, living in Government House, and indeed accompanied him to the negotiations on HMS *Tiger*, but he too eventually left as a result of his decision to ignore the Queen's reprieve of convicted murderers in March 1968. The acute conflict of loyalty for Government servants of all kinds which might have arisen was averted because Wilson, in statements in the House of Commons on 11 and 12 November 1965, told them to remain at their posts.[13] Although there were, doubtless, arguments to the effect that they should have all been instructed to resign, not only would this have been difficult to reconcile with the theoretical position which was that the Governor was still governing and that, having dismissed

Smith and his entire Government, all authority rested on his person to whom public servants owed their allegiance, but no one wished Rhodesia to degenerate into chaos: at the time it was thought that other measures would soon bring the recalcitrant Rhodesians to heel. In fact Smith was in firm control of his country. The Rhodesian Front Government had taken its decision and was most unlikely to change it, at least for some considerable time, unless it was forced to do so. With their leaders either in restriction or abroad, the Africans in Rhodesia were largely without a voice. It would be wrong, however, to disregard the psychological impact which UDI had on African minds, particularly among many of the more educated, who began to see clearly that they were on their own and that they would not achieve their freedom (as they saw it) without a very considerable effort including, perhaps, violence.

It was in Britain that the next moves were to be made. What, therefore, was the attitude of the British people to Rhodesia and, on a larger scale, towards the whole continent of Africa?

During the 1960s and 1970s affairs in Africa struck a deep chord in the British political consciousness. The population of the whole continent including North Africa was only half that of India, and Africa south of the Sahara was not an area of primary importance in the world scene. Black Africa was largely ignored by the United States, and African affairs were at that time not of any great interest to the Russians or to the Chinese when compared to other areas of potential or real conflict. Developments in Europe, the whole question of East/West relations, the Middle East, the relationship between the United States and Europe, Vietnam and its consequences, the implications of the rise of China, the conundrum of Japan – these were the red meat of foreign relations at the time. But Africa retained a capacity for arousing passions among the politically conscious in Britain to an extent which few, if any, of those other, far more important areas did. Even the war in the Middle East, with all the implications this had for the many Jews or Zionist sympathisers in Britain, did not touch the raw nerve of British political controversy quite so directly as did the problem of Rhodesia.

Part of the reason for this sensitivity lay, of course, in the fact that Britain still had a direct responsibility in Rhodesia. The love-affair with India, for instance with all its triumphs and agonies, faded surprisingly quickly once responsibility had passed. A certain nostalgia, confined almost entirely to the elderly, remained. But the romance, that over-powering sense of almost mystic affinity between two totally different races chronicled by Kipling, vanished without trace; and with it interest and political passion faded too. Britain never achieved a romantic relationship with Africa in the same sense as it did with India, partly because of the lack of any indigenous culture remotely comparable to that in India. There was a romance about the religious and cultures of the East to which Europeans, nurtured in an increasingly utilitarian age, were easily drawn. The witch doctor on the other hand was not a romantic figure. Colonialism in the East was a temporary phenomenon, an attempt to superimpose alien values on to existing cultures of ancient, although often cruel, sophistication. The East had a self-confidence which Africa lacked. Africa, indeed, had a pre-colonial heritage on which to build, but it lacked depth. And, furthermore, what Africa did possess – a structured tribal society – was anathema to many of the new African generation of Western orientated politicians and businessmen. The task of creating an African identity was, therefore, that much more difficult.

But in spite of all this, British interest in African affairs remained very considerable. The young politically conscious Briton felt deeply about what he considered to be injustice in Africa while largely ignoring similar injustices elsewhere. And this feeling was not confined to the young. There was guilt by association of colour – white with white – which was ripe for expiation by those in search of a cause, and there were many such in our society of comparative affluence.

As a nation we were still obsessed with the aftermath of Empire. The ubiquitous red splodges on the map may have gone but illusions of omnipotence remained, not least among those to whom the Empire was anathema. In Africa there was still some responsibility to which those on all sides of the political spectrum, who yearned for vanished power, could cling. The struggle between black and white in Africa became a symbol of other different conflicts in Britain which were often difficult to define and articulate because of the complexities and cross-currents which blurred the edges of controversy. The very remoteness of the reality of the Southern African dilemma from the experience of people in Britain brought a sharp and often distorted simplicity to problems which were in fact far from simple. Controversy thrives on caricature. There is a need for sharp definition for political passion to thrive, and the emotive spectacle of discrimination based on colour lent urgency to feelings of injustice which sometimes had their roots in other less obvious soil. Similarly the vision, equally simplistic and perhaps more distorted, of white civilisation, ordered and benevolent, at bay in the presence of black anarchy, predictable only in its corruption and personal self-seeking, had overtones of great emotional appeal to those who took a different view of the world and of Britain's place in it.

But until 1965 controversy over Rhodesia was largely conducted at an elitist level – the politically aware, the academic world, the civil service, the intellectual establishment and areas of the media. If the man in the street had been asked what he thought of the Federation, for instance, the answer would at best have been very hazy. It was at that time of UDI that the Rhodesian problem really began to make an impact on British politics at grass roots level. This was partly because Smith himself had made a remarkable public impact in television broadcasts when he was in Britain. But the primary reason for public interest was that Wilson had brought an air of great drama into the whole affair – and this was to continue. A last minute flight to Salisbury followed by a twelfth hour telephone call, dramatic appearances in the House of Commons and so on – this was all great news copy and there can have been few people in Britain who had not at least heard of the country and knew something, however inaccurate, about the issues at stake.

But what was to be done about Rhodesia now that UDI had actually happened? Although the Government's majority over all other parties was very small, its Parliamentary position on Rhodesia was reasonably secure because the nine Liberals under Jeremy Thorpe were if anything more radical in their general approach to Rhodesian affairs than was the Labour Party. As noted, the option of military intervention had been discarded already. There would have been two possibilities – a conventional invasion from Zambia or a quick descent from the skies on Salisbury Airport by a very small force – perhaps a company – in order to rally loyalist opinion. Both options were fraught with appalling dangers and difficulties. The logistic problems of a conventional invasion would have been very considerable: indeed this might well have been virtually impossible for Britain to achieve on her own. But even if it had been feasible to transport the mass of equipment of all kinds necessary for military action of this kind to Zambia without passing through Rhodesia, it would have taken considerable time and would have been seen as a highly provocative act at a time when the general view was that the ultimate step of UDI would not be taken. Indeed a move of this kind might well have precipitated UDI earlier than it in fact occurred, followed by Rhodesian military action against Lusaka Airfield. From the logistic point of view the introduction of a small-scale military presence into Salisbury immediately following UDI would have been much easier. But the gamble would have been enormous. There would have been no question of a military victory: if the Rhodesian Armed Forces had resisted, the British would have either had to surrender or be annihilated. The action would have been a political gesture, not a military operation. But it might have succeeded. It is possible that the Rhodesians would not have been prepared actually to shoot at British troops in these circumstances, that Government servants of all kinds would have rallied to the Governor and that Britain might have been able to establish control of the country. Alternatively, the result might have been a kind of stalemate with the British force isolated and ignored by the Rhodesian authorities – perhaps the most embarrassing of all outcomes.

But there were, of course, other considerations. Would the British Armed Services have been prepared to undertake such a mission at all? Many of them had friends or relations actually living in Rhodesia. The Curragh mutiny had left its mark and there were doubts at the highest level as to whether the British army would be prepared to launch an attack against an apparently peaceful Rhodesia. Furthermore, even if this hurdle could have been surmounted, there is no doubt that the Conservative Party in opposition would have been bitterly opposed to military operations in these circumstances. The nation would have been torn apart. It was clear that another

General Election was in the offing – Wilson could not have continued indefinitely with an overall majority at times of only one seat – and an invasion of Rhodesia would certainly have been a vote loser.

Lastly, whatever the rights and wrongs might have been, the Labour Government of the time was not psychologically attuned to the use of military force. It had been Conservative Governments which had taken the military actions in Suez, Jordan, Kenya, Uganda and Tanganyika. When Bevin was at the Foreign Office attitudes were more robust: the Berlin Airlift and the action in Palestine demonstrated the readiness of that Labour Government in the last resort to use the Services in pursuit of political objectives. It is difficult to imagine Wilson's Labour Government, which came to office in 1964, having the same firmness of purpose. There were indeed pacifist elements in the Labour Party in 1965. But these pacifist inclinations would not, in the main, have extended to opposing action against what they conceived to be right wing Fascist traitors. The crucial point was that Wilson seemed to believe that there was no problem which he could not solve, at least in the short term, by personal negotiation and this attitude was to persist later as he tried to reconcile the irreconcilable by dramatic personal intervention. It is possible, also, that he was still mesmerised by the aura of Macmillan, who had appeared to move effortlessly from success to success in foreign affairs. Relatively inexperienced himself in these matters, Wilson may not have appreciated that Macmillan had chosen issues in which to become personally involved with great care. Field-Marshal Lord Montgomery's maxim that the first rule of war was – 'Don't march on Moscow', meaning that it was a great mistake to become involved in impossible ventures, had, and has, much to commend it. Wilson's total personal involvement was a mistake.

To the Africans, Britain's failure to intervene confirmed their worst fears about the British attitude to its kith and kin in Rhodesia. They asserted that if a rebellion had taken place in any other British Colony where those who had rebelled were black, not white, the British would have intervened immediately. They simply refused to believe that Britain's failure to take military action was due to anything but a basic support by white Britain for her white colleagues in Rhodesia. When it came to the crunch, they believed, Britain was as racialist as were the Rhodesian settlers. The fact that the situation in Rhodesia was totally different from all other British Colonies because, uniquely, in that country Britain had no physical power of any kind, was ignored or treated as a euphemistic excuse for palpable connivance in racialism.

But, whether or not military force was a realistic option, why did Wilson and Bottomley announce well before UDI that there was no question of military action? It is true that there were persuasive arguments in favour of this announcement. One of the reasons for African dissidence within Rhodesia was that many Africans thought that Britain would be able to intervene and that by creating disturbances they would bring such pressure on Britain that she would be forced to do so. The decision not to use military force having been taken, it was argued, it was only right to make the situation clear so that the African population would not erupt, vainly hoping for immediate military intervention. There was also the domestic situation in Britain. A prior announcement that the military option was not in question would pre-empt left wing pressures for such action were UDI to take place.

In retrospect, however, the announcement was a mistake. It undoubtedly made the decision to take UDI much easier for the Smith Government, and the averting of UDI should have had priority over everything else.

When UDI came in November 1965 there was a sense of shock in political circles in Britain. The Conservative Party was aghast at the apparent near insanity of the Rhodesian action and apprehensive as to the potentially divisive consequences to its cohesion – an apprehension which was only too soon to be realised. The Labour Party was outraged and personal failure added some venom to Wilson's immediate reactions. The alternative to the use of force was clearly economic sanctions of one kind or another: it was inconceivable that Britain could possibly take no action of any kind. Indeed both Sandys, when Commonwealth Secretary, and Wilson had sent messages to Smith making it clear that UDI would be a very serious step leading to a strong British reaction. The immediate question was the extent to which sanctions should be imposed and to what ends they should be directed. One thing

57

is certain. Neither the Commonwealth Office nor Labour leaders nor indeed many Conservative politicians had grasped the depth of feeling in Rhodesia which had led to the Declaration. The result was that Goliath thought he could crush David with little difficulty and did not even reach for the largest bludgeon in his armoury. The original sanctions announced by Wilson on 12 November 1965 were paltry – the suspension of Commonwealth preference in trade, the removal of Rhodesia from the sterling area, the application of special exchange control restrictions and a ban on further purchase by Britain of Rhodesian sugar and tobacco.

There were two dilemmas for the British Government. First, economic sanctions could only have any hope of effectiveness if they were universal and this meant recourse to the United Nations. But it must follow from this that the problem would, to a greater or lesser extent, be taken out of the hands of Britain which had hitherto insisted that the Rhodesian affair was exclusively a British responsibility and that the United Nations had no standing in the matter. Furthermore, if sanctions were to be binding on member states, it was vital that they should be mandatory, and mandatory sanctions could only be imposed under the United Nations Charter (Chapter 7) if the Security Council decided that a 'threat to the peace' existed. But clearly the threat to the peace, if there was one, did not come from Rhodesia. The contortions which were gone through when eventually the Security Council did decide (in April 1966) that a threat to the peace existed[14] were well exposed by Reginald Maudling (the Conservative Shadow Commonwealth Secretary) when he said in debate – 'Another thing which troubles us very much is that there is no limit to the precedent of declaring this situation to be a threat to the peace. There is no threat to the peace whatever from Southern Rhodesia. There is no danger whatever of the people of Southern Rhodesia creating a threat to the peace. Other people say that so offensive to them is this regime that fighting may break out. But it is a very new concept that nations may say that because they so dislike what is going on in another country they can declare that there is a threat to the peace although it comes from themselves.' (Hansard, 27 April 1966, column 721).

Maudling's logic was impeccable. But it had no substance

in legal terms. The position was that if the Security Council declared that a certain situation constituted 'a threat to the peace', it did indeed do so and that was that. The law may have been a ass, but that was the law nonetheless. Wilson's embarrassment on this point had already become apparent when he was asked on 23 November 1965 whether the United Nations resolution calling for an economic embargo on Rhodesia was under Chapter 6 of the United Nations Charter, which was not mandatory and did not require the establishment of a threat to the peace, or under Chapter 7, which did. He replied that the resolution might well be interpreted 'as something between Chapter 6 and Chapter 7'.

Secondly, Wilson's original aim was undoubtedly to preserve what had in the main become an all-party approach to the problem. If he hoped for a quick surrender by Smith and his cabinet, and all the signs were that he did, political unity in Britain was an essential element of the background. Once Smith began to feel that he had extensive support on the Conservative benches, or indeed that the British Parliament was substantially divided on the issue, the temptation to persist would be irresistible. In order to preserve this all-party approach it was necessary not to go too far with what were certain to be considered punitive measures. Indeed in a revealing passage in his speech to the House on 11 November 1965 Wilson said – '*Our purpose is not punitive* [author's italics] ... our purpose is to restore a situation in Rhodesia in which there can be untrammelled loyalty and allegiance to the Crown and in which there can be, within whatever rules the House lays down, a free Government of Rhodesia acting in the interests of the people as a whole.' A certain restraint was important if he was to enable Heath to maintain his essential support of the Government without totally splitting his party. But the more restrained the sanctions were, the less effective they would be. The Parliamentary situation and the realities of the situation on the ground, therefore, were inevitably pulling in different directions.

The Conservative Party had problems of even greater magnitude. The fact was that it was hopelessly split. The two-party system does have, arguable, advantages in providing a ready-made alternative Government, thus helping to keep opposition to the existing Administration within the confines of a generally agreed constitutional framework. But it also means that each party has to straddle a very wide spectrum of national opinion. The electorate dislikes disunity in political parties, as the Labour Party had found to its cost in the Fifties (and as indeed it has found more recently). Blandly ignoring the paradox, voters wish their politicians to be at once honest, forthright and immune to the blandishments of the whips, but also to be capable of preserving the image of a united party. The views about Rhodesia of Nigel Fisher and Patrick Wall, for instance, were almost diametrically opposite, yet both were leading Conservative Parliamentary figures in the context of colonial affairs. Indeed one of the constant, and less admirable, features of Conservative Party attitudes towards Rhodesia has been an apparently compulsive opposition to anything advocated by the left wing of the party by those on the right and vice versa, almost regardless of the actual issues at stake. The Labour Party, in contrast, except for the maverick Reginald Paget, was united in its general approach of total opposition to Smith and to everything which it thought he stood for.

Edward Heath, recently elected in place of Douglas-Home, still had to win his political spurs as leader. Rhodesia was his first real test in this capacity. There was no question of persuading either the right or left wings of the Conservative Party to change their essentially divergent views of the situation: the only question was whether the division could be papered over, and this would be impossible if the issue was pushed to the point of overt decision by the escalation of sanctions.

In the event, the pressures from the Labour Party to extend sanctions quickly became irresistible. On 1 December 1965 Wilson announced a series of further economic measures against Rhodesia. Embargoes were placed on a large number of Rhodesian exports which, together with the already banned tobacco and sugar, amounted in total to over 95 per cent of Rhodesia's exports to Britain. A stop was placed on nearly all payments by UK residents to Rhodesia. It was originally intended to prevent even the paying of pensions to qualified residents in Rhodesia, but this decision was reversed after Conservative pressure.

The crunch was to come on the question of oil sanctions, which quickly attained a symbolic connotation. Oil was seen as the life blood of the Europeans in Rhodesia. Was Britain to attempt to cut it off in furtherance of her aims for that country or was she not? The question had arisen at an early stage. On 11 November, Wilson had said – 'Mr Heath asked about oil supplies. We have no proposals to make on this subject.' However on 23 November, Wilson slightly shifted his position. He said – 'The oil embargo is bristling with difficulties if it is going to be effective ... these matters will have to be very carefully studied and while we must insist that whatever sanctions are applied must be effective, we do not want those which are damaging and ineffective.' Then, on the evening of Friday, 17 December 1965, oil sanctions were imposed. Two orders were made: one banned the import of oil products into Rhodesia, and the other prohibited British nationals from supplying or carrying oil and oil products for Rhodesian use.

Without the support of a mandatory resolution of the United Nations, which all member states would be legally obliged to implement, and with the certainty that South Africa and Portugal would help Rhodesia to circumvent oil sanctions, this was in practice a virtually meaningless gesture in spite of the fact that the United States and some other countries had by that time agreed to join in the embargo. But gestures are important in national and international politics and Wilson clearly felt that he had to defer to the pressures on him. However, by imposing oil sanctions, the Labour Government made certain that the precarious political consensus in Britain was doomed, without in fact having any measurable effect on the situation on the ground in Rhodesia. That is not to say that Wilson had any other practical alternative: his party would undoubtedly have been totally split if he had not imposed oil sanctions, and that in its turn would have strengthened Heath's position while damaging the Government's situation at home. It might conceivably have been possible for Wilson to accept that situation if he had had a strong position in the House of Commons. But his majority was wafer thin and he could not afford to see his party rent by dissension on an issue which, after all, was not of vital domestic importance however much he elevated it to the centre of the stage. It is, of course, just possible that Wilson and his cabinet thought that oil sanctions, by Britain and by those countries who could be persuaded to join her, would be decisive but, if they did, the advice they were receiving from the Commonwealth Office and from the Department of Economic Affairs (DEA), a new Ministry (under the ebullient George Brown), whose officials, by and large, knew little, if anything, about Rhodesia, must have been so wildly out of tune with reality as to be almost ludicrous.

There can be little doubt that Commonwealth Office advice during this period did in fact leave a lot to be desired. Diplomats are not immune to the vice of wishful thinking. The Rhodesian situation presented a challenge to the whole philosophy of those who worked in the Commonwealth Office. The Empire had been shed with relatively little difficulty and the vision of a new Commonwealth, rising phoenix-like from the ashes of the Imperial past, had a powerful attraction to those who believed in the creative aspects of the British tradition. UDI was a spanner thrown in the works by a very small minority (about 250,000 people) of one British colony. Until the archives are opened up it is not possible to be certain, but the consistent over-optimism of Labour Ministers throughout their period of office as to the effectiveness of sanctions points to a cause beyond the undoubted tendency of those Ministers, and in particular of Wilson, to allow the wish to supersede reality. A well-known statement by Wilson which appeared in the communiqué issued after the Commonwealth Prime Ministers' Conference in Lagos in January 1966 to the effect that – 'On the expert advice available to him (Wilson) the cumulative effects of the economic and financial sanctions might well bring the rebellion to an end within a matter of weeks rather than months' – may have been the reactions of a man under heavy pressure and one who has often been accused of obsession with the short term – 'a week in politics is a long time'. But it is difficult to believe that a succession of Ministers would have been so over-optimistic about sanctions over such an extended period, if in fact they had been receiving directly contrary advice from those professionals whose task it should have been to approach these matters with dispassionate and hardheaded objectivity.

Of course it is easy to criticise in retrospect. Few people would have expected the small Rhodesian white population to hold out against virtually the whole world (less South Africa and, for a period, Portugal) for fourteen years. Certainly, in the context of the almost obsessive anti-colonialist atmosphere of world politics, this was a remarkable achievement, whatever the rights and wrongs of the matter may have been. But the British Government's case at that time was that Rhodesia would collapse under the pressures which could be exerted by Britain alone with only sporadic, and certainly not universal, external assistance.

The truth is that the attitude adopted was a mixture of overoptimism and necessity. There was a hope that oil sanctions, when added to the measures already taken, would be effective. And this hope was probably not shown to be a total illusion by the Commonwealth Office and the DEA, as it should have been. Secondly, for internal political reasons, it seemed essential to Wilson to offer further palliatives to party feeling in spite of the fact that this would certainly lead to national disunity and therefore work against the very purposes for which sanctions were imposed.

There is a further factor in considering the quality of Commonwealth Office advice. The fact is that Commonwealth Office officials were very different from those in the Foreign Office. They had been brought up under a different tradition, with different values requiring different attributes. In many cases their essential loyalties were to the Commonwealth, rather than directly to Britain. Unlike officials in the Foreign Office, those who worked in the Commonwealth Office had not been imbued with the belief that their raison d'être was solely to further the British interest and that situations should be looked at unemotionally with a hard-headed appreciation of where this interest lay followed by the emergence of a clear view as to how it could be secured. There was a residual, and indeed in many ways admirable, loyalty to the peoples which we had at one time governed and this at times came into conflict with loyalty to Britain. Foreign Office officials had no difficulties of this kind. There was no grain of paternalism in a Foreign Office diplomat. His intellectual standard was in general higher. He was more subtle and had a great political sophistication. Furthermore, many Commonwealth Office officials had been in the Colonial Office aspiring to the post of Colonial Governor. The qualities required of a Colonial Governor were very different from those which were needed by an Ambassador. A Governor had to be able to rule, but to be sympathetic to rising nationalism and even to become involved in it. Indeed, so successful were many at this task that they were freely chosen as the first Governors General in the newly independent countries. An Ambassador's task, in contrast, is to interpret his Government's policy to the country to which he is accredited and vice versa. At no stage does he wield power, and there is no question of divided loyalty.

The result of the character of the Commonwealth Office was that the advice it gave in the period leading up to and immediately after UDI was undoubtedly tinged with a bias against the Smith regime. There was a large element of subjectivity and wishful thinking. The contacts which the British High Commission had in Rhodesia were primarily with those who opposed Smith – businessmen, the intellectual establishment and so on – not with the hard-line Rhodesian Front. As a result there was a failure in really understanding the depth of the determination of the mass of the white population to resist all pressures in pursuit of what it considered to be a wholly just cause. Rhodesian businessmen were trying to prevent UDI by telling Smith that such action would lead to immediate disaster. These businessmen came to believe their own propaganda and convinced their friends in the High Commission that sanctions would have an immediate effect, and this view was almost certainly relayed to Britain. When the Foreign and Commonwealth Offices were merged, these issues were viewed more objectively. But the difference between the general approach to Commonwealth and Colonial affairs between those who had been brought up in the Foreign Office and those who came from the Commonwealth and the Colonial Offices remained very marked for some considerable time.

To add to the confusion, the fact that there were three Ministries involved – the CRO, the DEA and the Foreign Office – made the offering of coherent advice more difficult. Furthermore with the Prime Minister, in person, totally dominating the formulation of policy and deciding matters largely on the basis of the Parliamentary situation, even if civil servants had put forward contrary advice it was most unlikely that they would have been heeded.

The issue of oil sanctions came to a head in a two-day debate in the House of Commons on 20 and 21 December 1965 followed by a short debate on the oil order. These debates were crucial to the handling of Rhodesian affairs by Britain over the next few years and it is worth examining them in some detail.

There were difficulties concerning the procedures of the House of Commons. The apparent problem was that if the Government decided that the main debate would be on Rhodesia – and there was a motion on the Order Paper which could have been debated – then the whole two days would have to be devoted to the Rhodesian issue, and there were many other matters which members wished to debate. The alternative was to hold the main debate on what is known as the adjournment, in which case there could be a vote but there would be no precise words defining the issue. As is so often the case, a dispute about procedure concealed other deeper conflict. The Conservative Party hoped that the Government would indeed arrange to debate the motion which already existed, since it left open the possibility of the use of force in certain circumstances and this was an issue upon which the whole party would unite in opposition to the Government. The Government was reluctant to face its supporters with the need to vote against the use of force in any circumstances, because of the dangers of a split. It wished to centre the debate on oil sanctions, an issue on which it was united. But there was already a debate pending on the oil order and it was impossible to have two votes on the same subject. It was therefore to the Government's advantage that the debate should be on the adjournment. The Conservative Party, on the other hand, knew that it would probably split on oil sanctions but it it would be united on the issue of the use of force. In the event, the Government, which has the ultimate control in these matters, insisted that the vote should be on the adjournment.

The first day was mainly devoted to issues other than Rhodesia, although Michael Stewart, the Foreign Secretary, drew attention to the many countries which had agreed to sanctions of one kind or another against Rhodesia. The second day's debate was opened by Heath in one of the most difficult speeches he can ever have had to make. He had what turned out to be an impossible task. He had to attempt to differentiate his position from that of the Government sufficiently to allay the anxieties of many of his supporters that he was being led inexorably down a very dangerous road; but on the other hand he had to try to maintain national unity and to satisfy those on the left of the Conservative Party who were broadly in agreement with the Government's actions so far.

Heath started his speech with the strong and accurate point that there seemed to be a shift in the objective which the Government was pursuing. Their original aim had been to secure the return of Rhodesia to Constitutional rule. 'But a different objective was now beginning to arise. The Prime Minister was now equating the return of Rhodesia to legal rule with the objective of toppling Mr Smith and his entire regime.' Heath went on to say that there had been a contradiction in statements by Bottomley, the Commonwealth Secretary, in the House of Commons and Lord Gardiner, the Lord Chancellor, in the House of Lords on the same day. On 7 December 1965 Bottomley, speaking about Mr Smith, had said – 'He had lied not only to me but to others. This is one of the reasons why *we cannot deal with Smith in any way* [author's italics] because he is not a man to be trusted.' But Lord Gardiner had said – '*It is open to Mr Smith now, to put before the Government any proposals which he has to make* [author's italics] and any proposals will be carefully considered by Her Majesty's Government.' Heath made the point that this contradiction had been compounded by Wilson on 10 December when he, in his turn, had said – 'What I must make clear is that Her Majesty's Government are not prepared, directly or through the Governor, to enter into negotiations with Mr Smith on any basis which involves dealing with an illegal regime or on any conditions, other than procedure conditions, for a return to Constitutional methods ... we cannot negotiate with an illegal regime.'

Heath then went on to argue that he had supported the measures that the Government had taken but in the timing of them the Prime Minister had given the impression that he was succumbing to pressures and had no clearly thought out plan.

At this stage Heath came to oil sanctions, and his difficulties became apparent. What was he to say about an issue on which his party was totally divided? There was no question of his persuading most members of his party that oil sanctions should be imposed. Neither could he persuade a sizeable body of his supporters that they should not be imposed. Clearly, he was personally in favour of oil sanctions and believed that national unity should be maintained on this issue. But national unity would not be maintained if half his party deserted him. He took the only course open to him. He tried to shift the direction of the debate away from oil sanctions and on to other issues. Oil sanctions could help, he said, but what about the effect on Zambia? The danger of oil sanctions was that they might bring about the breakdown of law and order. For this to be avoided it was vital that the Government should keep in touch with the regime in Rhodesia. Furthermore, oil sanctions might escalate to the use of force. He did not share the view that this would necessarily follow but the danger was that the Prime Minister might in fact be prepared to use force. The clear line the Opposition would draw was on support for the use of force. They would oppose the Government, not on the question of the oil embargo, but because no adequate assurance had been given about the use of force.[15]

It was a brilliant Parliamentary speech which reads nearly as well now as it sounded at the time. Those who have denigrated Heath as a leader could certainly not fault this performance in a situation of great crisis for the Conservative Party.

Heath was followed by Wilson, equally experienced in the political battle and also facing great difficulties. In party political terms he knew that Heath was facing his first real test as a leader and if the Conservative Party split this would undoubtedly be to the advantage of the Labour Party which had plenty of difficulties of its own. He also knew that an election could not be long delayed. On the other hand, an end to national unity would clearly be disastrous to his hopes for an early solution to the Rhodesian problem. He made a very skilful speech adopting the tone of being more in sorrow than in anger. He said that Heath seemed to be departing from his position of maintaining national unity. Heath had not so far played party politics and had supported the measures which the Government had taken. He hoped this would continue. As far as Heath's spurious point about the use of force was concerned, Wilson said – 'We have ruled out the use of force for ending the situation in Rhodesia, I have said this time and time again.' It was essential to Wilson that he did not allow the Conservative Party to portray the Labour Government as being likely to invade Rhodesia. On the other hand he had to keep open the option of the possibility of blockading the port of Beira, the terminus of the Rhodesian oil pipeline, under the aegis of the United Nations (a development which actually occurred shortly afterwards). In the event he, too, had an impossible task since he could not give the absolute assurance which the Conservative Party required.

There were no particularly memorable back bench speeches during the debate except, perhaps, for that made by Gilbert Longden, a respected senior Conservative Member of Parliament without any strong prejudices either way. He made an appeal for national unity, but then went on with some remarks about the United Nations which were very representative of Conservative opinion. He said – 'The United Nations merely earns the contempt of all reasonable men of goodwill by the selective criteria which it adopts for visiting its wrath upon erring nations. No sanctions are even suggested to try to redeem the agony of Hungary, the martyrdom of Tibet, the appalling massacres in Zanzibar, Ruanda or the Sudan; but let a country be too weak to offer resistance or, like Britain, be the perpetual Aunt Sally for the abuse and vituperation of small countries which she has created and, rightly or wrongly, continues to succour; then it is another matter.' It was this attitude, widely held, which later made it very difficult for the Conservative Government to continue to support mandatory United Nations sanctions, once imposed.

During the course of the debate the real drama on the Conservative side of the House was taking place behind the scenes as the Conservative whips tried to persuade the party to follow the official advice which was to vote against the Government on the adjournment but to abstain on the oil order itself. There were great difficulties with both wings of the party.

Douglas-Home then wound up the debate for the Opposition. He said that the Conservative Party had tried to maintain national unity. They had leant over backwards to that end. They had accepted the 'consequential' sanctions, but – 'To make the lives of Europeans and Africans, friend and foe of Mr Smith, intolerable was a policy likely to harden the Rhodesian support for Mr Smith.' He went on to repeat Heath's charge that the Prime Minister seemed to have changed his mind under pressure. He then came to the issue on which the Conservative Party wished to vote. He was worried that the United Nations might push the Government into the use of force. There were still reservations in the Government's position, and there was no reason for them. A mandatory

United Nations resolution involving the use of force could always be prevented by the use of the veto we had in the Security Council. Why would the Government not give an assurance that Britain would not use force in any circumstances?

Wilson interjected to say that the use of a veto in these circumstances would be the end of the Commonwealth. This was a very weak argument and Wilson must have known it. Was Britain to go to war against her will under the threat of blackmail by the Commonwealth? If this was the position, the situation had become intolerable. On the other hand, Wilson was in a very difficult position. There were indeed threats to the continued existence of the Commonwealth, an institution in which the Labour Party believed profoundly. And it might well be that a limited use of force to police sanctions would be necessary. Douglas-Home seized on this weakness in the Government's case and said that the Conservative Party would vote on the adjournment because of the loophole which had been left on the use of force.

George Thomson wound up the debate for the Government. He was engagingly frank – 'The Right Honourable Gentleman complained that we have actually changed our position on this matter and that each time we have taken a decision there was a loophole for the next stage. But the behaviour of the Opposition has been one of constantly opposing each decision as it was taken, then coming to accept and then going on to oppose the next decision. I do not think we should be too critical of each other on this matter. We are facing an unprecedented position and one that is always changing.'

The fact of course was that the vacillations of both Government and Opposition had nothing to do either with the unprecedented nature of the position or with the changes which were indeed taking place from day to day. The leaders of both the Government and the Opposition were trying to maintain national unity and at the same time to prevent their Parliamentary parties from splitting, and these two aims were in each case conflicting. It was the Parliamentary situation which was dictating the course of events and leading to the apparent muddle and vacillation on both sides.

The vote on the adjournment was a straightforward split on party lines (299 for the Government and Liberal Parties, 272 for the Conservative Party). But this was followed immediately by the oil order. Opposition leaders hoped that there would be no debate, and no vote, but the body of the Conservative back benchers who opposed oil sanctions forced a debate and a vote. The result was a three-way split in the Conservative Party. Most Conservative members abstained, but 31 voted with the Government and 52 voted against it. The Conservative Party was in total disarray.

In retrospect, the split in the Conservative Party on this issue had very little, if any, fall out in domestic terms. But it undoubtedly did have an effect in Rhodesia where Smith and his Government must have been encouraged in their defiance. That is not to say that those Conservative rebels who voted against the advice of their party leadership were wrong to do so. There was a considerable body of opinion in Britain which was opposed to oil sanctions. And if Parliamentary democracy is to mean anything, it must be right that the various elements of the national view are reflected in Parliament, even if this can be embarrassing. Such are the implications of our system of democracy.

The year of 1966, therefore, began with the Labour Government in Britain taking the position that it would have no further dealings with Smith – 'Other than procedural conditions for a return to Constitutional methods'. The Conservative Party was split on oil sanctions. And in Rhodesia life went on much as it did before UDI. The prophecies of doom to the Rhodesian economy were not being borne out in practice. Indeed the initial impact of sanctions was probably to the benefit of the Rhodesian economy which had been over-reliant on the tobacco industry. Agriculture was diversified and import substitution industries were started up. In spite of their opposition to the Smith regime, businessmen devoted their considerable energies and ingenuity to the circumvention of sanctions with governmental blessing. Throughout the period of sanctions, inflation within Rhodesia was less than it was in Britain and the balance of payments problem was largely overcome. It was only very much later that difficulties in importing heavy engineering goods and the lack of outside investment began to raise real problems for a people united in its determination to resist outside pressures and indeed to prosper in the face of the disapproval of nearly the whole world.

It was clear that an attempt had to be made to unify the

Conservative Party on an issue which might well be of some importance in the General Election which was coming before long and Selwyn Lloyd, the Shadow Commonwealth Secretary, went out to Salisbury early in 1966. He had extensive talks with all shades of opinion and came back with the formula that a further attempt should urgently be made to reach a settlement with Smith. This was a policy upon which all shades of opinion within the Conservative Party could, with a sigh of relief, unite.

As the General Election approached in 1966, therefore, there was a clear cut differerence of policy between the two parties: the Conservatives were in favour of a further attempt at a settlement, while the Labour Government stood for no negotiations with a man whom they considered to be a traitor.

Both parties were to suffer from schizophrenia throughout the ensuing years. As far as the Labour Government was concerned it was, under Wilson, to embark on a series of attempts at a compromise solution which was of course a complete U-turn from its position at the 1966 election. Indeed it took Wilson only a few days after the election was over to announce (on 27 April 1966) that informal talks between officials had been arranged to examine whether a basis existed on which a solution of the problem could be reached. Any agreement which Wilson had reached with Smith would have come under bitter attack by a large and influential body of the Labour Party. There was no question of Smith resigning as Prime Minister and he was anathema to large sections of the Labour Party which believed that there should be no dealings of any kind with him. Indeed, the only solution which would have satisfied the Labour Party was one in which there could have been a hand over to a black Government with an interim period during which Britain would assume direct internal power. This was tantamount to the doctrine of No Independence Before Majority Rule (NIBMAR)[16] – a doctrine which, if adopted, must have put any negotiations out of the question. Indeed Thomson, when Labour Commonwealth Secretary, recognised this at a later date when he said on 22 October 1968 – 'I recognise that a number of my honourable friends sincerely take the view that under no circumstances should there be any departure from the principle of No Independence Before Majority Rule.... I ask them to recognise that they are com-

71

mitting themselves to the view that under no circumstances can there be a peaceful negotiated settlement of the Rhodesian problem. That is the hard truth of the matter.'

The Conservatives were similarly in a position of irreconcilable contradiction. Starting as it did from a basis of reverence for the Rule of Law, the Constitution and the Crown, the Conservative Party was confronted by a rebellion against all three. On the other hand, many of its members, including the bulk of its working-class supporters, had more than a sneaking admiration for Smith, who had refused to give way to what appeared to them to be the pressures of black anarchy and who had been extremely successful in projecting an image of calm reason on British television. There was a revulsion against what was seen as hypocritical posturings by leaders of ex-colonial territories who seemed to blame Britain for everything that went wrong in the world and took every opportunity to castigate and revile the country which, after all, had granted independence without trying to persist in an out-dated Imperial dream. Large areas of British society, normally slow to anger, were fed up with the new Commonwealth. Mass immigration into Britain stoked the fire. There was a deep division between the intellectual establishment and the view of the mass of the people which was not to be bridged. The attitude of many Conservatives had its roots deep in the gut-feelings of a high proportion of the British people.

Then there was the issue of economic sanctions. There were in essence two alternatives. Britain could either throw herself whole-heartedly behind the use of every possible weapon, short of military action, against the European Rhodesians and hope to force a political change: or it could merely show its disapproval by gestures with little practical effect in order to bring the British view of UDI to the continuing notice of the people of that country, black and white. The former option must entail recourse to the United Nations: the latter would have meant a continuing series of vetos in the Security Council of the United Nations and a readiness to be cast in the role of a Fascist supporter of white supremacy in Southern Africa. A policy on the former lines was deeply opposed by a majority of the party: the latter course was unacceptable to a considerable body of liberal opinion within the party which, although smaller in numbers, did represent a view, sincerely held by many Conservatives of impeccable Conservative credentials, which the leadership could only ignore at its peril. In the event, during the period of Labour power up to 1970, the Conservative Party opposed the introduction of mandatory United Nations sanctions though not their continuance once imposed (see page 77).

The talks which Wilson initiated with the Rhodesians immediately after the 1966 election soon ran into difficulties. The Rhodesians demanded a braking mechanism on the speed of advance to majority rule. The British insisted on a return to legality and the formation of an interim Government *before* a Royal Commission could operate to determine whether the people of Rhodesia as a whole would approve an agreed Constitution under the fifth principle. The British also reserved the right to provide military assistance to the Governor 'not only to deal with domestic disturbances, but also to prevent a repetition of unconstitutional action'. This was, understandably in the circumstances, totally unacceptable to the Rhodesians. The talks were in any case broken off in August when it was announced that the Rhodesians were introducing a Bill under the 1965 Constitution (which Smith had produced after UDI) to make preventive detention a permanent feature of Rhodesian law whether a State of Emergency had been declared or not.

The second Commonwealth Prime Ministers' Conference to be held in 1966 assembled in London on 6 September. It soon became clear that Rhodesia was to be the main topic at the Conference and, in spite of assurances to the contrary, Britain was to be placed in the dock. A series of speeches was made attacking British policy towards Rhodesia and, in spite of the fact that the proceedings were supposed to be confidential, the texts of the speeches were leaked to the Press and indeed sometimes announced at subsequent press conferences.

An agreed communiqué was eventually issued which set out the various decisions of the British Government. There were two key points: first, 'after the illegal regime is ended' the Governor would appoint a 'broadly based interim administration' and during its period of office the armed forces and police would be responsible to him, 'the Constitution would be negotiated with that administration and then submitted to a Test of Acceptability by the people of Rhodesia as a whole:

73

and second, that if an agreement on these lines was not negotiated 'the British Government would not be prepared to
submit to the British Parliament any settlement which
involves independence before majority rule' but would
sponsor 'effective and selective mandatory sanctions against
Rhodesia at the United Nations.'

Armed with this document which, of course, heavily circumscribed his room for manoeuvre, Wilson sent Herbert Bowden,
the new Commonwealth Secretary – a figure of far more political weight than the previous incumbent, Bottomley – to Salisbury in September and again in November 1966 to see if a
meeting with Smith could be arranged on the basis of the Commonwealth communiqué. He was successful.

The talks in December 1966 on HMS *Tiger* in the Mediter-
ranean – a dramatic and, in the event, uncomfortable venue
(the sea was very rough) – appeared at one time to be on the
threshold of success. One of the points at issue was whether or
not Smith had agreed that he would bring with him plenipo-
tentiary powers to settle. Wilson said that he had accepted this
as a pre-condition at a meeting with Sir Morrice James, Permanent Under Secretary at the Commonwealth Relations
Office, in Salisbury, Smith denied it. There may well have
been a misunderstanding: it seems almost incredible that
Smith could have agreed to the possibility of a renunciation of
UDI on terms which his cabinet would not have the chance
even to see, let alone discuss and decide upon.

The 'Working Document' which Smith insisted on taking
back to Salisbury for consultation with his cabinet, envisaged
that the existing Legislature in Rhodesia would be dissolved.
The Governor would appoint a broad-based interim Government headed by Smith. There was no mention of consultation
with Smith as to the members of this Government, who would
be appointed by the Governor at his discretion. During the
tenure of the interim Government the agreed Constitution
would be submitted to the Test of Acceptability to the people
of Rhodesia as a whole by a Royal Commission. Censorship
would be removed and normal political activities permitted
provided there was no intimidation. Not later than four
months from the dissolution, elections would be held. The
Governor would be invested with legislative powers to be used
on the advice of Ministers, except in those cases where he was

empowered to act at his own discretion. It was not clear what those cases would be. During the interim Government, the armed forces would be responsible to the Governor who would be advised 'in his capacity as Commander-in-Chief of the Defence Forces, by a Defence Security Council, comprising the responsible Ministers, together with the heads of the Defence Forces, the Chief of Police and a representative of the British Government.' There was no stipulation that the Governor would have to take this advice. A Treaty guaranteeing the independence Constitution and a Defence Agreement would be negotiated between the two Governments. If the Royal Commission found against the Constitution, the two Governments would confer to devise alternative proposals.

In circumstances of high drama, Smith flew back to Salisbury for cabinet consultations. There are conflicting reports as to exactly what happened, even from some of those who were present. One thing is certain: Smith did not try to sell the proposals or to invest them with any of his authority. He produced them and waited for the reaction, which he must have known would be hostile.

Those who were opposed to any deal with Britain had much to bite on. The Constitution was acceptable (in effect the existing fifty European seats were to remain and there were to be seventeen, as opposed to the existing fifteen African seats). But the difficulty lay in what was known as the 'return to legality'. It could be, and was, argued that the Rhodesians were being asked to hand over power, lock, stock and barrel, to a Governor who would in fact be able to take any action he chose during the vital interim period. He could act in what they, in their terms, would consider to be a highly irresponsible manner and they would not be able to prevent it. In fact the British had no such intention and it was a pity that a British Cabinet Minister did not accompany Smith to Salisbury to explain this – and, if necessary, to negotiate further safeguards.[17] But without any strong protagonist of the proposals in Salisbury a negative answer was inevitable. The Rhodesian cabinet was in a highly suspicious frame of mind, the country appeared to be flourishing in spite of sanctions and there was no overriding and immediate reason for compromise. The answer was – 'No'.

A two-day debate was held in the House of Commons on 7

75

and 8 December 1966 on the following motion: 'That this House endorses the decision of Her Majesty's Government to accept the Working Document worked out by the Prime Minister and Mr Ian Smith on the 3rd December, deplores its rejection by the illegal regime in Rhodesia, and supports the decision of Her Majesty's Government now to implement the undertakings given in the Commonwealth Prime Ministers' communiqué.' The decisions mentioned were to withdraw all previous offers, never to give Rhodesia independence before majority rule and to ask the Security Council for selective mandatory sanctions (which were imposed on 16 December).

Wilson made a highly successful speech in party political terms. He cast the Conservative Party in the role of near-traitors, going so far as to suggest that by voting against the Government the Conservative Party was condoning treason. 'If they do that (vote against the Government) then they must accept responsibility for every action of the Salisbury regime from now on.' Wilson was successful in creating an atmosphere of emotional unity within the Labour Party and in obscuring the failure on HMS *Tiger* by a strong counter-attack on his political opponents.

The arguments against United Nations mandatory sanctions were neatly and succinctly expressed by Maudling – 'Our four points against mandatory sactions ... have always remained the same. First, there will be a loss of control by Britain. Secondly, they will not work unless other countries do the same thing. Thirdly, they will certainly not work without South African support. Fourthly, they will consolidate opinion behind the right wing in Rhodesia and make the position of the moderates and a would-be moderate alternative Government totally impossible.'[18]

But there were obvious difficulties about this position. First, why impose sanctions at all if the aim was not to make them effective in economic terms? And this could only be done if United Nations assistance was involved. A gesture of disapproval could cut little ice with a regime which had taken the massive decision of UDI. Secondly, what if Mr Smith was not prepared to reach an acceptable settlement with Britain? Was not eventual recognition the logical conclusion of confining British reaction to a few mild gestures? And, thirdly what would the international repercussions be when the Afro/Asian group in the United Nations and other countries realised that Britain was not prepared to take any meaningful steps against a white rebellion, an action which struck at the very roots of what they considered to be the prime issue in international affairs?

There was a further problem which the Conservative Party had to face later. Under the procedure adopted by the Labour Government (this need not necessarily have been so and the acceptance of continuing Parliamentary control was a concession to Conservative pressures) sanctions had to be renewed by Parliament every year in November. What should the Conservative reaction be to the renewal of sanctions, once imposed? Would it continue to vote against them? Clearly a different situation arose once mandatory sanctions were enforced under resolutions of the Security Council of the United Nations. Britain, as a country, was committed to them regardless of which Government was in power when they were imposed. There were, in some Conservative circles, doubts about the legality of the resolutions, but on examination these doubts proved to have no legal foundation. Was the Conservative Party to advocate a unilateral breach of the most binding section of the United Nations Charter (Chapter 7)? And if it did so, how did this square with its attacks on the Labour Government for alleged breaches of other international agreements? Furthermore, once sanctions were enforced, their removal would, rightly, have been interpreted as surrender to Smith.

In the event the Conservatives in the House of Commons never voted as a party against the renewal of sanctions, although there was a protest vote of about forty members on every occasion when a vote was taken. But this attitude was not without considerable difficulties, particularly at the Party Conferences. As will be seen later, it was almost entirely due to the personality and enormous political skill of Douglas-Home that the Conservative Party retained any cohesion at all on this most emotive and divisive matter.

In spite of Wilson's NIBMAR pledge to the Commonwealth, it was not to be long before negotiations were reopened on the basis of independence before majority rule. Visits to Salisbury by Lord Alport in January 1967 and Thomson in November of the same year, together with a visit by Douglas-Home in February 1968 seemed to offer some hope of further substantive talks but all progress came to a halt when three murderers, convicted of particularly bestial crimes, were hanged in Salisbury in spite of the granting of a reprieve by the Queen, on the advice of the Commonwealth Secretary. However, in October 1968, a further meeting between Smith and Wilson was held on HMS *Fearless*, this time firmly secured to the quay in Gibraltar with Smith having comfortable quarters in another naval ship (HMS *Kent*) in contrast to the doctor's cabin he had had to make do with in HMS *Tiger*. Wilson's attitude towards Smith was relaxed and friendly as compared to the rather harsh and dogmatic tone he had adopted on HMS *Tiger*. Furthermore, unlike at the previous meeting, on this occasion the Rhodesians were not given a time limit in which to agree or reject the proposals. The main sticking point turned out to be the British proposals that there should be a second safeguard against amendments to the Constitution in addition to that which was already embodied. This was to be provided in the form of appeal to the Judicial Committee of the Privy Council in Britain. As is so often the case it was not so much the substance of the proposal which irked but its psychological connotations. As the Rhodesians saw it, their country, although independent in name, would in fact be in pawn to some crusty old lawyers belonging to an organisation of which they knew nothing, sitting in London, remote and totally divorced from reality. Smith made a disparaging remark to Elwyn Jones, the British Attorney-General, about the Privy Council and this was near blasphemy to a man steeped in the British legal tradition, serving only to entrench his determination to retain this particular provision of the proposed overall settlement. In the event, the British Government did make amendments to its proposals in this respect but the role of the Privy Council was nevertheless to remain, both in regard to constitutional and other cases. There were a number of other differences between the two Governments and, in spite of a further visit by Thomson to Salisbury, the initiative collapsed.

There seemed now to be no hope of a rapprochement with Britain and Smith introduced proposals for a new Constitution and the adoption of Republican status.

The 1969 Constitution ruled out majority rule. It had provisions for eventual parity of black and white representation in Parliament but since the rate of increase in African seats was tied to the overall level of African income tax contributions, this would not occur in the foreseeable future (it was reckoned that, at the existing rate of increase in African economic prospects, parity would occur after 460 years). Voting rolls were totally separated on racial lines. The Constitutional Council was abolished and the Declaration of Rights was made non-justiciable. The proposals for the Constitution and for the Declaration of Republican Status were put to the electorate in a referendum. 75 per cent voted for the Constitution and 81 per cent for Republican Status. The Constitution which permanently entrenched white power came into effect on 1 March 1970.

In a further move away from co-operation with the Africans, the Land Apportionment Act was replaced by the Land Tenure Act which worsened yet further the position of Africans in regard to the ownership and occupation of land.

Could a solution to the Rhodesian problem have been found during the period from UDI to the defeat of the Labour Government in 1970? Wilson certainly had great difficulties to contend with in his own party, with the Commonwealth and the United Nations. At times he reached the point of total exasperation with the unrealistic demands with which he was confronted at successive Commonwealth Conferences, and he made this clear in his memoirs (*The Labour Government 1964–1970*, p. 285). As for the United Nations, Wilson's attitude to the posturings of many of its members was made clear in a remark he made in the House of Commons on 1 November 1968 (Hansard, column 336) – 'As for the General Assembly resolution ... that has now been followed by a further resolution, saying, as usual, that Britain must use force and settle it that way. I am sure that the Right Honourable Gentleman (Mr Thorpe) will agree that it is one thing for the United Nations to pass irresponsible resolutions of that kind, leaving us to do the dirty work. It is quite another thing for Britain to carry out her responsibility to the people of Rhodesia, including four million Africans, which is what we are doing.' Exasperation both with the Commonwealth and the United Nations was not confined to the Conservative Party. But criticisms of Wilson on the grounds that he should have conceded more to the Rhodesians are misplaced. He could not have gone further than he did in trying to produce an acceptable formula. And it must be remembered that even if agreement had been reached with Smith, the consequential Test of Acceptability might well have produced a negative answer and possibly, if a British Governor had been installed, a further UDI. Indeed if Wilson is to be criticised it must be on the grounds that in his efforts to come to an agreement he reneged on the promises he had made to the Commonwealth. He was wide open to charges of inconsistency, if not deliberate subterfuge.

Having subscribed to the doctrine of NIBMAR before the 1964 election in the letter to Dr Mutasa already mentioned, Wilson then abandoned it in his talks with Smith before UDI, readopted it for the 1966 election, dropped it for the talks on HMS *Tiger* in December 1966, readopted it after the failure of these negotiations – in accordance with the explicit pledge to this effect he had made at the Commonwealth Prime Ministers' Conference in September 1966 – dropped it again for the talks on HMS *Fearless* and then finally readopted it again after the failure of those negotiations.

At one stage (between the *Tiger* and *Fearless* talks) Wilson did produce a formula in an attempt to get himself out of his difficulties. 'If circumstances changed,' he said, he would 'go back to the Commonwealth about NIBMAR', but this was far from convincing since it was inconceivable that the Commonwealth would release him from his pledge, and there would have been no point in negotiating at all if the Commonwealth had a veto which it would undoubtedly use. No wonder the good faith of Britain was questioned, not only in Africa, black and white – and particularly in Zambia which had to bear the burden of the day – but also at the United Nations.

As for Smith, he too had his difficulties with his own party. But the verdict must be that he did not appreciate the long-term impossibility of the white position. He appeared to imagine that the whites could hang on to a total power indefinitely. The guerillas were not a real threat to the whites during this period and he reacted by an attitude of intransigence, failing to realise that this was the moment to make considerable concessions in order to reach agreement before the existence of strong and well-organised guerilla armies would be able to prevent any solution short of immediate majority rule. But, again, Smith was representative of white opinion which itself was in a highly intransigent mood. And, even if he had had real vision and statesmanship, it must remain very doubtful that he could have carried his fellow white countrymen with him.

CHAPTER FOUR

Continuing Frustration, 1970–4

During his period as Prime Minister from 1970 to 1974, Heath did not involve himself in the Rhodesian affair on anything like the same scale as had Wilson. As far as foreign affairs were concerned, his interests were primarily in Europe, although he did already have a wide knowledge of the whole range of problems. In Douglas-Home, he had a Foreign and Commonwealth Secretary whose experience of African affairs was very considerable. Furthermore Douglas-Home, as Prime Minister, had been dealing with the self-same Rhodesian issue when his Government had been defeated in 1964. It has been said that Heath saw little possibility of a successful conclusion to the Rhodesian problem and therefore left it to Douglas-Home, thereby avoiding the inevitable opprobrium of failure. But this is totally to misunderstand Heath's character. Combative and supremely self-confident to the point of arrogance, he did not avoid difficult issues; if anything he was drawn to them. Criticisms of his intolerance, his failure to understand people, his forbidding air of intellectual superiority may have had some validity; but he certainly did not lack courage. The truth was that he had many other pressing preoccupations and he largely left Rhodesia to Douglas-Home, confident in his judgement.

At this point it may be of interest to examine in some detail the nature of political leadership in Britain and the way in which Douglas-Home controlled the Foreign and Commonwealth Office.

The public is apt to see almost everything in terms of personality, particularly in these days of television when political leaders are projected straight into the living room.

Parties are personified in terms of the personality of their leaders when, in fact, the leader is only one, albeit an important, element in the extremely complicated equation which makes up the corporate essence of a political party or Government. In fact, of course, political leaders are the apex of a pyramid made up of those whom they represent; indeed in democratic countries they are chosen for the very reason that they do represent a point of view which has a large-scale acceptance. But it is far easier for the public to grasp the nature of one man's personality and to react to it – this is a function which they undertake the whole time in their daily lives – than to try to understand the real issues at stake in all their complexity.

On the other hand, personality does have a considerable effect on events. The style of a political party or government department will stem from the man at the top, and style is a vitally important element in any organisation. Policies may or may not change but the effectiveness and general impression of purpose and decision of a department can be altered almost overnight by a change of Minister. The same applies in national terms. So much depends upon confidence and this intangible but vital factor is gained or lost largely through the personality of the leader. In trying to judge the real reasons for events in retrospect, the impact of personality should be seen not only in terms of the decisions the leader may or may not make – and the possible options may well in fact be very limited and in any case subject to extraneous factors which may later seem of minor importance although at the time appearing to be overriding – but also in terms of the general effect a leader has on his (or her) colleagues, adversaries and subordinates.

The leader conditions the atmosphere in which decisions are taken. In fact many decisions in Government are far more haphazard than is generally realised. However perfect the machinery of advice, the final decision may well depend on which advisors are around at the crucial moment and how persuasive they happen to be. There are many chance factors such as whether a particular Cabinet Minister is or is not present at a crucial meeting, whether a newspaper happens to have made much of the issue, what personal experiences those who take the decisions happen to have had – and so on. But atmosphere is not chance: it stems directly from personality. Situations are conditioned in such a way that certain courses become unthinkable. The eventual decision emerges often not so much as a conscious act of will as an inevitable consequence of the general atmosphere which a Minister and his colleagues have created, not consciously but by virtue of their personality and character.

Reputations depend on success. But the success or failure of a Government is relative, not absolute. To a large extent it exists in the minds of the public and is conditioned by expectations which are often irrational. A balance sheet is struck not so much in terms of the possible but of the hopes which have been aroused by the politicians themselves, the media and the public itself. Much less is there a precise balance sheet to be struck in foreign affairs. There is no ready gauge for success or failure such as the standard of living, the balance of payments, the number of houses, hospitals and roads built and the rest. Success depends largely on the amount of influence a country wields, and influence is almost by definition an intangible thing. Diplomacy is best conducted behind the scenes and successes normally pass unnoticed because often to give them publicity would lead to reactions which would turn them into failures. One of the greatest successes in foreign affairs of the Conservative Government of 1970 to 1974 – the settlement of the Islands Dispute in the Persian Gulf (engineered by Sir William Luce – the father of Richard Luce, a Foreign Office Minister in Mrs Thatcher's 1979 Government) – went virtually unnoticed. But had there been failure, the result would have been either the bitter hatred of the Shah or of the Arab world, either of which would at that time have been greatly to the economic and political detriment of Britain. Foreign affairs should not be conducted with a view to the enhancement of the domestic political status of either the Foreign Secretary or the Prime Minister or of the Government as a whole.

The temptations of conducting foreign affairs with an eye primarily to the domestic political status of the Minister concerned are great; neither Wilson nor, later, Dr Owen, are entirely immune to criticism on this score.

The personality of the Foreign Secretary, therefore, has great importance, both in the style which he projects into his Department and in the general tone and atmosphere with which he conducts his contacts with the leaders of foreign countries. Of course a Foreign Secretary takes a great number of decisions, but this is not done in isolation. The corporate spirit and general approach to affairs of the Department or of the Government lead to the type of decision taken and this in its turn is created by the personality of all those in it. The higher in the hierarchy, the greater the impact of the personality in question and clearly the man at the top is the most important of all.

It is difficult to describe Douglas-Home's character and achievements without relapsing into platitudes. This is not because he was a stereotyped figure, a conventional product of his class, predictable in his reactions and attitudes. He was, in many respects, unconventional. He questioned received assumptions, enjoyed the consternation occasioned by the maverick idea on closed minds and got an impish pleasure out of seeing pomposity deflated. He was very rarely angry. He had a serenity which must have been almost unique. This stemmed from a certain detachment, perhaps in part due to his long period of illness as a young man, which he preserved in both personal and public relations. He did not become involved in disputes, public or private, in any personal sense and could view the vagaries of human nature from the security of an inner self-confidence. There was more to this than the conventional amused tolerance of the aristocrat, secure in his unassailable social position. He was in a certain sense untouchable. He did not start from the premise that, if something had gone wrong, some individual was to blame. He accepted what had happened and wondered what, if anything, could be done to rectify it. This was most striking in his relations with his personal staff. An apology for error was received with embarrassment, not gratification, A major error was accepted as a joint, if unfortunate, responsibility. The original premise was that everyone was trying to do his best. Similarly in his dealings with the representatives of foreign countries, he made a total distinction between the man and the policies of the country he represented. He might like him or he might not. He might be bored or amused by him. But he would not project a policy on the personality. He accepted that the world we live in is as it is and did not kick against the pricks.

On the other hand he had few illusions. He was not easily

taken in. He had seen too much not to appreciate the effect of greed, ambition, fear or even lust on personality. But he was not immune to a certain settled view, largely inherited from his background, of national and international society. He had no class or colour prejudice in the sense of believing in the inherent and unalterable superiority of one class or colour. But he instinctively felt that at any particular moment in time there existed certain people who, because of their background or achievements, had the capacity to govern and lead and that they should do so. He did not believe in equality. He distrusted those who would make violent and convulsive changes to the existing order. He maintained a profound dislike of Communism, seeing it as an inexorable challenge to the way of life of the West of which he was inevitably a part.

Douglas-Home was not an intellectual. That is not to say that he was not interested in abstract concepts. He was. He would instantly recognise the true intellectual and give him or her due attention and a measure of admiration provided there was a lightness of touch which was essential for any kind of meeting of minds. But he had frequent intuitive flashes of insight which arrived at the truth apparently almost by accident. He was cautious in asserting his views immediately a subject was raised. He listened carefully to the views of others and, being an essentially humble man, was always very open to argument. However, having lived a great part of his life in positions of power, he was more interested in what could be done than in what should be done. When there was no immediate decision to be taken – and these occasions were few and far between – he would toy with academic arguments. But the academic approach, to him almost an attractive but irrelevant vice, would be banished when the realities of decision arrived. He was not in the least frightened by the consequences of a decision once taken and wasted little time or sleep in worrying about the future, or indeed the present.

There was one occasion when he was faced by a number of particularly difficult questions in the House of Commons. He spent a whole hour or more going through the questions in the morning, trying to foresee difficult supplementaries and arriving at the best possible answers to them ready for his appearance which was due at 2.30 p.m. He went to lunch at his Club and when he came out at about 2.15 p.m. he told his driver that he thought he would get his hair cut. He had forgotten all about the questions. Luckily his driver knew his programme and he appeared on time. There can be few other Ministers who would have been so unworried by the prospect of questions in the House of Commons, particularly when difficult issues were pending, that they would have forgotten all about it.

But he was prepared to spend a great deal of time and effort in avoiding the need for harsh decisions if humanly possible. He searched indefatigably for consensus. He veered away from confrontation, whether personal, national or international. He would invariably try for a third course between two opposing entrenched views, and he had what almost amounted to a genius for finding it. His experience led him to the belief that the consequences of conflict were nearly always worse than the consequences of compromise even if that involved a certain loss of face. He would hold on to an optimistic view of almost any situation long after other people had become pessimistic. On the other hand, an apparent paradox, he was not an easy prey to wishful thinking. He very quickly saw the weakness in the case as must any Minister who has to stand up to Parliamentary questions. He would not accept at their face value the bland evasions sometimes produced for him by civil servants or, if he did accept them, he did so knowing them for what they were. He had a mixture of optimism and realism which served him well.

But he could also be very tough when the issue warranted it. He expelled 105 Russian spies masquerading as diplomats of one kind or another and enjoying diplomatic immunity. Britain was the only country which had the nerve to take action of this kind in spite of the fact that a similar situation existed throughout the free world. In the event the outcome was that, after an initial flurry, Britain gained a new respect in Soviet eyes and, a year or so later, Douglas-Home was asked to visit Moscow. In the event, when the announcement was made at the press conference called by the Head of the Foreign Office News Department – John Leahy – the correspondents at first misheard him. Of the 105, ninety were actually in Britain and fifteen were out of the country and would not be allowed back. When Leahy said that Britain was expelling ninety people, someone in the packed room asked if he could say who the nine were. When he said that it was not 'nine' but 'nine O' there was a gasp and a rush for the door in order to break the news. But, since Leahy wished to ensure that the journalists stayed to hear the whole story, the precaution had been taken of locking the door, and they could not get out.

Douglas-Home had a remarkable facility for humanising the official language served up to him by some civil servants. He did it with remarkable speed. He could put his own unique stamp on a long speech in a matter of minutes, turning the platitude into the arresting phrase with a few quick strokes of his spidery red biro. He could find humour in almost any situation and – a great gift – could find just the right phrase to bring an air of endearing informality to the very many occasions he attended which could easily degenerate into pomposity. He would always start a meeting of any kind, no matter how serious and difficult the topic, with a joke of some kind which dispelled any tension there might have been. His political opponents were instantly disarmed in spite of themselves; his staff relaxed, his political friends recognised again his serenity and poise. His air of concerned detachment, tinged with humour, brought a sense of proportion. He was always particularly effective with fire-brands of the Left who came to see him expecting to find a pompous and rigid, if not haughty, aristocrat. When they found that they were dealing with a very human and open-minded man with a near irresistible sense of humour, they became calmer and less extreme.

He had an immense capacity for work and a totally rigid self-discipline. Rising early, he would sift through the deplorable mass of paper with which any modern Foreign Secretary has to deal and dispose of it with remarkable speed. He would never complain if the papers he saw were not organised as they should be (a rare occurrence) and would read in full everything put in front of him. If he had not fully grasped the point, and this would become apparent in his remarks written on the paper, he would not in the least mind if this was drawn to his attention. He would generally have two or three main ideas or themes on each subject and would return to these ideas again and again. Once he had really grasped a point, and he found this easiest to do in verbal communication, he would not forget it easily.

To those who have not seen it at close quarters, the range

and intensity of subject matter which must be grasped day in and day out by any Foreign Secretary is difficult to understand. Visits by other Foreign and Prime Ministers to Britain, Parliamentary appearances, visits abroad, interviews with foreign Ambassadors and High Commissioners, complicated and urgent decisions in a multitude of fields press urgently and insistently in bewildering complexity day by day and sometimes almost minute by minute. There is little, if any, time to see the wood for the trees. And on top of all this there is the constant round of receptions, luncheons, dinners and speeches to say nothing of cabinet meetings and cabinet committees for all of which preparation is necessary.

Douglas-Home's health and stamina were remarkable. When he returned from Rhodesia in December 1971 he had been negotiating hard for a week. He had an all-night flight, arriving at London Airport at 5.30 a.m. He saw the Prime Minister in the morning and attended a cabinet meeting. He then made a statement in the House of Commons at 3.30 p.m. followed by half an hour's questioning, made separate statements to the 1922 Committee of Conservative back-bench Members of Parliament, the Commonwealth High Commissioners and the press, then appeared on BBC and ITV television and finished the day with a dinner at which he made a speech. He was sixty-eight at the time. He did get tired on occasion, and this was one, but he had a very great capacity for recuperation. The explanation for this was threefold. He had good basic health, he did not worry and he enjoyed public affairs.

Douglas-Home was an unusual mixture of the sensitive and insensitive: sensitive because he was acutely socially aware of unease or unhappiness when he was focusing on that aspect of life, but insensitive to extraneous atmosphere when he was concentrating on one particular problem. Like most British people, he was easily embarrassed by overt emotion and would try to avoid either showing it or being in the presence of it.

He was a bad speaker in a technical sense. He could not rouse an audience and he made his speeches in staccato fashion, often losing the rhythm, and occasionally even the sense, in midstream. But he had the overriding gift of communicating sincerity and this carried him through with apparently effortless ease. He disliked adulation, of which he had almost a surfeit. He was always embarrassed by the customary standing ovations at Party Conferences and some other meetings. On one such occasion he made a remark to the effect that adulation could too easily turn into scorn.

He disliked the House of Commons and, although he enjoyed scoring the occasional political point, he did not relish the cut and thrust of debate and in particular he loathed the baying of the Parliamentary bloodhounds sniffing blood – his own or anybody else's. On one occasion, for instance, as Shadow Foreign Secretary, he virtually saved George Brown's political career (only temporarily as it turned out) by producing a disarmingly friendly remark in the House of Commons after one of the worst indiscretions of that ebullient figure. What was threatening to blow up into a major issue – and would indeed have been blown up deliberately by 99 out of 100 Parliamentarians of any party – dissolved immediately in the gentle air of Douglas-Home's unique personality.

Douglas-Home's attitude towards politics was severely practical. His political nose and his ability to see issues from a political point of view – he had been in politics all his life – would have amazed those of his supporters who saw him in some way as standing above politics. Nothing could be further from the truth. He was very much a part of the political scene, aware of the volatile but relentless and often cruel demands and pressures which our system of democracy inevitably entails, ready to play down the embarrassing and to emphasise the favourable factors of any situation but not to twist or distort – although the dividing line between these two activities is thin indeed.

His political views, on the whole right of centre, stemmed largely from his background. He could never have been a Socialist, not because he did not feel for the underprivileged but because it would never have occurred to him to believe in Socialism. Like all of us, he started from an essentially emotional position and then rationalised his beliefs later. But he had an instinctive understanding of people which often eluded those who approached politics in a more intellectual way. He had an almost devastating facility for putting his finger on the essentially human point of any proposed policy and this is an invaluable asset of the greatest value to any administration.

Douglas-Home had an extraordinary gift for getting away

with things, and this is perhaps one of the most important attributes of any politician. He constantly used to alarm members of his staff by the frank and sometimes extremely outspoken remarks he made to the press and others. There was one occasion at a Party Conference when Lord Carrington, no less, had made a speech which had occasioned a great deal of controversy. Douglas-Home met the lobby correspondents the next evening and they were all ready with pencils poised to get his reactions, obviously hoping for a break through the official silence which was a sign of embarrassment. Of course the lobby will not quote a Minister directly, but well-worn phrases of 'official sources' or 'sources close to the Minister' or some such euphemism immediately alert the experienced reader to the truth. Douglas-Home entered the small room crowded with correspondents agog to hear what he would say. After a few initial pleasantries, the fateful question was asked – 'I was a bit puzzled by Lord Carrington's speech yesterday. I wonder if you can give us your views.' Pencils were poised, pads at the ready, the telephone booths open outside the room. Without any hesitation, Douglas-Home answered – 'So was I.' There was an aghast silence, followed by a delighted roar of laughter. It was impossible to pursue the subject any further and the questions moved on to other more mundane and less politically sensitive matters. The fact was that Douglas-Home's response was not the contrived ready answer of the consummate politician, the soft reply designed to turn away wrath: it was the honest reply. He had been puzzled and he said so. He disarmed the hard-boiled journalists and no further reference was made to the incident.

Douglas-Home's impact at the Foreign Office was not immediate and instantly apparent. He did not demand this or that, or order people about. He must have been very different from George Brown or Anthony Eden or even Selwyn Lloyd. The ideas he had and his general approach to affairs seeped down from the top until virtually everybody in the building understood the official line and, more important, what the atmosphere was. Of course there were many officials who disagreed with various aspects of Government policy and there were arguments, often heated, at official level. But the arguments were rarely, if ever, conducted by him. He decided the general approach within the limits of the politically possible and

91

listened to his officials arguing in front of him. Out of the discussion or argument a policy would emerge at first imperceptibly and then gradually with greater clarity to be noted and followed up by his private secretaries.

The methods used by Douglas-Home, which emerged of course from his own personality, undoubtedly had great advantages, not least in that he retained the respect and liking of his officials while not neglecting any of the arguments so persuasively deployed because people were not frightened of putting contrary views. Of course he would constantly point out difficulties which had not been touched upon and suggest alternatives. But this was not done in any sense as if he was producing the ultimate wisdom. He welcomed argument. He made the conduct of foreign affairs amusing and stimulating; this was a remarkable achievement when the world was bedevilled by so many intractable problems, and responsibilities could weigh heavy.

Of great relevance to the part Douglas-Home played in both national and international affairs was the hold he had over the Conservative Party. This was particularly important in connection with Rhodesia. It is customary to portray him as the darling of those Conservative ladies with hats, upon whom the BBC loves to dwell with its cameras at party rallies – thus deliberately fostering a half-truth if not sheer myth about the nature of the Conservative Party. Of course, he was the darling of the Conservative Party Conference. Quite apart from his other qualities, the magnanimity and selflessness with which he had accepted his displacement as leader was enough in itself to endear him to those, and there were many of them, who felt unhappy or even ashamed about his resignation.

Douglas-Home was also regarded with enormous respect and esteem by large sections of society which would never dream of attending a party political function of any kind. Many of these were Conservative voters. But he had a considerable respect and even affection from his political antagonists. Very few Labour Members of Parliament would attack him personally. He set a high moral standard, not consciously or priggishly, but by the very fact of his personality; and this was communicated to millions of people, thereby enriching public life and, incidentally, giving him a standing, nationally and internationally, which enabled him to exert considerable influence.

On its return to power the Conservative Government faced great difficulties in its Rhodesian policies. The Rhodesians had survived the impact of sanctions to a remarkable degree. The sanctions net was proving to be ineffectual and there was little sign of governmental action in a number of countries to enforce their own laws. The Africans were cynical about the British attitude under the Labour Government and apprehensive about the new Conservative Government's intentions. They were determined to obstruct any move which they saw as an approach to what they feared would be a 'sell-out'. There was no chance of any settlement being achieved without a major international upheaval. When the news of any contact with Smith broke, this was certain to spark off deep suspicions and bitter accusations of bad faith. There were extreme reactions to the possibility of the Conservative Government selling arms to South Africa (in the event this did not happen except for the provision of six maritime helicopters which, in the view of the Conservative Attorney-General, Britain was legally bound to supply under the Simonstown Agreement). Any agreement with Smith would add fuel to the already considerable fire. However the Conservative Government was committed to another attempt and after a lull, during which Heath made a considerable and robust impact at the Commonwealth Prime Ministers' Conference in Singapore, the first approaches were made.

The original talks were entrusted to the redoubtable Lord Goodman. This was a brilliant choice as not only was Goodman a supreme practitioner of the art of negotiation, but he had performed a similar function for Wilson, and Labour Party political criticism of his role could not be strident.

Apart from his intellectual ability which was very considerable, Goodman had three invaluable attributes. He was consistently optimistic and never downcast by an apparently total impasse; he had a great sense of humour which again and again brought a sense of proportion at the vital moment; and he was a very nice man, courteous, understanding and friendly to everybody whatever their views or position – he was as polite to the African servant scrubbing the floor outside his room at Meikles Hotel as he was to Smith or to Douglas-Home.

Of course Smith had his difficulties, which were probably as great as those of the British Government. The mass of his supporters were determined not to concede majority rule at all, and certainly not in the foreseeable future. The country seemed to have a reasonable prosperity in spite of sanctions. The propaganda beamed out daily from the Government-controlled radio and television contrasting Communist anarchy to the north with the peace of Rhodesia had had the effect of entrenching rigidity of mind. The difficulties of travel had made the already introverted Europeans in Rhodesia even more so. Many businessmen making goods for import substitution were doing well. The business community as a whole, in the main strongly against the Rhodesian Front Government, had become discredited as its prophecies of imminent doom had not been borne out by events. At that stage violence seemed to be well under control. Why make any concessions at all?

But Smith wanted a settlement. His constant refusal over many years to turn his back on all hopes of a constitutional solution sprung essentially from his desire to become the legitimate Prime Minister of a legitimate country. He was never psychologically reconciled to being an international outcast. And this unpleasant feeling of isolation in a hostile world had echoes among many Rhodesians. Smith wished to be treated as an equal by the British Prime Minister and many Rhodesians had the same gut-feeling. It was only the British Parliament which could give Rhodesia what it wanted – legal independence – and this was realised. Hence the constant refusal to close the option of a negotiated settlement – an attitude which even persisted later after the result of the Pearce Commission had shattered the Agreement of November 1971. There was also a reluctance among many Europeans and Rhodesians to become too enmeshed with South Africa. Many Rhodesians were proud of their own traditions. They did not wish to become a part of South Africa or indeed of any other foreign country, any more than did their forbears in 1923.

Smith has been the target of much criticism, some of it misplaced. The truth is that he was the product of his environment. He was born in Rhodesia (the first Rhodesian Prime Minister to be so) and acquired the attributes and prejudices of his contemporaries. He did indeed see the Europeans as having a civilising mission in Rhodesia. He did not believe that the Africans were capable of running the country effectively and he probably did regard Africans as inherently intellectually inferior to Europeans, at any rate in the foreseeable future.

But to blame the Rhodesian tragedy wholly on Smith is to misunderstand the situation. If he had not represented the views and attitudes of the majority of Europeans in Rhodesia, he would not have been Prime Minister.

The valid criticism of Smith as a politician is that, while giving an impression of decision and firmness of purpose, he was in fact very unsure of himself. His immediate reaction to almost any proposal, whatever its merits, was negative. He waited for reactions before committing himself and followed the general view: he was not a real leader. His original accession to power was manipulated by others, and his room for manoeuvre in the early stages was small, but over the years he did acquire a vast reputation among the bulk of the whites, partly indeed because he was obdurate and reflected their mood but also because he was highly successful in projecting himself as the no-nonsense protector of the white cause. 'Good old Smithy' was the cry, and he did personify the thoughtless intransigence of those he represented. Having achieved that position of widespread trust he could have disregarded pressures from the political right to a far greater degree than he in fact did. But he shrank from radical decisions or strong leadership. Even the announcement of UDI, apparently the act of a strong man, was in fact a weak move: it would have been far more difficult not to take that step in the circumstances than it was to take it. The decision flowed from an inexorable build-up starting from the moment when he was given the job of Prime Minister precisely in order to bring it about. When the moment came, unlike nearly all his cabinet colleagues, he was in a highly nervy frame of mind, full of hesitation and self-doubt.

Smith was a very political animal, aware of nuances and shades of meaning, articulate in a Rhodesian style with the dogged suspicions bred of the essential inferiority complex of some, although not all, of those brought up in a colony. He was apt to think and speak in clichés – 'trouble makers', 'Communists', and by very virtue of the isolation of his position,

95

unaware that the world was moving and changing and that he was being left behind in a very insecure backwater. He had a mixture of high sophistication in terms of the political realities in his own country (he could be ruthless in domestic politics) and of great naivety in the wider affairs of the world. He lacked the essential ingredient of an unshackled imagination, the capacity to project the situation of his country into a future which must eventually bring impossible pressures on the Europeans in Rhodesia whom he represented and, having done so, to formulate policies, accept compromises and create an atmosphere in which his people could flourish in the long term.

Like so many of his kind, Smith was basically afraid of the Africans and he reacted to this fear by ignoring them as people. Until a late stage in the proceedings he was ignorant of the personalities of the leading Africans in his own country. He had never met them. He was therefore incapable of understanding them and of realising that they were just as human as he was, open to argument, capable of distinterested patriotism as of selfish ambition – as fallible or as capable of nobility as the rest of humanity. To Smith, Africans were in general either 'good' – prepared to accept indefinitely European leadership; or 'bad' – with revolutionary and disruptive ideas. Smith had his virtues, but human understanding, particularly of Africans, was not one of them.

The point of departure for the negotiations which the Conservative Government undertook with the Smith Government was radically different from that of the previous negotiations. There were similarities: the Conservative Party had accepted the famous five principles (the sixth caused no difficulty).[19] But the Rhodesians had adopted their 1969 Constitution under which the concept of eventual African rule (clearly present under the 1961 Constitution upon which the negotiations on *Tiger* and *Fearless* were conducted) had vanished, to be replaced by the idea of eventual parity of racial representation in Parliament. But the date when parity would be reached was so remote in the future that even this concept lacked any meaning. The first, and the most important aspect of the negotiations was, therefore, to get the Rhodesian Government to accept the concept of eventual African rule in a framework which, if not precisely measurable in terms of years, would be at least foreseeable as a practical proposition. The Rhodesians did accept this principle and this was a major step forward. There were many other issues of principle which led to the long period of negotiations in which the ingenuity of Lord Goodman and the two Foreign Office officials who accompanied him – Philip Mansfield and Philip Adams – was exercised to the full. But, when the moment came for the final negotiations by Douglas-Home in Salisbury in November 1971, there were still a number of crucial issues to be resolved.

As well as Douglas-Home, Goodman and the Foreign Office officials who had been principally concerned with Rhodesia, the party included Sir Peter Rawlinson (the Attorney-General) and Sir Denis Greenhill (the Permanent Under Secretary). It was a hectic period. Douglas-Home was still in control of the Foreign and Commonwealth Office and apart from the negotiations in which he was totally engaged he constantly had to take decisions on other matters.

A negotiation of this kind is rather like being in a ship in the sense that the rest of the world becomes curiously unreal. Everyone is bound up in the effort to reach agreement. The precise wording of the text of the document to be agreed becomes of absorbing importance and interest. Decisions have to be taken constantly as to where to stand firm and where to compromise. Each side has to guess at the likelihood that the other may be prepared to accept failure rather than give way over certain points. A will to succeed by both sides is of course vital. But for final success, each side must identify those points on which it is not prepared to give way and convince the other that this is indeed so. The tone adopted by the negotiators, therefore, becomes extremely important. As far as Douglas-Home was concerned it was clearly vital that he could carry with him those forty Conservative MPs on the left of the party, led by Nicholas Scott, who had already fired a warning shot in a letter to him before he left. Any agreement reached with Smith would certainly be voted against by the whole Labour Party (less the maverick Paget) and the Liberal Party. If sufficient Conservative MPs either abstained or voted against the proposals, the Government would be defeated. Similarly Smith had to gauge the likely strength of opposition within Rhodesia to the compromises he would clearly be forced to make if the negotiations were to succeed. Finally, any draft agreement had to be agreed by the British cabinet, remote from the scene and inevitably unable to gauge the atmosphere in Salisbury. There must always be a danger that those involved in a negotiation can become so bound up in it and so determined to succeed that they will lose a sense of proportion and concede more than is wise. Cabinet ratification is therefore essential.

As the negotiations proceeded, the various points which had been left for decision were gradually eliminated until only one or two were left. The atmosphere became electric. The stories, appearing in some newspapers, that the negotiations were a charade and that the whole thing had been fixed before the delegation arrived in Salisbury, were total nonsense. Even at that stage success was not at all certain and on one occasion, towards the end, the British delegation actually packed its bags to leave, prepared to accept failure if the necessary concessions were not made.

At the final meeting of the negotiations it became apparent that success was imminent and, after a haggle over the last outstanding point, the draft was agreed by both sides. The British dislike of drama then took over. Smith, entirely British in this respect, said – 'Well, that's it I suppose.' Douglas-Home replied – 'I suppose it is,' and the conversation then turned to the arrangements for the final signing ceremony followed by a rather embarrassed drinking of (French!) champagne. It seemed to those present that the long saga of deadlock between Britain and Rhodesia was at an end, but there was no euphoria or show of emotion. Goodman had bought a 'beautiful new blue suit' which he hoped to wear at the final signing ceremony – but he had to leave for London before this took place. Douglas-Home, of course, knew he would have to bear the burden of the day on his return to England where he was certain to come under heavy attack from the Labour Party. But the achievement had been considerable and the representatives of most other nations would certainly have made much more of the occasion.

Any agreement concluded between a Conservative Government and Smith was certain to be opposed by the whole of black Africa and by the Labour Party in Britain, and it was immediately labelled as a total sell out by both. There would be a blocking mechanism in the hands of the Africans to prevent retrogressive amendments to the Constitution and a justiciable Declaration of Rights but it was true that concessions had been made which went beyond anything contemplated under the previous Government: in particular Douglas-Home had not insisted on the so-called second guarantee under which the Constitution would have had some kind of safeguard beyond that provided within Rhodesia itself. It was also true that majority rule, although certain in the long run, was a distant prospect.

The main argument for the agreement was that the Rhodesian Front Government had accepted a change of direction. Had the agreement been accepted by the Africans, it was said, the atmosphere in Rhodesia would undoubtedly have been totally altered. Instead of moving as she was towards further apartheid, Rhodesia would have had to move in the other direction. Instead of political discussion within that country being about how far Rhodesia should move to the right, the argument would have been about how far she should move to the left. In the proposed Constitution the Rhodesian Government would have accepted the basic truth that all men were born equal: eventually Rhodesian society would have had to organise itself so that this was accepted as a part of political, economic and social life.

Those in the Labour Party who said that Smith was not honest and would ignore or change the Constitution, once it was granted, were arguing against the undertaking of any negotiations at all, not against the Constitution which had been agreed. If there was to be any agreed basis for independence, it was necessary at some stage to negotiate with Smith, and indeed this was precisely what the previous Labour Government had done. Britain had ample experience of the legitimisation of revolt. In any case the agreement was subject to the fifth principle – 'The overriding requirement that Britain must be satisfied that any proposed basis for independence would be acceptable to the Rhodesian people as a whole.' If this principle was satisfied, who was to argue that Britain should desist from granting independence? This was a powerful point, and interest was shifted to the method of arriving at the answer to the question which was now to be put to the Rhodesian people.

The Commission set up under Lord Pearce, a respected

senior judge, to answer this question had an extremely difficult task.[20] It was indeed rather slow to get off the ground, and the British Government was not entirely without blame for this. There is an inevitable tendency with all Governments, once a problem is no longer urgent, for attention to be diverted to other pressing matters and to leave details of the follow-through to officials who, without the constant spur of political direction, can drag their feet. Once the Commission arrived in Rhodesia, advice from the Rhodesian Government as to how to conduct its affairs was largely ignored, for very under-standable reasons – it certainly did not wish to be labelled a Rhodesian Government puppet.

There were differences of opinion in Britain about the precise question to be asked and the context in which it would be put. Liberal opinion in Britain, including, to its shame, the British Council of Churches, put the maximum pressures on the Africans to say 'No'. Pamphlets were produced and distri-buted in Rhodesia which grossly distorted the proposed Con-stitution. On the signature of the tentative agreement, there had been an initial euphoria which was widespread among both Africans and Europeans. But the African National Council, formed under the chairmanship of the then obscure figure of Bishop Muzorewa, in order to oppose the proposals, managed to change the direction of popular African opinion and the band wagon, a phenomenon to which the Africans with their tradition of tribal consensus are particularly prone, became one of opposition to the agreement. Intimidation, however one defines that imprecise word, undoubtedly took place. But the Pearce Commissioners were no fools, they spent two months in Rhodesia seeing as much as 6 per cent of the entire population and they produced a masterly report which fully covered intimidation and all other relevant matters. The answer they gave was that the bulk of the Africans did not accept the agreement.[21] Even if the Commission had operated in a different manner, and had started its work earlier, the outcome would, in all probability, have been the same. The Rhodesian Front Government had been in power for many years and it was understandably unpopular in many quarters as is any Government after a long period of office. To this was added the vital fact that the mass of Africans had had no say in its appointment. However carefully the matter was presented,

100

the issue was virtually certain to turn into a vote of confidence in the Rhodesian Government, and the response to that was certain to be an African 'No'.

The European Rhodesians had undoubtedly expected the response to be an overwhelming 'Yes', especially as they thought that the tribal Africans were massively behind the Government. They were shattered by the eventual answer.

When the report was made, all the efforts made by Douglas-Home, Goodman and the officials of the Foreign and Commonwealth Office who had been concerned with this matter, seemed to have come to nought. Smith believed that he had been totally let down because the Commission had not operated in the manner in which he expected it to do. He had allowed considerable political activity during the operation of the Commission, there were many disturbances and he felt that he had let the stopper off the bottle unnecessarily. However, the fact was that the gap between what the Rhodesian Government thought to be the opinion of the Africans, and what it clearly was, represented a most damaging blow to the self-esteem of Smith and his colleagues. The situation in Rhodesia could never be the same again. For the first time the Africans had actually been consulted on their future. They could never henceforth be ignored.

World reactions to the findings of the Pearce Commission were predictable. Many Africans and others had said in public that the Commission was a tool in the hands of the British Government, set up to provide a façade of respectability for a 'sell out'. They had to eat their words and Britain had a fleeting and unusual moment of glory in African and progressive circles.

In Britain, the Labour Party kept very quiet, but the Conservative Party was bitterly disappointed. If the Pearce Commission had reported that the Africans were in favour of the proposed Constitution this would have been accepted by all shades of Conservative Party opinion and Rhodesia would have had her independence regardless of the inevitable uproar in Parliament and the United Nations. Britain would have dropped sanctions under the argument that the situation that had given rise to mandatory sanctions in the first place – the rebellion – had come to an end and that it followed that sanctions should lapse. But this had not happened and many right wing Conservative politicians concentrated their wrath on the Pearce Commission, attacking it for its dilatory and perverse procedures and the bias they thought had been shown by its members and, particularly, the officials who serviced it.

The truth was that no agreement could have stuck in the long run without African participation. There were three parties to the dispute – the British Government, the Rhodesian Government and the African population of Rhodesia. But the negotiations were conducted between the British and Rhodesian Governments and the Africans were then expected to endorse an agreement in which they had not been involved. This had been inherent in the approach by all British Governments concerned with this matter for many years. The real difficulty lay in convincing the Africans that any settlement agreed was in their interest, not in coming to an agreement in the first place. But the lesser obstacle of coming to a provisional agreement between the British and Rhodesian Governments was so great that both sides became increasingly preoccupied with this and tended to ignore the second and more important stage of the procedure. There had been very little talk either on HMS *Tiger* or on HMS *Fearless* about the Test of Acceptability and this matter was to receive scant attention in the subsequent discussions. It became to be accepted by both sides that there would be a Commission to test the views of the people of Rhodesia. There were so many points of difficulty in the negotiations that the one issue on which there was agreement – the Test of Acceptability – was relegated to second place. It was not realised that, given a free chance to express their views, the Africans would probably reject any agreement in which they had not been involved. But, even if this essential point had been fully grasped, the fact was that there was no African political party, either inside or outside Rhodesia, which could have authoritatively represented all the African people of that country. During the negotiations in Salisbury, among many other people, black and white, Douglas-Home had seen Nkomo, who was brought to Salisbury from detention, but there was no question of his taking part in the negotiations. Had the Nationalists been prepared to work within the Constitution back in 1962 there might well have been an African Nationalist party which could have claimed to represent the African people as a whole but, as already noted, they had turned away from constitutional progress and towards violence. As a result they had not been allowed to operate freely within the country and in any case they were hopelessly split. Certainly in the conditions existing in 1972, Smith would have refused to accept as part of the negotiating team any representative of Rhodesian opinion except himself and those he nominated. The options were either to negotiate with Smith alone or not to negotiate at all, and the Conservative Government had been inexorably tied to a further attempt at negotiation at the election which brought it to power. In the political circumstances of the time it would have been impossible not to have included some such commitment in the Conservative Party Manifesto.

The question now was – what next? There were various possibilities. There was much pressure from the right wing of the Conservative Party to go ahead with the agreement regardless of Lord Pearce's report. The fact was that the proposed Constitution did represent a considerable advance for the Africans; Britain could not bring Smith to heel; the Rhodesian economy had undoubtedly survived sanctions; and there was no question of using force. Why not, the argument went, make the best of a bad job, take what was available and cut the Gordian knot? But, quite apart from the fact that it would have been extremely doubtful if the Government could have won a majority in the House of Commons for action on these lines, to ask Lord Pearce to report and then to ignore his findings would have been an act of such blatant cynicism that it could hardly be contemplated by any British Foreign Secretary.

A further alternative, which was canvassed in many circles, was to disown Rhodesia and to relinquish colonial responsibility for her. There would undoubtedly have been some legal difficulties in doing this, although these might not have been insurmountable. But the result would inevitably have been that the United Nations would have filled the vacuum left by Britain's disappearance from the scene. A Government in exile would have been set up, recognised by the United Nations, and this would have been very difficult for Britain to veto in the Security Council. The likelihood of a multi-racial society in Rhodesia emerging from a scenario of this kind must have been very small indeed.

However, there were some glimmerings of light in an otherwise murky scene. At least in Rhodesia there was, for the first time in years, a body of African opinion, the African National Council, with which negotiation could henceforth be conducted and this body was led by a moderate – Bishop Muzorewa. If the Rhodesian Government could be persuaded to negotiate with him, it was possible that a solution might eventually emerge. It was decided that Britain would leave the proposals agreed with Smith on the table as a basis for negotiations between Rhodesians, black and white. The ball was thrown firmly into the Rhodesian court. Greenhill was sent out to Rhodesia to talk to both sides – Smith and the Bishop – in order to probe the ground. A very accomplished diplomat, Greenhill was superb in his handling of all the very different kinds of people he met. Understanding, kind, unhurried, but firm and knowledgeable, he immediately gained widespread confidence and respect. It may well have been partly as a result of this visit that Smith did eventually start talks with Bishop Muzorewa.

The mass of the Conservative Party had never really been reconciled to sanctions. Very many Conservatives felt that the Rhodesian Government was infinitely preferable to many autocratic regimes elsewhere in Africa. They despised what they believed to be the hypocrisy of almost all African leaders. They had little time for the United Nations, under whose auspices sanctions were imposed and, anyway, they could not understand why sanctions, which had clearly failed, should be maintained indefinitely. They pointed out that Britain had recognised many rebels in the past – in fact most Commonwealth leaders had at some stage committed acts of rebellion. And they were deeply affronted by the fact that Britain was almost the only country which was properly observing sanctions.[22]

These views had been expressed forcibly at Party Conference after Party Conference. The Conservative leadership had had difficulties on Rhodesia at the Party Conferences in 1965, 1966, 1967, 1968 and 1970.

In 1973 the motion for debate was short and simple – 'That this Conference urges Her Majesty's Government to recognise Rhodesia as an Independent State and to withdraw all sanctions.' There was no question of the Government accepting the terms of the motion and, even if it had been carried, the

Government would not have been commited to the policies it advocated. But the repercussions, both in Britain and, perhaps more importantly, abroad, of a defeat for the Government at a Party Conference on this issue would have been very considerable. Furthermore, a clear statement by the Conservative Party Conference to the effect that Smith's Government should be recognised and sanctions should be dropped would undoubtedly exert a powerful influence on Conservative MPs when they voted on the renewal of sanctions which was due in November.

During the week before the Conference Douglas-Home had, most unusually, been ill. He had an infection which left him barely able to speak and it was doubtful if he would be able to perform on the day. However he was determined to speak, come what may.

As the debate proceeded it became clear that a very considerable majority of those in the hall were supporting the motion. Speeches advocating the dropping of sanctions and the recognition of Smith's Government were loudly cheered. Those supporting the Government's position were listened to either in silence or were barracked. The whole atmosphere was one of baffled anger against the Government's policies. There was a feeling that the time had come to call a halt to the slide and to abandon what seemed to be a Socialist policy of permanent and futile vendetta against Smith. The Conservative Party, as represented at Blackpool, felt that it had been prevented again and again from expressing this feeling, first in the attempt to maintain a bi-partisan policy in 1965, then because it had been said that a settlement was just around the corner on HMS *Tiger* in 1966 and HMS *Fearless* in 1968, and then during Douglas-Home's negotiations in November 1971. There was overwhelming support for the motion. That was the atmosphere which confronted Douglas-Home when he rose to speak.

Douglas-Home did have some very strong points to make. The objective of British policy was to bring Rhodesia back into a legal relationship with the United Kingdom and to give her independence which would be acceptable to all Rhodesians, black and white. Only in this way could Rhodesia have international recognition. 'Nothing which falls short of these two goals – that is the restoration of the British/Rhodesian relationship and the independence which will gain for Rhodesia recognition as a country in its own right – nothing less is any good to Rhodesians or to us if we care, not about our own emotions, but for the future Rhodesians, black and white. No Rhodesian – European or African – would thank us if we left them high and dry without international recognition, ostracised in a hostile world.'

Douglas-Home then came to a very powerful point. 'But the British Government of the day put its signature to a resolution of the Security Council of the United Nations which is binding on its members. We are a permanent member and we are in the habit of keeping Britain's word. We do not, and the Conservatives do not, pick and choose which laws we obey and which we do not, nationally or internationally. When others do so we rightly complain.'

As Douglas-Home was speaking, it was clear that opinions were being altered. The atmosphere was changing minute by minute. Those who had been convinced in one direction before he spoke were being convinced in the other as he proceeded. It was a very remarkable performance. The vote at the end was almost a formality and there was a massive majority against the motion. The speech was indeed one of Douglas-Home's best. But if it had been delivered by anyone else the motion would almost certainly have been carried, to the Government's extreme embarrassment. There are very few political occasions when the quality of a speech or of the speaker can totally transform a situation. This was one.

This debate, however, did not alter the essential problem and the Conservative Government of 1970–74 ended its period of office as it had begun it, with the Rhodesian situation in a state of deadlock.

CHAPTER FIVE

Further Attempts at a Solution, 1974–7

The Nationalists can claim with much validity that it was the gun and not sanctions or non-recognition which brought victory in the end. It is also true that the interminable internecine squabbling between the various political and tribal factions greatly inhibited the effectiveness of the guerillas for many years. Furthermore, the methods they used were barbaric in the extreme and certainly steeled the resolve of the whites not to capitulate.

When ZAPU and ZANU were banned they set up their headquarters in Lusaka, and in 1964 the initial infiltrations over the Zambezi took place. In 1966 there were further incursions and in May a white farmer, Hendrik Viljoen, was killed. In 1967 there was a comparative heightening of the tempo with ZAPU in alliance with the South African Nationalist Congress (SANC). This led to the South Africans sending in police and helicopters, a development which was to have profound repercussions later. Further moves across the Zambezi by a joint ZAPU/SANC force were made in 1968. None of these forays were successful. The guerillas had been trained in Ghana, Russia, China, Tanzania, North Korea, and some other Communist states. They had no real contact with the indigenous inhabitants and were no match for the well-organised and well-led Rhodesian Security Forces. At that time, also the local tribesmen were not disposed to give them help.

As has already been mentioned, the 1963 split in the Nationalist leadership resulting in the formation of ZANU under Ndabaningi Sithole, had not been motivated by tribalism (tribal areas are shown at Appendix 1). It is true that the

ZANU leadership had been primarily Shona, but it did have an Ndebele (Enos Nkala) on its central committee. As for the PCC (ZAPU), the central committee was evenly divided between Ndebele and Shona, and Nkomo's main -support came from Salisbury, the capital of Mashonaland. In 1970 (with both Nkomo and Sithole detained inside Rhodesia) the establishments in exile in Lusaka of both ZAPU and ZANU broke up in bitter and violent tribal rivalry. As for ZAPU, Chikerema, the acting President and a Zezuru (Shona), and Nyandoro, the Secretary General and also a Zezuru (Shona), lost control of their party to Jason Moyo, Edward Ndhlovu and George Silundika – all Ndebele (Kalanga). ZANU was also in a state of factional tribal disarray and Godfrey Savanhu, Lovemore Chihota and Nathan Shamuyarira – all Shona (Zezuru) joined the dissident ZAPU leaders of their tribe to form a new party – the Front for the Liberation of Zimbabwe (FROLIZI) in October 1971 under the chairmanship of Shelton Siwela, a Shona (Ndau) who was replaced by Chikerema in August 1972. ZAPU in exile therefore became primarily an Ndebele party and ZANU under Herbert Chitepo – a highly intelligent and determined leader – was totally dominated by the Manyika and Karanga (Shona) tribes. Kaunda, the President of the unfortunate country in which all this bloody in-fighting was taking place, tried in vain to persuade the rival factions to come together. He became increasingly disillusioned.

ZANU now changed its tactics. First, it decided that the ground within Rhodesia must be much more thoroughly prepared before guerillas could operate in comparative safety. An intensified campaign of intimidation began in tribal areas in the North-East. And, secondly, it decided to enter Rhodesia through the Tete province of Mozambique in which FRELIMO, the dissident movement which was active in the country, was having considerable success. From this latter move was to come the eventual line-up – ZAPU/Zambia and ZANU/Mozambique which was later to become highly important.

In December 1972 a European farm was attacked in the Centenary area and shortly afterwards a farmer, Kleynhaus, was wounded and his wife killed. It soon became clear that the guerillas had infiltrated much of the North-East of the country. The call-up was extended and on 9 January 1973 Smith announced that the border with Zambia would be closed. He hoped that this would bring the Zambians, who did indeed greatly rely on the road and rail route through Rhodesia for their trade, to heel. But he miscalculated badly. The South Africans and Portuguese were not pleased and the Rhodesian economy was affected by the loss of revenue. He announced that he had had satisfactory assurances from Kaunda about Zambia's future conduct and that he would re-open the border, but Kaunda refuted this and said that the border would remain closed.

The Rhodesian Government now turned to what it called 'firm measures'. It imposed collective fines and moved tribes-men from the border areas, resettling them eventually in 'pro-tected villages', a policy which later was to be greatly extended. The new tougher policies began to pay off but the guerillas, for their part, turned to greater brutality, murdering those who they believed to be informers and abducting chil-dren and others to Mozambique. The wretched tribesmen found themselves in an intolerable situation: if they did not help the Government they were in severe trouble with the authorities; if they did, they were liable to be murdered by the guerillas.

The impossible position in which the tribesmen in the rural areas found themselves was to be the general pattern through-out the subsequent guerilla campaign: right up to the end there was surprisingly little guerilla activity in the towns. The tribesmen wished to be left alone in peace to live normal lives. They undoubtedly had political views and were not deaf to the Nationalist arguments: indeed they were not happy with the general lines of Government policy on which they, rightly or wrongly, blamed many of the difficulties which they would have faced whatever Government was in power. Many, but by no means all, of the whites whom they saw treated them with scant respect. But all this paled into total insignificance when compared to the fear of death and disruption which was to turn their lives into a nightmare of misery and squalor. In these circumstances they supported, and who can blame them, the side which to them appeared at the time to have the upper hand. The struggle became not so much one for the classic 'hearts and minds' in the sense that either side could convince them that it had the better objective case: it was a physical struggle for domination on the ground. When the Security Forces had the upper hand, information about the guerillas flowed easily. When the guerillas were dominant, no information was forthcoming. The sword was mightier than the pen or whatever form of communication was to hand.

The guerilla war continued with the Government imposing tougher and tougher measures, evicting more and more tribesmen, curtailing the movement of food and generally controlling every facet of life with the objectives first, of putting the guerillas on the defensive and then forcing them to retreat out of the country. The guerillas responded with even more ghastly atrocities, nearly all against the African population. Some white consciences, particularly in the Catholic Church, were moved by some of the activities of the Security Forces which, undoubtedly, went far beyond the tenents of the Geneva or any other Convention.[23] However, the Government gradually began to get on top and by the end of 1974 the immediate threat to the North-East of the country had undoubtedly been contained, if not totally defeated.

Meanwhile the talks between Smith and Muzorewa, which had been initiated in July 1973, were stumbling on. The Rhodesian Government had hoped that African opinion would consolidate behind the 1971 proposals, and indeed there were a number of Africans who did favour this course. But the ANC had undoubtedly received majority African support in its fight for a 'No' answer to the Pearce Commission, and if any kind of agreed internal settlement was to get off the ground it was essential to come to terms with that body. Muzorewa was in a far stronger position than he realised. He could probably have obtained far more concessions from Smith than he in fact did. Smith needed him far more than he did Smith. And Smith failed to realise that his objective should not have been to pressurise Muzorewa, a weak negotiator, into accepting comparatively minor concessions but to construct an agreement which would be widely acceptable in Muzorewa's party. It had been agreed that the talks would be secret and this caused uneasiness in ANC circles. Eventually, in May 1974, Muzorewa did come to an agreement with Smith *ad referendum* to his Executive Committee. The agreement did have some minor improvements from the African point of view; in particular there would have been six more African seats in Parliament immediately. But the Executive Committee of the ANC turned down the proposals unanimously. The negotiations had, therefore, failed, and Muzorewa's personal position in his party was greatly weakened.

Just before the final meeting which sealed the fate of the Muzorewa negotiations, there occurred a momentous event which undoubtedly contributed to the ANC decision – the Portuguese coup d'état on 25 April 1974. As a result of the coup, the Portuguese abdicated power in Angola and Mozambique. Although the impact was not immediate, it was obvious that this event would in the long run totally change the equation in Rhodesia. The eventual loss of access to the sea through Mozambique and, above all, the great increase in the length of frontier over which guerillas could operate, clearly adding immense burdens to those already carried by the Rhodesian Security Forces, were a shattering blow to the Rhodesian Government. The writing on the wall was now easy to read even by the most short-sighted.

The impact was not confined to Rhodesia. South Africa, too, was confronted by a new and vastly more difficult situation. Vorster, the South African Prime Minister, was nothing if not a realist. He had hoped that Rhodesia and Portugal would provide a cordon sanitaire to the North, behind which his country could live in peace. With the Portuguese collapse, not only would African Nationalism reach right up to his borders with Angola and Mozambique but a white controlled Rhodesia was probably doomed too in the long run. He decided to work for an arrangement with Mozambique whereby he would help the new regime to overcome the enormous difficulties it faced and to try to achieve the advent to power of a moderate black regime in Rhodesia, thus giving him continued protection from the North, albeit with black instead of white faces in Government.

South African policy towards Rhodesia since UDI had always been equivocal. On the one hand South Africa certainly did not wish the white position in Rhodesia to collapse: the implications for the long-term future of white domination in her own country were clear. But, also, she did not wish unnecessarily to exacerbate anti-apartheid feeling in black Africa or indeed in the rest of the world by too overt support of white

Rhodesia. On numerous occasions she brought pressures to bear on Smith to settle with Britain. But the Rhodesians held a trump card which they did not hesitate to threaten to use – an appeal over the heads of its own Government to the South African electorate which had many emotional and other ties with the whites in Rhodesia. The South Africans could only go a limited way, therefore, in pressurising Smith and both sides knew this. As far as sanctions were concerned, the South African policy was, in theory, one of normal trade. But this became a farce, particularly after the collapse of Portugal when Rhodesia became entirely dependent on South African middle-men for virtually all her imports and exports. The hypocrisy of the South African attitude was infuriating to many Rhodesians. While taking their percentage cut of nearly all Rhodesian trade, the South Africans were pressing Rhodesia to move to majority rule when they themselves were practising a form of government which went far beyond anything ever contemplated by Rhodesia in the way of excluding the Africans from any political role. The South Africans were playing naked power politics without any semblance of moral justification for their actions, even in their own terms.

President Kaunda of Zambia, too, had very strong reasons for seeking a settlement. The economy of his country was in dire straits. The closure of the border had had an increasingly disastrous effect. The other routes to the sea were unreliable and slow. Dar-es-Salaam as a port left a lot to be desired. And the Benguela railway through Angola was closed by the fighting in that country. Furthermore, the Rhodesian Nationalists in his country were a very great nuisance, spending much of their time squabbling and fighting each other and seeming to be making no progress at all in what should have been their primary aim – the successful conclusion of the war in Rhodesia.

All the elements were present, therefore, for a strange alliance between Vorster and Kaunda aimed at the transfer of power within Rhodesia to a moderate black Government and an end to the guerilla war. The two had been in correspondence in 1968 but this had come to nothing, ending in mutual recrimination when the correspondence was published. Now the time had come to try again. After a series of meetings between representatives of the two Governments, general

112

agreement was reached under which the South Africans would withdraw their police (the numbers of which had been increased to deal with the greater tempo of the guerilla war), both would put pressure on their respective sides – Vorster on Smith, Kaunda on the Nationalists – to accept a transitional period to majority rule and a common voters' roll, and the war would cease. After a meeting between Vorster and Smith, it was agreed that the Nationalist leaders in Rhodesia would be released, a Constitutional Conference would be held and terrorism would cease.

It seemed that here was a real chance for a settlement. It remained for Kaunda to get the Nationalist leaders together, to arrive at a common front and to start negotiations in earnest. But the task of reconciliation between ZAPU and ZANU was made immensely more difficult because ZANU was by now hopelessly divided. Sithole was in prison, having been convicted of incitement to murder (of Smith among others). Chitepo, the ZANU Director of Operations, based in Lusaka, was against any form of negotiations with Smith. Mugabe, who was also in detention in Rhodesia, was also opposed. Tribal differences within the Shona, of which ZANU was primarily composed, led to bitter conflict within the ZANU military wing (the Zimbabwe African National Liberation Army (ZANLA)) between the two main tribal groups still supporting ZANU – the Karanga and the Manyika. No less than 250 ZANU supporters were killed.

This was hardly an auspicious background to the meeting in Lusaka in early December 1974 between Sithole (released from prison for the occasion), Nkomo, Muzorewa, Kaunda, President Nyerere of Tanzania and President Seretse Khama from Botswana. After very considerable discussion at this and subsequent meetings, during which Chitepo apparently resisted any form of unity, an agreement was made whereby ZAPU, ZANU and FROLIZI would join under the umbrella of the ANC, led by Muzorewa. On 11 December, a cease-fire and the release of the Nationalist detainees was announced. But, not surprisingly in the circumstances, the cease-fire did not hold for long. Mugabe, in particular, never accepted either a cease-fire or a Constitutional Conference and his supporters set about the finding of more recruits for ZANLA within Rhodesia.

113

It was subsequently argued that the cease-fire, coming at a moment when there were less than one hundred guerillas left in Rhodesia, gave a respite to the militant Nationalists at a crucial moment and that they were thereby able to regroup and re-organise for further advances later. There is probably much truth in this and it certainly explains the reluctance of Rhodesian military commanders to agree to further cease-fires when subsequently proposed. But it is difficult to argue that this apparent opportunity for a peaceful solution should have been rejected by the Rhodesian Government. The prize of peace was certainly worth the risk.

Negotiations continued between the ANC and Smith in order to pave the way for a Constitutional Conference. These were complicated by the re-arrest of Sithole in March 1975 and his detention on the grounds of plotting to assassinate some political rivals, including Nkomo and Muzorewa. No evidence to this effect was produced, and the charge was changed to that of being the head of ZANU and therefore responsible for many acts of terrorism. Shortly afterwards Chitepo was assassinated in Lusaka. This greatly upset Kaunda who detained a number of ZANU officials and closed down their offices. An international Commission was set up to establish responsibility for the murder: it announced that Chitepo had been killed on the orders of the ZANU High Command under the chairmanship of Josiah Tongogara who had emerged as a strong and efficient military leader. In Rhodesia, Sithole's case was reviewed by a special tribunal which found his detention fully warranted, but in response to strong representations by Muzorewa, the South African Government and other African Heads of State he was released on 6 April in order to attend an OAU meeting in Tanzania. In spite of all this and an attempt by Nkomo to oust Muzorewa from the leadership of ANC, talks continued in order to establish conditions for a Constitutional Conference. Much to the dismay of the white Rhodesians, the South Africans withdrew their forces from Rhodesia in an attempt to force the pace. Eventually, on 25 August, a meeting was held in a railway compartment halfway between Zambia and Rhodesia on the railway bridge at Victoria Falls. It was attended by Vorster, Kaunda, Smith, Muzorewa, Nkomo and Sithole. It was a dramatic venue, but it was a total failure.

114

It is difficult to know whether Smith was ever really serious about these negotiations. He had certainly never conceded the principle of majority rule and, without that, the prospect of agreement was nil: the Nationalists would accept nothing else. However, the almost incredible divisions and bitterness on the Nationalist side, the despair of the Front Line Presidents, put a very strong card in Smith's hands in his dealings with Vorster. How could Rhodesia possibly be handed over to such a rag-bag of squabbling mutual enemies? If the Nationalists had had one undisputed leader and one clear policy it might have been that Vorster could have put such pressure on Smith that he would have had to capitulate.

In most other British colonies in Africa the decision as to whom power should be handed over had been comparatively simple. The process was gradual and a leader emerged, often after elections. The Africans were encouraged to participate in the Government of their country before independence. They therefore had experience of the political process. In Rhodesia, however, things were very different. The Africans had the task of agreeing on a leader either straight from detention or prison, or from exile. The opportunities for tribal and personal rivalries in this situation were vast. Furthermore, in other African colonies where Britain had the ultimate power it was to the advantage of the Administration that a single undisputed leader should emerge. In Rhodesia, as long as the whites were intending to hold on to power indefinitely, the apparent balance of advantage for them lay in perpetuating Nationalist divisions. In fact, of course, in the long run it would have been to the white advantage even in Rhodesia to deal with one Nationalist leader, and this may well have been appreciated by some elements in the Rhodesian Administration. But it was certainly not clear to all and much of the thrust of white Rhodesian policy was directed towards perpetuating and exacerbating Nationalist divisions.

Apart from their very considerable tribal differences, the main conflict within the Nationalist ranks lay between those who were in favour of a negotiated settlement and those who believed that only perpetuation of the war would gain the real prize. Some, including Nkomo, seemed to veer from one view to the other. Mugabe, certainly, never changed his view that victory could only come through a continued and constantly

115

intensifying war. This was to give him an authority which many of his rivals lacked.

Should the Nationalist leaders be blamed for not achieving unity? There was no difference between them as to the eventual aim. Certainly in an ideal world they should have put aside all tribal and other differences and subsumed their personal ambitions in the cause of freedom as they saw it. They certainly should, and perhaps could, have come to an agreed policy and stuck to it. Had the outside powers – the Front Line Presidents, South Africa and Britain (although her role at this stage was minor) – been able to identify one leader, then perhaps the problem could have been solved by negotiation much earlier and the loss of thousands of lives and great misery could have been averted. We will never know. But whatever the reasons, or excuses, were for the failure of the Nationalists to unite, it is certainly true that there was a large element of culpable human weakness which can be blamed directly on the Nationalist leaders themselves. They did not live up to their responsibilities even in their own terms. Most of them were self-seeking and obsessed by personal power.

The murder of Chitepo was to have far-reaching implications. Kaunda's subsequent decision to arrest many ZANU leaders and to shut down their office in Lusaka led to that party shifting its entire effort to Mozambique. In military terms, operations into Rhodesia from that country were far easier than from Zambia because of the difficulties of crossing the Zambezi and Lake Kariba. ZAPU, which remained in Zambia, did subsequently mount operations from Botswana but this had its difficulties, while the long Mozambique border – much of it in mountainous and difficult terrain – was ideal for guerilla incursions. ZANU was therefore able to penetrate the whole of Mashonaland and even in some cases to push into Matabeleland whereas ZAPU was, by reason of geography, greatly inhibited in the amount of territory it could dominate. A further factor behind the comparative quiescence of ZAPU was that Nkomo was reluctant to commit the bulk of his army to the battle, no doubt believing that it would be to his advantage to retain a disciplined and effective force in Zambia for use if civil war broke out in Zimbabwe after victory. But the net result of all this was that Nkomo's support in Mashonaland was greatly eroded, that the basic Shona (ZANU)/

Ndebele (ZAPU) division was confirmed at grass roots level (the leadership of both parties was not so rigidly defined) and that, as a consequence, Nkomo's claim to national leadership virtually disappeared. Indeed the result of the 1980 election, when Nkomo's votes came overwhelmingly from Matabeleland, stemmed directly from these events.

The next move in the drama was to consist of bilateral negotiations between Smith and Nkomo. Nkomo had great advantages from the white point of view. He was not dogmatic in a political sense, he was experienced and any agreement arrived at with him would have a good chance of acceptance by the international community. As far as Nkomo was concerned, he had seen his stature as the acknowledged leader of African Nationalism gradually diminish. The split with Sithole, the growing support for Mugabe and the great prestige which Muzorewa had obtained through his successful campaign against the Home/Smith proposals meant that unless he could force himself to the centre of the stage he would be unlikely to finish up as leader of a united Zimbabwe.

The endless shifts in the kaleidoscope of Nationalist infighting continued unabated. Sithole, with Muzorewa's approval, formed yet another organisation – the Zimbabwe Liberation Council – as the external wing of the ANC which in theory still existed as an umbrella organisation comprising both ZANU and ZAPU. Nkomo attempted to depose Muzorewa as leader of the ANC who promptly announced that Nkomo was expelled. Nkomo refused to accept this and engineered his own election as President of the ANC at a meeting in Salisbury attended only by his own followers. The guerillas in camps in Zambia and Mozambique by this time were thoroughly disillusioned with their leaders and a further organisation – the Zimbabwe People's Army – was formed under Rex Nhongo, a guerilla leader, which in theory was to merge the ZANU and ZAPU armies. This force looked to Mugabe, who had remained adamant throughout that the only solution to the problem lay in armed force, as its leader. At that time, also, Mugabe had the advantage, as far as many of the guerillas were concerned, of his uncompromising Marxism.

Mugabe's inexorable rise to power culminating in his appointment as the first Prime Minister of Zimbabwe had three main causes: first, his intellectual pre-eminence among

117

his contemporaries; second, his refusal to compromise; and, third, his ability to appear to be the one leader who transcended the interminable internecine squabbling within his own party.

He had been involved in the higher echelons of the Nationalist movement since 1960 when he became Publicity Secretary of the NDP on his return from Ghana where he had been teaching and where he met his wife, who was to be of great help to him throughout. He had the same post in ZAPU, the party which replaced the NDP when it was banned. When criticism of Nkomo's alleged lack of leadership came to the boil in 1963, Mugabe was in Dar-es-Salaam and his suspension, together with that of Sithole, by Nkomo led to the formation of ZANU of which he became Secretary General. He was detained in 1964 and remained in detention for no less than ten years during which time he obtained a further three university degrees to add to the three he already had. During this period, too, he studied Marxism and became intellectually convinced of that economic and philosophic doctrine, although throughout he has insisted that the application of it in his country must take account of Zimbabwean circumstances (whatever that may mean in practice). His displacement of Sithole and his emergence as the leader of ZANU was a gradual process over the years with many setbacks – Nyerere at first distrusted him, and President Machel of Mozambique actually put him in detention for a short period in the early days. Furthermore, at no stage prior to independence, did he exert direct personal authority over ZANU on anything like the same scale as did Nkomo over ZAPU: his task was vastly more difficult and, indeed, at times his problem was to retain any power at all. As has already been said, the Shona tradition was far less authoritarian than was the Ndebele, and the inter-tribal rivalries (almost entirely lacking within the Ndebele) among the Shona were acute. Furthermore, Mugabe did not have much personal magnetism: his appeal as a leader stemmed from the head, not the heart. But he had great determination, he was vastly skilful and he did emerge as the one figure who could possibly hold together the many conflicting elements within the Shona Nationalist movement. He eventually established a close relationship with Machel which was to be of the greatest value to his party.

118

With almost total Nationalist disunity in the background, talks between Smith and Nkomo began in December 1975. They were to drag on until March 1976. There never was the slightest chance that they would succeed. The issue, which could not be evaded, was simplicity itself. Smith would not concede majority rule; Nkomo would settle for nothing else. There was talk about a qualified franchise, about the transitional period and a whole range of other matters. But the time when such comparative irrelevancies had any importance at all had long since passed. Nkomo could not possibly have conceded the main issue even if he had wished to: had he done so, he would not have lasted a week. And Smith was not yet prepared to surrender the essential point. The guerilla war had indeed escalated: there were many incursions along the whole length of the Mozambique border. However, the violence was certainly not yet at the stage when the whites had no alternative to an immediate concession of majority rule, in spite of the closure of the Mozambique border in early March.

Since it came to power in February 1974, the Labour Government in Britain had played little or no part in events in Rhodesia. It had not been overtly involved in the détente exercise or in the negotiations between Smith and Nkomo. There was indeed little it could do except to hope that a settlement of some kind would emerge inside Rhodesia which would rid it of the turbulent Smith. The fact that Rhodesia was still a British responsibility and that only Britain could grant it independence seemed almost irrelevant when Kaunda, Vorster, Nkomo, Smith and others were negotiating. It was not as if the Labour Government had much respect either from Smith or from his Nationalist opponents. Smith thought Wilson to be a twister: the Nationalists, and especially Kaunda, were convinced that Britain could have solved the issue by the use of force but had deliberately engineered affairs so that Smith was still in power. Any British initiative at that stage would have had little credibility.

The Americans, on the other hand, were beginning to take an interest. Africa had been very low on their list of priorities in the past. As Britain withdrew from its world-wide responsibilities, they had gradually been sucked into more and more situations of conflict in the Middle and Far East in particular. But they had managed to avoid any major role in Africa south of the Sahara. They knew very little about the dark continent. They were prepared to support Britain over Rhodesia, but hoped that they would not themselves become involved. There was very little in it for them. They did indeed have considerable trade with South Africa and relied on raw materials from the whole of Southern Africa. But they did not wish to appear as champions of white supremacy. The internal and external implications of such a posture would have been considerable.

However, when Nixon became President as a result of the 1968 election, Kissinger – at the time his National Security Adviser – decided that United States policy towards Africa should be reviewed. The result, the National Security Study Memorandum No. 39 – was leaked to the press later (in 1972). The Study produced five options, ranging from strong support of the whites to total commitment to the Nationalists. Kissinger and Nixon chose option two which envisaged modifications in American attitudes towards the whites on the one hand, including relaxations in trade embargoes of one kind or another, while giving enhanced economic help to the black African states. This became known as the 'Tar Baby' option. As far as Rhodesia was concerned, the prime result was the adoption of the Byrd amendment in November 1971 whereby the United States broke sanctions in respect of the purchase of chrome and other metals. If Nixon had used all his considerable powers of persuasion he could undoubtedly have prevented this amendment being accepted. He chose not to do so, and this certainly helped Rhodesia in its fight for economic survival. It also added to Smith's personal intransigence. When the argument was put to him that Rhodesia stood virtually alone in the world and that black majority rule was therefore inevitable in the long run, he could, and did, point to the Byrd amendment as evidence of American support.

With far more serious implications for American policy in the future, however, were the events in Angola. The impending Portuguese withdrawal of November 1975 led to a struggle for power between the Marxist MPLA and the two pro-Western parties – UNITA and the FNLA. Kissinger, by now Secretary of State to President Ford, saw this in terms of a direct struggle for power between the Communists and the West. He gave as much covert support as he could to the two pro-Western parties and encouraged the South Africans to intervene. They did so and advanced on the capital, Luanda. However, when the issue came before Congress, it refused to authorise any money to help UNITA and the FNLA in their fight. The South Africans were deserted and withdrew in ignominy. Kissinger's policy lay in ruins.

These events were typical of the dilemma which confronted the West during the whole of the process of the transition of power from white to black in Southern Africa, and which will continue to do so in the future. On the one side, the argument runs, to support pro-Western elements, black or white, would be to damn the West in the eyes of the Nationalists and inevitably to force them straight into the arms of the Communists. On the other, it is argued, not to help those who are anti-Communist would be to hand Southern Africa to the Communists on a plate and to confirm in the minds of those throughout the world who would otherwise resist Communism that in the final analysis the Western nations, and the United States in particular, were unreliable allies. One thing was certain: to promise support and then to renege on it was to get the worst of all worlds, and this was what, in effect, the Americans did in Angola. It was surprising that Kissinger and Ford did not more accurately judge the mood of Congress, chastened by Vietnam and determined not to embark on any more, as they saw it, damaging foreign adventures.

Kissinger was nothing if not flexible and, having lost in Angola, he clearly determined to recoup the American position in Africa by giving public support to the Nationalists. He went on a tour of Africa in April 1976 and pledged American support for majority rule in Angola, Mozambique and, above all, Rhodesia.

Meanwhile the war inside Rhodesia was greatly intensified. ZAPU began to operate into Rhodesia from Botswana, thereby opening up yet another front; and ZANU incursions from Mozambique increased. It became necessary to extend the call-up in Rhodesia yet further, the economy came under even greater strain and white emigration increased. The Rhodesian Security Forces started to hit back across the Mozambique border and this culminated in August 1976 in a major attack on a large guerilla camp at Nyadzonya when hundreds of guerillas were killed. This was a major military success, but it was not welcome to Vorster who was worried about any escalation of the conflict. It was condemned by Waldheim, the United Nations Secretary General, and the British Foreign Office issued its customary euphemisms about violence. The hypocritical utterances of those not involved in the conflict which were to flow whenever the Rhodesian Security Forces hit back at their enemy only served, in the eyes of the white Rhodesians, to discredit those who made them. It may have been true that the white Rhodesians should have agreed to majority rule far earlier and that they had brought violence upon themselves by their intransigent attitude. This was a perfectly tenable thesis. But to argue that, given the situation in which they found themselves, they should not attack their enemies who were in camps in Mozambique and Zambia, crossing the border with the active assistance of those countries, was an obviously absurd proposition, not even valid in international law. What were they supposed to do? It would have been military folly not to attack the guerilla bases and, in fact, the attacks on the guerillas in Mozambique and, later, in Zambia did have a marked effect in reducing the impact of the guerilla assault.

Although the Vorster/Kaunda axis had been a failure, Vorster was still determined to achieve the advent to power of a moderate black Government in Rhodesia. His next ally was to be Kissinger. The United States had abandoned South Africa in Angola and the wound still hurt. But the South Africans were extremely worried about the future of their part of the African continent. They saw that unless Smith was prepared to make a deal, including majority rule, the situation would get steadily worse from their point of view. They also realised that, in the last resort, they had the whip hand: they could cut Rhodesia's economic life-line if they wished in spite of the very considerable internal repercussions that would ensue. However, if the pressure came from Kissinger, the Rhodesia lobby in South Africa would not be able to blame Vorster. Vorster had met Kissinger in Bavaria in June when these matters had been discussed. It was clear that the interests of the two coincided. The question was how pressure was to be applied.

Vorster initiated the first moves by withdrawing the residual helicopter pilots and technicians who were still in Rhodesia and by slowing down the rate at which oil, arms and ammunition were reaching that country. These were the real levers of power which could not be ignored by the Rhodesians. Kissinger met Vorster in Zurich in September 1976 and eight days later set out on his fateful journey to Africa.

The African Nationalists were in their usual state of total disunity. ZIPA, which was supposed to comprise the combined ZAPU and ZANU forces, existed in little but name since few ZAPU guerillas had joined it. In effect ZANU was operating from Mozambique and ZAPU, quite independently, from Zambia and Botswana, albeit on a much reduced scale. In the political sphere, the eventual line-up was gradually emerging with Nkomo leading ZAPU and Mugabe becoming the acknowledged leader of ZANU. The two armies ZIPRA (ZAPU) and ZANLA (ZANU) were opposed to each other and this division resulted occasionally in armed clashes. Muzorewa was still leader of the ANC which in theory comprised all the Nationalist movements, but this had become a charade. Sithole still considered himself the leader of ZANU but this, too, was a farcical claim; his support existed only in Rhodesia itself and even there it was waning fast. The Front Line Presidents again tried to reconcile the various factions at a meeting in Dar-es-Salaam, but this failed.

In Rhodesia, Smith's position, for the first time, had become a little precarious. There were many whites who had been suspicious of his negotiations with Nkomo and who were extremely worried about the possible implications of the Kissinger/Vorster initiative. Smith had made some concessions to the Africans by including four chiefs in his cabinet, and he announced that he was prepared to accept more. He had also adopted some of the less radical proposals of a Commission under Sir Vincent Quénet which had been set up to look into racial discrimination: in particular the higher reaches of the civil service, the army and the police were to be opened up to the Africans if they could qualify. However, he turned down the only two recommendations which were of real substance – reform of the Land Tenure Act and the adoption of a common voters' roll. Even the modest changes he had made were anathema to many of his right wing supporters. He was, however, able to ride off criticism at his Party Conference in September with the assistance of David Smith, the able and balanced Finance Minister, who was emerging as the principal moderate in the Rhodesian Front Government.

After visiting Tanzania and Zambia, Kissinger arrived in Pretoria on 17 September. His first meeting with Smith took place on 19 September. Kissinger's prestige was immense and the impact of his analytical mind on Smith was profound. His arguments as to the impossibility of the Rhodesians continuing as they were, with the economic and military situation steadily deteriorating, were irrefutable, particularly if South African support was to be in question. After an agonising discussion with his principal advisers the break came. Smith had to concede the principle of majority rule within two years. However, there were other elements in the package deal with which he was confronted which were more encouraging from his point of view. There would be an interim Government consisting of a Council of Ministers and a Council of State. As soon as these two bodies came into existence the war would stop and sanctions would be lifted. The Council of Ministers would have a majority of Africans with an African Prime Minister. But the Council of State would be half white and half black and it would be that body which would draft the new Consitution. With a divided Nationalist movement, the whites would still probably be able to shape the Constitution in a direction which would suit them. Smith asked that the Chairman of the Council of State should be white and that the portfolios of defence, law and order and finance in the Council of Ministers should be given to whites.

Smith persuaded his cabinet to support the package and made his fateful broadcast to the Rhodesian people on 24 September in which he accepted, for the first time, the principle of majority rule. The psychological effect of this total volte-face was profound. Although opposition to the statement was widespread, such was Smith's personal prestige that the majority of whites accepted it as inevitable. They could not believe that Smith could have put his name to the package unless it was really necessary. Furthermore, there was always the hope that, with his considerable diplomatic skills, he would be able to salvage a great deal out of the consequent negotiations on the Constitution.

Far from accepting the Kissinger package, the Front Line Presidents now demanded a Conference which would be charged with deciding on the form and structure of the interim

124

administration. The British agreed to set up a Conference, but with no pre-conditions. Smith protested that he had only agreed to majority rule on the basis of the Kissinger package and that there was no question of re-negotiation. He was supported by Vorster in this.

So much is clear. There are, however, doubts as to what extent, if at all, Kissinger led Smith to believe that the Front Line Presidents had accepted the package, and indeed in how much detail he had discussed the proposed deal with Kaunda and Nyerere. One view is that Kissinger deliberately duped Smith, that he had not come to any agreement with Kaunda and Nyerere as to the package involved, but gave the impression that he had, thereby leading Smith to make his broadcast on a false assumption in the hope that the breaking of the log jam would result in an agreement later. Another is that Nyerere and Kaunda had agreed to the package but subsequently reneged on it. A third is that Smith realised that the package had not been agreed but decided to make the broadcast nevertheless in the hope that, the main issue of majority rule having been settled, an acceptable deal based on Kissinger's package could be negotiated. The truth is obscure and all those involved in the affair tell different stories.

Muzorewa returned to Salisbury and received an overwhelming welcome, thereby confirming him in his view that he, unlike the other Nationalist leaders who were outside the country, really represented the people of his country. At this point, too, there occurred the event which was to be a major, if not determining, factor in the eventual outcome. Nkomo and Mugabe finally came to an agreement to unite under the name of the 'Patriotic Front'.

The African picture was, therefore, at last achieving some clarity: the Patriotic Front, which was in control of the guerillas inside and outside Rhodesia, was the radical arm of African Nationalism; while Muzorewa, with very considerable support among the Africans inside the country, apart from the bulk of the Ndebele who remained loyal to Nkomo, represented a more moderate approach although he, too, was adamant in his demand for majority rule. The split between Mugabe, who was in control of the mainly Karanga and Zezuru external elements of ZANU, and Sithole was total. Both claimed to be the leader of ZANU, but Sithole's claim to this position was becoming increasingly meaningless.

Eventually it was agreed to hold a Conference, opening in Geneva in October, to be chaired by a British representative and attended by Smith, Muzorewa, Nkomo, Mugabe and Sithole.

Britain was again at the centre of the stage for the first time since the Pearce Report. Callaghan had been very involved in the preparations for the Kissinger initiative. But Britain had not been in the headlines. Smith, Kaunda, Nkomo, Vorster and Kissinger – these were the men who had been in the public eye. Rhodesia occasioned no great public interest in Britain: the drama had, temporarily as it turned out, outrun its audience. Party political controversy in Britain was concerned with other matters; if anything the Conservatives were relieved not to have to deal with a problem which seemed to be insoluble and they had little to offer in the way of an alternative policy.

However, the Kissinger initiative and the fact that the Rhodesians had accepted the inevitability of majority rule, whether under false pretences or not, led the British Government to take a more active interest. Crosland, by now the British Foreign Secretary, decided not to play a personal role in the Conference and appointed Ivor Richard, a clever lawyer who had been a Labour MP and who was in charge of the British Mission to the United Nations, as Chairman. It was to be a thankless task. The most radical of the African delegations was that of Mugabe, who was not prepared to compromise in any way. He persuaded Kaunda to release Tongogara, who was still under arrest in Zambia charged with the murder of Chitepo, and called for the immediate establishment of a Socialist State with no protection whatsoever for the white minority. He quickly established himself in the white minds as being the most dangerous adversary they had. Nkomo found himself pulled along by Mugabe's extreme statements. There were interminable arguments about procedure, status and who was to pay for the extremely expensive accommodation in Geneva – about almost everything except the real issues which everybody realised were virtually insoluble. Negotiations eventually centred on the date for independence rather than the far more important issue of the form of the interim Government and how the Constitution was to be agreed. Ivor Richard remained defiantly optimistic but the Conference eventually ground to a halt on 14 December. Failure was inevitable from the start. Smith saw it in terms of implementing the Kissinger package. The Africans, still very divided, saw it in terms of negotiating a new agreement. The two positions were, and remained, totally irreconcilable.

Richard set off on a tour of Southern Africa to try to retrieve something out of the wreckage. The British had produced a plan under which there would be a British Commissioner having a casting vote. This was totally unacceptable to the white Rhodesians because, in effect, it meant handing over power without any safeguards for the future. Richard tried to maintain his optimism as he shuttled to and fro in Southern Africa on the now familiar route, but it quickly became apparent that the plan had no chance of success.

At this stage it might be worth examining the constantly re-iterated Rhodesian charge that, even after the merger of the Foreign and Commonwealth Relations Offices, the British officials concerned with these matters were deeply prejudiced and that it was their, almost paranoic, opposition to the whites in Rhodesia which had bedevilled all attempts at a settlement. This was believed profoundly by much of the white Rhodesian population at that time and this belief was to persist right through until the election won by Mugabe in 1980.

The first point to make is that it is not true that officials are wholly unbiased. They are human and of course they are conditioned by the same kind of prejudices and preconceived ideas, based on a whole variety of actual and received experience, as the rest of us. Their views, too, are an important factor in the formulation of policy. Some Ministers take more notice of them than others, but, almost always, official advice does have some bearing on the policy which is eventually adopted. Facts are facts, but the way they are presented can be crucial.

It is, however, also true that the white Rhodesians had little or no conception of the difficulties which faced the British Government. They were easily persuaded by their own propaganda and they were not exposed to the realities of the world scene either by way of their own media, which was heavily controlled or, because of the many difficulties which existed due to sanctions, by personal visits abroad except to South Africa and, before the Portuguese coup, to Mozambique. One of the functions, certainly, of Foreign Office officials was to point out to their political masters the international repercussions of any particular course of action and if Britain had granted independence to Rhodesia on easy terms from the white point of view, these repercussions would have been very considerable. The Commonwealth may indeed have broken up, Britain may well have had damaging trade sanctions to contend with and all kinds of other problems would undoubtedly have arisen. Foreign Office officials of course drew the attention of their political masters to these facts, but in itself this did not denote any bias one way or the other.

One of the problems for the British Government was that it had no permanent representation in Salisbury. Its information about the real state of affairs inside Rhodesia was, therefore, apart from the occasional visits made by Ministers and officials,[24] necessarily second hand. This was an enormous drawback to a proper evaluation of the situation. Information was constantly flowing in about the likely reactions of every country in the world to any initiative, but from the one country most intimately involved came little, except what could be gleaned from a whole range of unofficial contacts. The Rhodesians had refused to accept a British diplomatic presence in Rhodesia unless Britain in its turn accepted a Rhodesian presence in London, which would have been contrary to the spirit, and indeed the letter, of United Nations mandatory sanctions to which Britain was a party. There was no way out of this dilemma, but lack of direct contact was a considerable drawback to both sides.

It is true that some British officials were more hard line than others: this was inevitable. Those whose responsibilities were further from the scene of action were apt to be more radical than those who actually had to cope with the situation: to those not actually deeply involved in any problem the solution is always apt to look simple. To an official whose responsibility was the Commonwealth or the United Nations or Europe, for instance, the Rhodesian situation was indeed an embarrassing irrelevancy. But those officials who actually dealt with Rhodesian affairs did on the whole understand a great deal about the problem in all its complexity – far more than is commonly supposed. Furthermore, with rare exceptions, they were not swayed by personal feelings of dislike for the white

Rhodesians.

There was a large element of self-delusion in the white Rhodesian strictures on the Foreign Office. They thought that their case was self-evident: they could not understand why successive British Governments, and particularly Conservative Governments, did not accept it and act accordingly. They therefore searched for hidden and even conspiratorial causes behind what to them was the astonishing British behaviour. Foreign Office official advice was apparently the one constant factor in an otherwise changing political scene in Britain, and they became convinced that this must be the reason for the British attitude.

There were possible problems attached to the formulation of British policy but these were nothing to do with the quality of official advice. The difficulties came if there was a conflict between the interests of Rhodesia and Britain.

But what were the interests of Rhodesia? The white Rhodesians saw their Government as representing their country and they thought Britain should accept its evaluation of the Rhodesian interest. However, successive British Governments (and their official advisers) did not see it in that ways. To them, the Rhodesian Front Government, particularly after UDI, did not represent all the people of Rhodesia and the British still had the overall responsibility for affairs in that country. And, in any case, the British view was that the interests of the two did not conflict at any stage. The long-term interests of both coincided – that an orderly transfer of power from white to black should take place with international recognition.

These matters are highly emotive and the opposing views cannot be reconciled. But to blame British governmental policy on nefarious Foreign Office advice is to misunderstand the British political system. The overall political approach to the Rhodesian affair was, throughout, in the hands of politicians, not civil servants.

The Foreign Office was certainly not responsible for many of the policy decisions made by Dr David Owen, who became Foreign Secretary in February 1977. Certainly as far as the Rhodesian issue was concerned, he was a disastrous choice. Brash, intellectually arrogant and lacking in experience, he was greatly disliked by Foreign Office officials whom he

129

treated with scant respect. He thought he knew it all, and he certainly did not. Foreign Office dislike of Owen was not because he often disregarded their advice: it was because he frequently did not listen to it at all. He tried to bulldoze his way through difficulties without really taking into account either the views of those whose whole lives had been spent in evaluating the likely responses of other countries to possible policy options or of those who would actually be affected. He frequently changed his mind and blamed officials for the consequent muddle. Of all the Foreign Secretaries since 1945, he was the one with whom the Foreign Office found it most difficult to work.

It was, of course, inherently far more difficult for a Labour than for a Conservative Government to bring about a settlement in Rhodesia. If a solution was to be reached it was essential for some concessions to be made to Smith, and the internal party political pressures within the Labour Party meant that any such concessions would come under heavy attack from the Government's own supporters. This would not have been the case, at least not on anything like the same scale, in the Conservative Party. A Government can accept, and defeat, criticism from the Opposition: it cannot permanently ride off virulent attacks from its own party. This situation weakened Owen's position as an intermediary and was partly, but only partly, responsible for some of the errors of judgement he made.

Apart from Owen, there was a further – and most important – twist to the political kaleidoscope. Carter had succeeded Ford as President of the United States and this had profound implications for Rhodesia. Kissinger, who dominated American foreign policy, had at least been very aware of the dangers of Communist advance in Southern Africa and was prepared to focus his considerable powers of rigorous analysis on the matter without any prejudice or wishy-washy emotional tie-ups. Carter was very different. He was obsessed by human rights and appeared to think that issues could be decided on the basis of imagined moral imperatives, divorced from the harsh realities of power. His advisers in the White House, too, were very much on the left of the political spectrum. He appointed Andrew Young, who had delivered to him a large part of the black vote in the elections, as his Ambassador to the

United Nations. Because he was black, Young seemed to think that he understood the Southern African problem. He did not. He committed a series of appalling diplomatic gaffes to the great embarrassment of Cyrus Vance, the Secretary of State, who himself also had little understanding of Southern Africa.

The cardinal mistake which the British Government made at this stage, was to involve the Americans in the various further initiatives made. It seemed at the time, no doubt, that Britain did not have enough political muscle to bring about an agreement on her own and that American help would be a great advantage. But the task of reconciling black and white objectives within Rhodesia, together with the enormous added complication of the Front Line Presidents, to say nothing of the South Africans, was difficult enough without adding yet another complicating factor – the Americans – particularly since American policy seemed to be largely directed by Andrew Young, who clearly had no idea whatever of what was happening on the ground.

For instance, in an interview in *The Times* on 22 May 1978 Young delivered himself of the following conclusion: 'Non-violence is in many ways being practised by the Patriotic Front ... I asked one of their commanders, Tongogara, what they actually do in Rhodesia, and he said they're not doing much fighting, except when they are fired upon, or when the Rhodesian Defence Forces find them and try to run them out. Basically, what they're doing is moving around the villages and conducting political seminars and singing songs – which is exactly what we (Civil Rights fighters in the United States) did'.

Reading this, a white Rhodesian who knew, or had even had personal experience, of the appalling guerilla atrocities was not likely to think that Young would be a perceptive and useful intermediary.

Carter had the Byrd amendment, whereby the United States had been importing chrome and other metals from Rhodesia, repealed, and talks between the United States and Britain as to the way forward began. Owen went on a tour of Southern Africa and arrived in Rhodesia in mid-April 1977. Owen's idea was that since previous initiatives had broken down on the issue of the transitional period before a new Constitution came into effect, it might be better to start with the

Constitution. If that goal could be achieved, then the way to arrive there could be easier to settle. The proposals envisaged the setting up of yet another Conference in order to agree on an Independence Constitution, and that some kind of neutral administration would run the country in the interim period during which it would organise an election to be held under the new agreed Constitution. Owen's talks seemed to offer some hope of success and a group of officials led by John Graham, a senior Foreign Office official, and Stephen Low, the American Ambassador to Zambia, were sent round the main capitals of Southern Africa with the task of producing an arrangement which could satisfy both sides.

Further progress was made and Owen and Young, now in tandem, set off in August on a further tour of Southern Africa. Owen, who had made a good impression on the white Rhodesians on his first visit, did not this time endear himself to his hosts in Salisbury. It seemed to them that he had failed to grasp their point of view, and went out of his way to flout it. For instance, the Rhodesians took great exception to the word 'surrender' which was used in the phrase 'surrender of power' – a tactless formulation in the circumstances. It is also, however, possible that the Rhodesian Government was already intent on bringing off an internal settlement and was pleased to seize on any evidence of tactlessness and blow it up into a major issue.

The proposals were published on 1 September. One of the main problems concerned the Security Forces. The white Rhodesians were not prepared to have their forces disbanded or merged with the guerilla army. The Nationalists would settle for nothing but guerilla control during the interim period. The British produced the idea of a British Resident Commissioner who would effectively rule Rhodesia for six months during this time and Field-Marshal Lord Carver, who had retired as Chief of the Defence Staff in Britain, was appointed. The plan, which also envisaged a United Nations force inside Rhodesia, was opposed by both the Rhodesian Government and the Nationalists, but it was nevertheless proceeded with and in late October Carver set out on yet another tour of the area. Highly intelligent, but humourless and limited in political know-how, he was an unfortunate choice. He arrived at Salisbury Airport in full military uniform, an extremely tactless gesture in the circumstances. He was soon sent packing. Neither was he successful in his meetings with the African Nationalists who saw him as an irrelevancy.

The internal situation in Rhodesia meantime had been deteriorating further. Guerilla activity had spread over virtually the whole country. Many schools had been forced to close. African farmers and Councillors were harrassed and often murdered. White farmers were killed. Hospitals and clinics were destroyed or shut down. Children were abducted. The Security Force reaction was to take ever stronger measures against Africans thought to be helping the guerillas. The economic situation was also deteriorating fast. Smith, who had tréd to move marginally towards the Nationalist demands by amending the Land Tenure Act, was being attacked on his right flank by a new die-hard party, the Rhodesia Action Party, to which twelve of his Rhodesia Front Members of Parliament defected. Smith challenged this attack by holding yet another general election in August in which he again made a clean sweep of the seats with 85 per cent of the vote. Once again the Nationalists were at odds with each other as a result of a meeting between Smith and Kaunda arranged by Tiny Rowland, the powerful Chairman of Lonrho. Mugabe suspected, almost certainly rightly, that Smith was trying, through Kaunda, to persuade Nkomo to take part in an internal settlement. But the central fact in the situation at that time was that, although neither the British nor the Americans accepted it, the Anglo-American initiative was as good as dead. Negotiations continued at official level for a time, but Smith's eyes were already on a deal with Muzorewa.

Vorster/Kaunda, Kissinger, Richard/Crosland, Owen/Young – they had all failed. The war continued. Was there no way out of the agony? And could there have been a solution if any of the principal actors in the drama had behaved differently?

Certainly, many mistakes had been made. The absence of African Nationalist unity had been a major factor in the failure of the Vorster/Kaunda initiative. As far as Smith was concerned, although he had been forced to make the broadcast in which he accepted the principle of majority rule, he had refused to face the implications of this volte-face. He was constantly trying to avoid the consequences by what amounted to

133

sleight of hand, and this added great force to the arguments of those Africans who were determined to continue with the war and not to look for compromise. It followed that when, later, Muzorewa did become Prime Minister of a black dominated Government but with Smith still retaining his position as a Cabinet Minister, many Africans could not believe that power really had been transferred. Kissinger, for his part, had indeed made a contribution in persuading Smith publicly to accept the principle of majority rule, but this initiative had foundered in a miasma of mutual incomprehension. As far as Britain was concerned, while Callaghan was Foreign Secretary, its policy on Rhodesia was sensible.[25] But Owen's attempts at personalised diplomacy in tandem with Young were inept and fruitless.

But, in spite of all this, given the circumstances, it is unlikely that a peaceful solution could have been found during this period whatever policies had been adopted by the various political leaders concerned. Expectations among the guerillas, outside and inside Rhodesia, were such that, even if they had been united, their leaders could not have accepted compromises which would have been tolerable to the mass of the white population. The legacy of the decisions in 1962 when, by their vote against Whitehead, the whites had deliberately eschewed partnership and co-operation with the blacks, and the African Nationalists had, by refusing to take part in the elections, deliberately turned to violence, was still the predominating factor. A further period of misery and bloodshed was probably necessary before conditions could possibly exist in which a solution could be found.

CHAPTER SIX

The Internal Settlement, 1977–9

The last hope for the whites now was to try again to come to an agreement with those moderate black leaders who were prepared to do a separate deal, to sell the agreement to international opinion and then to persuade as many guerillas as possible to surrender or to 'come on side' as the current phrase was.

The whites had accepted 'majority rule', but this had different meanings for different people. For the Nationalists it meant rule by the black majority race. It was therefore a racialist concept. It certainly did not mean rule by the majority of the people. Every African country would claim to have 'majority rule' but there were very few which had Governments elected in free elections in which anyone representing any party could stand as a candidate, a pre-requirement if the claim to be ruled by the majority of the people could be substantiated. To many of the whites, however, the phrase had a different meaning and Smith played on the ambiguity. There were of course racial overtones in the white interpretation of the phrase, too. For them, 'majority rule' would have been conceded when there was a black majority in Parliament. But the Constitution could be set about with so many safeguards that the black majority could not in practice do very much without the support of some white members of Parliament. Furthermore, the franchise could be set at a level which would allow only the African middle class to participate in elections so that, although there was a black majority in Parliament, this certainly would not represent the majority of the people.

One of the great cries of the whites throughout had been the call for 'responsible rule' which would ensure the 'mainten-

135

ance of standards'. The difficulty was that, in the white mind, 'responsible' rule meant 'white' rule or at least a situation where the whites had a power of veto. They had much justification for their belief. Black rule to the North had, indeed, led to a very considerable lowering of standards. Corruption and inefficiency were indeed rife in nearly all African countries. Law and order had indeed broken down in many African countries. There were many examples of extreme cruelty and self-seeking aggrandisement by the leaders of African states.

The problem which faced Smith, therefore, was somehow to bring about a situation in which the transition to 'majority rule', whatever interpretation was put on that phrase, was achieved without destroying the general structure of administration which had been built up over the years by the whites and of course, from his point of view, to safeguard as far as possible the white standard of living.

The Africans, too, did have an interest in avoiding actions which would lead to a white exodus. If all the whites left immediately, the chaos would be absolute. All the public services, the bulk – and certainly the most efficient – of the agricultural sector and the whole of the industrial and commercial sectors were firmly in white hands. Africans could not possibly hope to replace the whites in these key positions at a stroke. If a considerable proportion of the whites were not prepared to remain, the advent of 'majority rule' would be followed almost immediately by 'majority starvation'. The problem for the Africans, therefore, was to get an agreement which would satisfy black opinion that a real transfer of power had taken place but yet would leave enough safeguards in white hands to ensure that the whites did not all pack up their bags and leave. In fact, therefore, although arising from the opposite end of the spectrum, the black and white objectives were very similar.

The difficulty, of course, was that the bulk of the guerillas and most of their leaders refused to be involved in any dealings with Smith, and even those African leaders who were prepared to participate in internal negotiations were themselves, too, very divided.

Negotiations were started in December 1977 between Smith, Muzorewa, Sithole and Chirau. Muzorewa had very considerable internal support. It was he who had successfully led opposition to the Home agreement. He had not been associated with the war and, already, there was an overwhelming desire for peace: indeed, he was seen as a man of peace. It was not thought that he was personally motivated by pure ambition. Although he was rather lost in the atmosphere of political bargaining and *quid pro quo*, which was to be the principal feature of constitutional negotiations from now on, and often appeared to be vacillating and indecisive, he was more astute than was realised by many whites. He was not a charismatic figure who could possibly dominate any situation and he was certainly not a man of high intellectual calibre, but he was in the end generally able to bring about a consensus within his party and then to enunciate it, which was the traditional method adopted by Shona leaders.

Sithole had lost a great deal of ground. His intelligence was considerable but he was a scheming seeker after personal power who had been bypassed by other more politically adept men. He did, nevertheless, still retain a certain following.

Chirau, a dignified but not very intelligent chief, who had been pushed forward by Smith, was rather lost in this kind of milieu. He was the leader of a new party – ZUPO – which never really got off the ground. Smith had continually tried to use the chiefs as political agents for the Rhodesian Front, but he clearly did not understand their role, which was to protect traditional values in the Tribal Trust Lands. To pitch-fork the chiefs into the political battle in Salisbury was at once to diminish their authority and to ask them to undertake activities for which they were not at all personally qualified.

David Smith, the Deputy Prime Minister, who was personally popular with the Africans, played a leading role in the negotiations and agreement was reached surprisingly quickly, although not without considerable difficulty and much bargaining. For the first time, the whites agreed to elections with 'one-man-one-vote' – a massive concession. Until the elections were held, a Transitional Government was to be set up with a Ministerial Council consisting of nine whites and nine blacks (three from each of the black parties) paired off as co-Ministers. An Executive Council was to be in overall control composed of the four leaders who would alternate as Chairman. The Government was to draft a new Constitution. There would be seventy-two black seats in the House of Assembly.

137

Twenty white seats would be elected on a separate roll and the last eight seats would be elected on a common roll from sixteen candidates selected by those elected to the twenty white seats. There would be a justiciable Declaration of Rights, an independent judiciary, a public service board and a blocking mechanism (requiring the support of at least six white MPs) to prevent amendments to those key features of the Constitution which embodied white safeguards. The Transitional Government would abolish racial discrimination and hold an election so that the new Government would take over on 31 December 1978. The agreement was signed on 3 March 1978.

The whites had come a long way. The question was whether they had gone far enough to satisfy international opinion and to persuade the guerillas that 'majority rule' had indeed been achieved and that there was no point in continuing the war.

The signing of the internal agreement put the British Government in a quandary. In the political circumstances of the time they could not merely have accepted it and ditched the Nationalist leaders. On the other hand it was, clearly, a considerable achievement. It can be argued that they should have insisted that it provided a basis for discussion at a Conference, to which the Nationalist leaders would be invited, but with a threat to go ahead with it whether or not Nkomo and Mugabe turned up (it was this kind of procedure which was to be so successfully used by Lord Carrington later). It must, however, be very doubtful if, at that moment, either Nkomo or Mugabe would have attended – they still no doubt thought, probably rightly, that the guerilla war would weaken the Rhodesian Government still further and it is unlikely that Kaunda, Nyerere or Machel would have supported a British initiative of that nature at the time. Furthermore, as already explained, Owen's political position at home would probably have prevented him from mounting a credible threat to go ahead in negotiations with the Transitional Government in Rhodesia without Nkomo or Mugabe. It must also be realised that, the agreement having been signed, the four internal leaders would have been extremely reluctant to re-open negotiations. Muzorewa undoubtedly saw a great chance of obtaining power at the forthcoming election. At that time, too, the four internal leaders may well have genuinely believed that they could persuade a sizeable number of guerillas to surrender and that both Mugabe and Nkomo would find their support inside Rhodesia draining away.

In the event, the British Government gave only lukewarm support to the internal agreement and at first tried to persist with the outdated Anglo/American plan. The prospect of an internal agreement did bring some pressure to bear on Nkomo and Mugabe, and at a meeting in Malta in February 1978 some progress was made in modifying their demands. After further talks between the Graham/Low team and the Transitional Government in Salisbury, yet another mission, this time composed of Owen, Young, Vance and Carver set out in April 1978 on a further tour first to Dar-es-Salaam and then to Salisbury. It received the now routine rebuff. Thereafter, although the Anglo/American plan was still official policy, the British Government's efforts were directed to trying to get the internal and external leaders together. That failed too.

The British Government had made many mistakes: it should not have involved the Americans at all; it should not have persisted with a plan which, in spite of considerable progress on the Constitution, could not have been accepted by both sides; and its handling of the white Rhodesians was certainly not as tactful as it could have been. But there were very real difficulties for which it was not responsible. The whites must bear a heavy load of responsibility for the eventual failure of the internal agreement. Instead of accepting that control was to pass to the Africans and falling over backwards to demonstrate that real power was in black hands, they continued to prevaricate. There was no immediate and radical action on racial discrimination. Nothing was done about the Land Tenure Act. There was no immediate acceleration in black promotion in the public service. The whites missed an opportunity to make the reality of black power so apparent that international opinion would perforce have had to recognise that a completely new situation had arisen and perhaps to come to terms with it. This could have been achieved without giving away the few safeguards which were vital if a white exodus was to be avoided. Smith was largely to blame for this massive error. Perhaps for the first time he could have transformed the situation. He was the leading figure in the Transitional Government. It is true that a white referendum was necessary before the new Constitution could be enacted but if

139

Smith had insisted on immediate and radical change in the structure of government in Rhodesia during the transitional period, thrown his entire weight behind the new Constitution during the referendum campaign and then resigned before the elections were held, the situation would have been very different. The very continuance of Smith in the Government was an enormous obstacle to international recognition. However, as is so often the case with leaders who ought to retire, he thought himself to be indispensable, thus, in the long run, ensuring the victory of the very man who, to him at the time, represented the worst of all possible outcomes.

In the event the Transitional Government plodded on, not really achieving very much, finding it difficult even to stick together when Byron Hove, an astute lawyer and joint Minister for Law and Order, was dismissed because he spoke out against the lack of progress in Africanisation. Horror piled on horror in the course of the war, including a massacre of eight British missionaries and four children, one of which was a one-month-old baby, at Elim near Mozambique. The pattern of life in many of the Tribal Trust Lands now consisted mainly of a struggle for mere survival – no schools, no medical facilities, a strict curfew, martial law, starvation and the constant fear of death, only relieved in some areas by the existence of protected villages which could either be regarded as havens or prisons, depending on the eye of the beholder.

Smith was only too aware of the situation. All attempts by Muzorewa and Sithole to get the guerillas to 'come on side' had failed. The International community had clearly not accepted the internal settlement and the prospects for peace were very gloomy. He turned again to Nkomo as he had done so often in the past, hoping to get him to participate in the Transitional Government, perhaps as Chairman. Kaunda, whose support for Nkomo had been constant and whose country was in ever direr economic straits, agreed to organise a meeting. Smith and Nkomo met in secret in Lusaka on 14 August but an attempt, with Nigerian help, to cajole Mugabe into a tripartite meeting with Smith failed. Mugabe refused and published the proposal. There was a considerable furore and much recrimination. However, all hope of any kind of deal was ended when, on 3 September 1978, a Rhodesian Viscount aircraft full of holidaymakers returning from Kariba to Salisbury was shot down by ZIPRA (Nkomo's army) and ten of the eighteen survivors were massacred. In a radio interview heard in Rhodesia, Nkomo appeared to be pleased with what his soldiers had done, although denying responsibility for the subsequent massacre. The profound shock and disgust which swept over white Rhodesia made any further negotiation with Nkomo totally impossible (a second Viscount was shot down in February 1979).

The Rhodesians now turned to even stronger retaliation in cross-border raids and for the first time they really set about the task of attacking Nkomo's army in Zambia.[26] They killed large numbers of ZIPRA guerillas in their camps and made more highly successful raids on the ZANLA bases in Mozambique. Muzorewa and Sithole were allowed to set up their own private armies in Rhodesia, known as Auxiliaries, composed in part of surrendered guerillas. In the early stages these armies were very undisciplined and, although discipline was gradually improved and a measure of control was imposed on them, they added a further and highly complicating factor to an already confused situation (183 of Sithole's Auxiliaries were killed by the Security Forces in July 1979).

In November 1978 ZANU published a 'Death List' of Africans. Those on it were told that unless they stopped collaborating with the Transitional Government immediately they would be arrested or shot on sight. The list included Sithole, Muzorewa and Chirau and a large number of other names. The document was signed by Eddison Zvobgo, the Deputy Secretary for Information and Publicity. It is reproduced at Appendix 2. The ritual Communist jargon of the document gives a clear indication of the atmosphere in Maputo, the capital of Mozambique, at the time. In fact retribution on a large scale did not take place when Mugabe came to power and Zvobgo turned out to be an effective and moderate Minister, at least in the early stages of independence.

The elections had been due to take place before 31 December 1978, but here too there was delay. The new Constitution was not published until January and the date for the election was fixed for 20 April 1979.

The new Constitution was to come under heavy attack mainly on the grounds that, although it gave the appearance of black rule, in practice white power was entrenched in it. There were 28 white as against 72 black seats, a vastly disproportionate share to the whites. In fact, once the principle of special safeguards for the whites was accepted – and this principle was in the event also accepted at the Lancaster House Conference – the precise figure of white seats was of comparatively minor importance. What mattered was whether or not they could block alterations to the Constitution which would jeopardise their essential interests. They did have this power. But of far greater importance were the requirements for appointment to high positions in the Security Forces, the armed services and the police, and to the independent commissions which controlled these bodies. These were pitched at a level which meant that few Africans would be eligible for some considerable time. Those who framed the Constitution were undoubtedly faced by a dilemma on this point. Because the whites had, in the past, been so dilatory in training Africans for senior posts in the public service,[27] and because some Africans, though qualified, had refused to put themselves forward as candidates for even those posts which were available for fear of being dubbed 'Tshombes' or 'sell-outs', there were only two alternatives. Either Africans would be pitch-forked into positions for which they had had no proper training, thus inevitably leading to a general 'lowering of standards', or high standards would be maintained which meant that leading positions would remain in white hands for a considerable period. This would inevitably lead to accusations of continuing white power. It would probably have been better to compromise on this point and to allow a certain lowering of standards, but it could well be argued that, however the Constitution had been drafted, it would still have been attacked by the external Nationalists, and the fear of a white exodus was still a predominant feature in the minds of all those who drafted the Constitution.

One innovation which, also, was to be highly controversial was the provision of an automatic coalition Government after the election. The electoral system was to be one of proportional representation under the regional list system whereby in each province seats would be allocated to parties in accordance with the proportion of votes they obtained. This had not been adopted as a matter of principle but because it was impossible to delineate constituencies in the time available and, therefore, it was not practical to hold elections under the first

142

past the post system for the African seats[28] (white seats were to continue to be decided on the old system).

It was decided to institute a 'Government of National Unity'. The system to be adopted was that each party would obtain one cabinet post for every five seats it won in the election. The Prime Minister would be the leader of the party with the most seats and he would be responsible for allocating portfolios to the members of the cabinet. This arrangement was attacked on the grounds that it perpetuated white power. This particular criticism had no validity at all. The whites would only have five out of twenty cabinet seats, hardly a dominant position. On the other hand the system had great advantages. The Ndebele would be certain to have a number of cabinet seats thus, hopefully, avoiding tribal troubles. And the whites would feel that they still had a stake in the country – a vital element in the situation. It is interesting that when Mugabe eventually came to power he, too, formed his cabinet with much the same considerations in mind.

Neither was it true that the Ministers had no control over their respective Departments. For instance, in the case of the armed services, Section 103 (3) of the Constitution expressly stated that 'The Prime Minister may give to a Commander referred to in Sub-Section 1 (The Head of the Armed Services) such general directions of policy with respect to the defence of Zimbabwe/Rhodesia as he may consider necessary *and that Commander shall comply with such directions or cause them to be complied with* [author's italics]'.

There was a whole range of other criticisms most of which did not stand up to detailed examination. But it was indeed most unfortunate that when Muzorewa became Prime Minister he was not able to choose his own secretary of the cabinet in place of Jack Gaylard, the genial and immensely able incumbent of that post for many years under Smith, who had retired. This played right into the hands of the critics and was to be used most effectively later by those who argued that a real transfer of power had not taken place.

However, the real objection to the Constitution was not based on its terms. It was that Mugabe and Nkomo had not been a party to it and had refused to take any part in the consequent election, and therefore it could not possibly be said to represent the aspirations of the whole Rhodesian people. The

OAU and the Front Line Presidents had said that the Patriotic Front represented the Rhodesian people and, if the Patriotic Front was not involved, it was argued, it followed that the Constitution was a farcical and unjust imposition by Smith and his stooges. This was the attitude adopted by the Security Council of the United Nations on 14 March, when it approved a resolution to the effect that any Rhodesian internal settlement produced under the auspices of the present Salisbury Administration was illegal and unacceptable. This motion was passed by ten votes to nil with five abstentions (Britain, the United States, Canada, France and West Germany). The fact that the Patriotic Front had been asked to take part in the negotiations leading to the adoption of the Constitution, but had refused to do so, had little impact on the bulk of international opinion which by now seemed to accept that Mugabe and Nkomo did indeed represent the overwhelming majority of Africans in Rhodesia and, therefore, had the right to dictate the terms of white surrender.

In the referendum held on 30 January 1979, the Constitution was accepted by the white electorate after a bitter campaign with Smith defending it strongly on the grounds that it was the best that could be obtained in the circumstances. There was an 85 per cent vote in favour of the Constitution in a poll of 71 per cent of the electorate. One of the white opponents of the Constitution was, surprisingly, a right wing Cabinet Minister, Hayman, who resigned and argued that it would not be recognised by the international community and would therefore be ineffective. He turned out to be right.

Meanwhile, in Britain, party political controversy over Rhodesia was increasing. A general election was due before very long and the question of the Conservative reaction to the internal settlement was clearly of great importance. What would the Conservative Party's attitude towards Rhodesia be if it was returned to power?

One of the features of democracy, certainly as practised in Britain, is the great pressure which is put on any Opposition to oppose the Government's policies in as many areas as possible and to do so with the maximum vehemence. The very essence of any democratic system of Government is the provision of an alternative administration. As far as Britain is concerned, our 'elective dictatorship', as Lord Hailsham puts it, does at least provide for a possible change at least every five years. But, unless there is a clear choice, the electorate will indeed wonder why it should vote for a new Government. Political parties are in business in order to exercise power – not to languish in Opposition. The pressures on Oppositions to produce alternative policy in every field become most apparent during the actual election period when the party spokesmen are questioned by Robin Day or whoever on their party's policy in the respective spheres for which they are responsible. The question asked of Opposition spokesmen is – 'What would you do if you were in power?' If the Shadow Minister has no alternative to the Government's existing policy he will find himself in great difficulty. This inevitably leads to a compulsion to advocate changes of policy in every field. On the other hand, in practice there may well be no real alternative other than a marginal alteration of emphasis. The temptation to put forward more radical changes of policy is overwhelming, and this can often lead to the new Government finding itself lumbered with policies which are either impossible to carry out or will actually be damaging to the national interest. A further, and very considerable, complication is that Oppositions are not in possession of the facts upon which balanced judgements can be made. As far as foreign affairs are concerned, they do not have access to all the telegrams and reports which flow into Whitehall daily from British Embassies and High Commissions: neither are they privy to the conversations which Ministers have with foreign leaders, week by week. Even if, therefore, Oppositions do act with the highest sense of responsibility and eschew all opposition except where they genuinely believe that the Government is wrong, they may well find themselves unable to carry out policies adopted in good faith.

Undoubtedly, from the point of view of good government, it is best for Oppositions to give no pledges of any kind and to confine themselves to vague generalisations. But this is not the way to win elections. The electorate demands definition and by so doing damages the national interest in the long run.

A further factor is that, during election campaigns, party activists wish to tie their parties to firm policies which cannot be upset after victory by what they conceive to be the dead and obstructive hand of officialdom. When a new Government takes office, activists in both major parties are apt to blame

Whitehall for diluting the pure stream of party dogma. There is some validity in these criticisms; officials do indeed sometimes resist radical change almost on principle, but in the majority of cases they do no more than draw the attention of new Ministers to facts which cannot be gainsaid.

As far as Rhodesia is concerned, the Conservative Party had watched affairs with ever increasing dismay. It was becoming more and more difficult to persuade Conservative MPs to vote for the renewal of sanctions every year in November. The House of Lords was out of control to an even greater extent. There was great sympathy for Smith whom, it was thought, had been duped by Kissinger. He had conceded majority rule and one-man-one-vote. He had satisfied all the principles except for the fifth – the acceptability of the Constitution to the nation as a whole – and, in order to satisfy that principle, he was prepared for elections to be held in which anyone could take part who was prepared to eschew violence. His opponents were not only committing the most appalling atrocities, but were trained and armed by Communists of one form or another. Sanctions appeared to have failed and, except for the United States, the only country which was really trying to carry them out was Britain. The arguments for recognising the new Government, which would be formed after the election in Rhodesia, and dropping sanctions appeared to be overwhelming. Furthermore, such a policy would undoubtedly have been popular in Britain. As was the case at the time of Suez, the working class was certainly, if anything, on the right of the political spectrum on this matter.

The Conservative leadership was in a quandary. Neither Mrs Thatcher nor John Davies, the Shadow Foreign Secretary, had much personal experience of African affairs. There were, however, other leading Conservatives who did know a great deal about the subject. The situation was changing week by week and, clearly, the fewer commitments a new Conservative Government had on its accession to power the better. Once it had access to all the facts it might decide to move in one direction or the other, but deliberately to close one whole range of options would certainly be a great mistake. It was not as if policy on Rhodesia would decide the result of an election anyway: there were other and, in the British domestic context, immensely more important issues at stake. On the other hand the party was under considerable pressure both from its right wing and from its grass roots supporters to accept the new situation in Rhodesia as satisfying all the requirements laid down for recognition.

In December 1977, Davies had publicly written off the Anglo/American proposals as having totally failed and, in February 1978 he welcomed the move to an internal settlement, 'if it complies with the principles to which we have previously agreed.' He criticised Owen for his cold attitude towards the internal Transitional Government. He went himself to Rhodesia and Zambia in July to learn about the situation at first hand and tried to persuade Nkomo to take part in the internal settlement, without success. He refused, however, to commit the Conservative Party either to unqualified recognition of the Transitional Government or to the dropping of sanctions, and in this he undoubtedly had the support of his Shadow Cabinet colleagues. As a result he came under heavy criticism from the right wing of his party and this became very apparent during the Party Conference in October 1978 when – a most unusual event for a Conservative Party Conference – he was heavily barracked. The delegates did not realise that he was very ill at the time, and he died shortly afterwards.

In his defence of what he deeply believed to be right, Davies was a heroic and misunderstood figure. A very sincere, gentle and honourable man, he suffered greatly at the end of his political life from having to stand fast against the bulk of his own party at grass roots level which was advocating policies that, as he and his cabinet colleagues saw it, would be greatly against the British interest. He was not a great orator and he did not command the affection or loyalty of large sections of the Conservative Party (unlike Douglas-Home who had similar problems earlier). And when the crunch came, he was seriously ill. Those who castigate politicians for self-seeking, double-dealing and hypocrisy should, whatever they believed to be the rights or wrongs of Davies' stand, consider whether, had they held his views, they themselves would have acted as did this honourable and, in the end, tragic figure.

Davies was succeeded by Francis Pym, a man of great charm and integrity, who had been a highly successful chief whip but who had had little experience of running a Department of State – his only major Ministerial post had been as Secretary of State for Northern Ireland for some six weeks before the demise of Heath's Government. He had also been Shadow Minister of Agriculture but had little experience of foreign affairs. The general election was clearly approaching and the Conservative Party had to decide on its attitude towards Rhodesia and, in particular, what should appear in the Manifesto on that subject.

As far as the forthcoming election in Rhodesia was concerned the Government had refused to send observers, as had the United States. Mrs Thatcher announced that she would send a team of observers and that they would report to her.[29]

But when it came to the Manifesto there was every sign that the Rhodesian section of it was drafted without full realisation of its implications for a Conservative Government, and since neither the Shadow Foreign Secretary nor the Shadow Prime Minister knew much about the problem, this is perhaps not surprising.

The relevant paragraph of the Conservative Manifesto which appeared on 6 February 1979 was as follows – 'The Conservative Party will aim to achieve a lasting settlement to the Rhodesia problem based on the democratic wishes of the people of that country. If the six principles, which all British Governments have supported for the last fifteen years, are fully satisfied following the present Rhodesian elections the next Government will have the duty to return Rhodesia to a state of legality, move to lift sanctions, and do its utmost to ensure that the new independent state gains international recognition.'

The precise words of the Manifesto were to have very great importance and it is worth analysing them in some detail. There were three elements. First, an unexceptional and generalised commitment to adhere to the democratic wishes of the people of Rhodesia. Second, a requirement to be met and, finally, action to be taken if that requirement was satisfied. It was the last two elements which were to be crucial.

The requirement was that the six principles (set out on page 46) should be implemented in the structure of Government in Rhodesia after the election had been held. There was no argument about five of them. They were undoubtedly all embodied in the new Constitution and many Conservative spokesmen said so. The one remaining obstacle was the 'Test of Accepta-

148

bility' (this was the fifth principle, although to confuse the issue Mrs Thatcher, Pym, Carrington and even Wilson all insisted on calling it, in error, the last or sixth principle). Mrs Thatcher, in a major speech at Solihull on 24 March made the position clear – 'For the last fifteen years all British Governments supported the six principles. The election holds out hope of the last of those principles being satisfied. If the election takes place in the freest and fairest conditions possible for a country beset by terrorism, that last principle – that Britain must be satisfied that any proposed basis for independence would be acceptable to the Rhodesian population as a whole – would have been met.

'Unlike Dr Owen, we do not intend to prejudge the issue either way. That is for the Rhodesian people, not him, to decide whether the Constitution represents a satisfactory form of majority rule. We will send observers to the election and we will form a balanced judgement on the basis of their report.

'If the six principles are met it will be the paramount duty of any British Government to return Rhodesia to a state of legality, to move to lift sanctions and do our utmost to ensure that the new independent state gains international recognition.'

This was repeated by Pym in a speech on 9 April. He did introduce a slight modification of Mrs Thatcher's words by adding the proviso that there should be a reasonable turn-out.

The position therefore was that if the new Government, having received the report of the observers, decided that the elections had been held in 'the freest and fairest conditions possible for a country beset by terrorism', then the requirement had been met.

As regards the action to be taken if the principles were satisfied, the manifesto is also clear. Rhodesia was to be returned to a state of legality and sanctions would be lifted. The new British Government would also do its utmost to secure international recognition for Rhodesia. But there was no question of recognition and the dropping of sanctions not taking place if this international recognition was not forthcoming. If that had been the intention, the wording would have been quite different. The Manifesto clearly stated that the first step was to recognise and drop sanctions and, simultaneously but *not as a precondition*, an attempt would be made to gain international

149

recognition. Indeed the words 'do its utmost' explicitly make it clear that the possibility of failure in gaining international recognition was envisaged, but that such a failure was not to prejudice the other actions. Furthermore, the words 'new independent state' must mean that independence would be granted either before or simultaneously with attempts to gain international recognition.

As the election proceeded there were signs that the Conservative leadership was becoming worried about the situation. In speeches on 15 and 23 April, Pym tried to modify the position. On the 15th he said – 'It will not be possible to make a snap judgement immediately the result of the Rhodesian election is known, nor would it be right to do so. The whole issue will require full consideration once we have the resources of Government behind us. It may also be appropriate to have detailed discussions with our European and American allies and the Commonwealth.' In his speech on the 23rd he repeated these words and went on to say – 'Our response must be carefully planned and thoroughly considered.'

Carrington, who had not been personally concerned with the drafting of the Manifesto since he had other responsibilities, was also extremely cautious in a radio broadcast on 25 April when he said – 'If this election is free and fair, then those principles will have been satisfied and consequently it is the job of the British Government to bring them back to legality and move to international recognition and the lifting of sanctions ... I think you also have to take account of the fact that if you are going to bring Rhodesia back to legality it will be necessary to get the support and agreement of the international community and so that would have to be done too.' These words were, of course, quite incompatible with the Manifesto.

There is every sign, therefore, that the Conservative leadership in early April suddenly began to realise the implications of the Manifesto and tried to pull back from the commitment in it in order to leave their hands free when they achieved power. However, whatever they said during the election campaign, the actual commitment lay in the Manifesto and could not be changed. In fact the six principles were largely out of date. They were produced back in 1965 to deal with a totally different situation from that obtaining in 1979. For instance, the first principle referred to the 1961 Constitution which had already been abandoned as a basis for agreement by Douglas-Home in his 1971 negotiations and there were other anomalies. The principles had become a talisman of orthodoxy but they bore no relation whatever to the situation on the ground. Their advantage, as far as the Conservative Party was concerned, was that they had been broadly accepted by virtually all the party. If they were changed, this would inevitably stir up controversy in a party which remained deeply divided on the Rhodesia issue. If they were kept, however out of date they might have been, the party would not be rent asunder.

As always, the Labour Party had far fewer internal differences over Rhodesia than did the Conservative Party. The Anglo/American plan was still party dogma. The only leading Labour figure who seemed to dissent – and his day was done – was Wilson who, in a broadcast on 13 March, took the view that observers should be sent and that if the elections were free and fair the Rhodesian Government should be recognised and sanctions dropped.

The elections held on 20 April were a triumph for the Rhodesian Government. In spite of massive intimidation by the guerillas, directed against the exercise of the vote, there was a very high turnout indeed (62.16 per cent of the electorate cast valid votes). It is true that all the organs of Government had been deployed for some time in trying to persuade the people to vote. There were also, certainly, pressures by many farmers on their workers to get them to the polls. It is also the case that there was no organised peaceful propaganda against participation in the election and, although the authorities denied this, such a campaign might well have found itself faced with official obstruction. But the pressures not to vote were provided by the 13,000 guerillas who were actually in the country at the time using the gun and not the microphone as their persuader.

All these arguments are largely irrelevant, however. There was an atmosphere of carnival as nearly two million Africans went peacefully to the polls, sometimes in queues of a mile in length, in a massive demonstration of support for the elections which they hoped would lead them out of the fear and misery to which they had by now become accustomed. It was the atmosphere which was important and foreign observers were, almost without exception, highly impressed. Virtually the only observer to reject the election was Lord Chitnis, a Liberal Peer. His attitude was entirely predictable. The organisation he represented in this particular task was miles to the left of the political spectrum. It was well financed and the glossy report that he produced contrasted markedly with the scruffy document produced by the British Government in which Lord Boyd's Mission announced its conclusion, which was that the elections had been fair and as free as possible in the circumstances.[30] But Lord Chitnis' report was important. It gave an excuse to those who were determined to reject the election come what might – and there were very many such.

Muzorewa was the predictable winner of the election with fifty-one seats. Sithole, who got twelve seats, was incapable of recovering his position and he compounded his difficulties by announcing during the election that he had been responsible for starting the violence. Chirau's party was annihilated and Ndiweni, who was trying to gain the Ndebele vote in Nkomo's place, obtained nine seats. Some papers were spoilt, many of them perhaps deliberately in Ndebele areas because of Nkomo's absence, but the mass of the voters understood exactly what they were doing, thus confounding those who had argued that African tribesmen would be incapable of taking part in the democratic process. The white Rhodesians had mounted a massive effort, calling up virtually all able bodied men in order to see the election through. It was the final fling of a people clinging desperately to what they believed to be their last hope against darkness and death.

The mass of the Africans in Rhodesia were delighted that they were, at last, to have a black Prime Minister and a black Government. Few of them understood the intricacies of the Constitution but they realised the truth that there was to be a great and irrevocable shift of power into black hands. However, this was a secondary reason for their actions. The vote was a massive gesture against the war. Poignant, direct and springing from the deep revulsion which the overwhelming majority of the people had against the continuing and escalating misery with which they had been afflicted, it was a cry for peace. Comparatively few Africans had themselves been involved in all the comings and goings, the interminable con-

152

ferences and the internecine squabbling which had been deciding their fate. Here was a chance for them to play a part themselves. Nothing was to prevent them from doing so, and they braved considerable Nationalist intimidation in their hundreds of thousands. If the war could be stopped, they would certainly settle for what had been achieved and that is what they were saying with all the vehemence they could muster. If Mugabe and/or Nkomo had been on the ballot paper no doubt many would have voted for them, but they were not able to do so and they turned to Muzorewa who had widespread respect. They hoped that the advent to office of his Government would lead to peace. They were satisfied with the shift of power which had been achieved. They were rejecting the use of further force as a way of extracting yet further concessions from the whites. They had had enough.

The case for recognition was powerful indeed. Leaving aside all the pettifogging criticisms of the Constitution, the fact was that the vast mass of the people of Rhodesia, black and white, undoubtedly wished the international community to recognise Rhodesia, drop sanctions and stop the guerillas from continuing the war. That is what the vote was about. It is of course easy to make judgements of this kind which are not capable of statistical proof, but anyone who was present during the election, and who had an open mind, would inevitably have been drawn to that conclusion. The Nationalists realised that this would be the inference if there was a high turn-out. That, of course, is why they tried to prevent it. Certainly if the poll had been low, the general conclusion would have been that the people as a whole were rejecting the Constitution. But when there was a high poll the whole left wing propaganda machine was directed to discrediting the election. The OAU, the United Nations, the Front Line Presidents – the whole array of organisations pledged to seeing that the wishes of the people of Rhodesia should be implemented – joined together in a determined effort to prevent just that happening. They were successful.

Until after the election, it was not clear who would be the Foreign Secretary in the new Conservative Administration. Pym and Carrington were both contenders. Carrington was chosen. Immensely able and decisive with enormous charm and a great sense of humour – that vital attribute in any man

153

with heavy responsibilities – he was the ideal choice. He could cut through irrelevancies and move with apparently effortless ease straight to the essential point of almost any problem. He was prepared to take hard decisions and stick to them. Greatly experienced – Heath had unloaded problem after problem on him during the previous Conservative Administration – he had a feel for foreign affairs and an instinctive appreciation of what was possible and what was not which gave him an authority that had been sadly lacking in his predecessor. He was to be one of the great successes of the new Government. Foreign Office officials were delighted with their new master and a new spirit of hope and confidence spread rapidly through the Department, where morale had been at a very low ebb indeed.

The election of a Conservative Administration, too, brought great hopes in Rhodesia. The whole of the white community and most of the Africans hoped that this would lead to recognition, the dropping of sanctions and an end to the war. Because of the wording of the Conservative Manifesto they had good reason to expect it.

However, the problem was far from simple as seen from Britain. As luck would have it there was to be a Commonwealth Prime Ministers' Conference in Lusaka, the capital of Zambia, in August to be opened by the Queen in person. Any immediate move of the new Conservative Administration towards recognition would undoubtedly throw the Commonwealth into total confusion and it was very much on the cards that it really would break up: certainly the British position at the Conference would be one of extreme difficulty. It would not exactly have been to the credit of the new Conservative Government if its advent to power had been followed by the disintegration of the Commonwealth within a month. Stringent trade sanctions would certainly be imposed against Britain, particularly by Nigeria, whose trade with Britain was of considerable importance. All this argued for caution. But there were even more pressing arguments against recognition. Leaving aside all considerations of the narrow British interest, what would have been the repercussions within Rhodesia if Britain had gone ahead? The new British Government quickly learnt that no foreign country would follow its lead in recognition or dropping sanctions. The United States, France, Germany – all made it perfectly clear that they would oppose

154

any such move. Stories to the contrary which were put about by the Rhodesian Government and by some right wing Conservatives were not based on fact. Promises made by individuals, however important, were one thing. Official communications at governmental level were another. That being so, would the war in fact stop? Or would it escalate with further Communist involvement? Would Britain, therefore, be putting its international position in jeopardy, to say nothing of the dangers to its trade – however much those dangers might have been exaggerated – for no useful purpose?

These were the questions which had to be answered, and quickly, by Carrington and Mrs Thatcher. Apart from the commitments in the Conservative Manifesto, the argument for recognition was based on two basic premises: first, that the Rhodesian people, black and white, actually favoured this action. And, secondly, that recognition and the dropping of sanctions by Britain would transform the internal situation. For the first time since 1965 the Rhodesian Government would be legitimate. This would undoubtedly give an enormous psychological boost to the administration. The argument was that the mass of the people would refuse to continue to countenance the guerillas, who for their part would realise that they had in fact gained all they were fighting for. The war would tail off and gradually other countries would be forced to accept the situation.

It is extremely difficult to know with certainty which prognosis was correct. Mrs Thatcher may well have been tempted to recognise – after all that is what she had clearly been advocating during the election campaign. But the arguments against radical action were very strong and she was convinced otherwise, as was Carrington. Furthermore, although Rhodesia was of course most important – and one of her first major appearances on the international stage was to be at the Commonwealth Prime Ministers' Conference where this issue was certain to predominate – there were other problems of even greater importance which she was determined to face up to. Rhodesia was not an essential element in her overall strategy which was related primarily to the vast task of bringing about a radical change of attitudes within Britain.

But how about the Manifesto commitment? One way out of the difficulty would have been to cast doubt on the findings of the Boyd Report. If the Government was not convinced that the elections had been fair and as free as possible, it would follow that recognition and the dropping of sanctions were no longer mandatory on it. To do this would, however, have been to question the judgement of Lord Boyd – a vastly experienced ex-Colonial Secretary whose integrity was entirely beyond question – and the other members of his team (see n. 29). In the event, at no stage were the conclusions of the Boyd Mission questioned by any Conservative leader. It followed that the Government did believe that the elections were fair and as free as possible and therefore that the requirements set out in the Manifesto had been satisfied. The commitment to recognise and drop sanctions was absolute.

The unenviable choice which, therefore, faced the British Government was either to break its Manifesto commitment or to embark on a policy which it believed would be disastrous both for Rhodesia and for Britain. There may have been some wishful thinking to the effect that the Manifesto commitment was not clear and that the words used could be interpreted differently. Indeed, official Foreign Office replies to questions about the commitment used the palpably false argument that the words of the Manifesto implied that recognition depended on international acceptance of the Rhodesian regime which would have to come first. But, in their hearts, Conservative leaders must have known where the truth lay. The issue could not be balked.

There was no possibility of delaying the decision. 'If it were done when 'tis done, then 'twere well it were done quickly'. Once the possibility of temporising was seen to be in the British Government's mind, the pressures would escalate, and recognition and the dropping of sanctions would no longer be a viable option.

On balance, and he certainly did not think so at the time, it is the author's opinion that the Government was probably right in the circumstances to do what it did, in spite of its Manifesto commitment. If the Rhodesian Government had been recognised and sanctions had been dropped, the war probably would not have ceased. Britain would not have been able to convene, let alone bring to a successful conclusion, a new Conference whether at Lancaster House or anywhere else. In the end, after even more bloodshed than actually occurred,

Mugabe would probably have come to power with a great grudge against Britain whose international position would have been much undermined. It is, however, difficult to excuse the drafting of the words of the Conservative Manifesto and the phrases in the speeches of Conservative leaders during the election campaign which meant that, in the event, the pledges given had to be flagrantly broken.

Other, even deeper, issues are also raised here. Is there a distinction between public and private morality? Most people would agree that if a private person makes a promise, he should stick to it even if doing so turns out to be to his own detriment to a greater degree than appeared likely when he made it. Does this hold true in public affairs? A Government is elected to safeguard the interests of its citizens. What if these interests are to be thrown in jeopardy by a promise made under wrong assumptions? And what if a Government has responsibility both to its own citizens and to those of another country and those interests conflict? Furthermore, supposing a Government concludes that even the interests of that other country would be best served by breaking a promise? Who is to be the judge? In an ideal world a private person in this dilemma would go to the recipient of the promise and, by argument, try to be relieved of his obligation: if this was not forthcoming, he would stick to his word. Does the same morality hold good in public affairs? If the answer is 'No', the danger is that any form of obligation by a state, however solemnly entered into, can only be of very transitory value. And if this is generally acknowledged, then the whole conduct of foreign relations becomes extremely difficult, related not to any firm basis of continuing obligation but to the needs of the moment as seen by those fallible and changeable human beings who happen to be leaders at any particular moment. Treaties and statements of policy will have value only in so far as they define an attitude at a particular moment: whatever the form of words used at the time, they will not have relevance to any future situation. They will indeed be 'scraps of paper' to be despatched to the dustbin without remorse.

But in this case it can well be argued, and the author agrees, that it would have been wrong for the British Government to embark on a course of action which it believed to be greatly against the interests, not only of its own country but of those whom that policy was designed to protect. If there is a moral, it is that political parties should resist all pressures, however strident, to make clear commitments in Opposition upon which they might have to renege when in power.

The decision having, rightly or wrongly, been taken not to recognise Muzorewa's Government, Carrington took an immediate and firm grip on the situation. With Sir Anthony Duff and Robin Renwick, the two Foreign Office officials in charge, he had a brilliant team. There was to be no question of the Americans or anyone else directing British Foreign policy, which was to be made in the British Foreign Office. The Front Line Presidents, the United Nations, the Commonwealth and the European Community were, of course, all factors in the equation; but none of them was to have any kind of veto on British actions which were directed towards a smooth handover of British responsibilities to a Government formed after elections in Rhodesia. There was a new sense of purpose to British policy. Mrs Thatcher, too, played a strong role. She trusted her Foreign Secretary and, without her unequivocal support throughout, the outcome would have been very different. The situation within Britain was, therefore, ideal. An excellent Foreign Office staff was led by a man upon whom they could rely implicitly not to deviate from policy once agreed, and the Foreign Secretary had a Prime Minister who was staunch and not liable to cave in under pressure. At this stage the pressures were from the Conservative right, but these were easily surmounted in the first flush of Conservative victory at the polls.

At a press conference on 14 May Carrington signalled the climb down from the Manifesto commitment beyond any doubt by announcing that policy would be formulated after talks with the Commonwealth, the United States, Rhodesia and the European Community. Sir Anthony Duff was sent to Salisbury to talk to Muzorewa on 15 May and shortly afterwards it was announced that Lord Harlech, the highly experienced, urbane and civilised ex-Ambassador to the United States who had been a Deputy Chairman of the Pearce Commission, would make a tour of Africa including Zambia, Nigeria and Tanzania, to make contact with the leaders of those countries.

The six principles were supplemented by a whole range of

other conditions which seemed to emerge almost day by day – international acceptance, the end of hostilities, the granting of a Constitution comparable to the other Constitutions granted to ex-colonial territories, and so on. It seemed to the white Rhodesians and indeed to the Africans in the Rhodesian Government that, whatever they did, Britain added yet another hurdle to be surmounted. There was much, and very understandable, bitterness.

United States policy makers were, too, in a dilemma. Carter was surrounded by foreign policy advisers who were surprisingly far to the left in the political spectrum. Some of them openly supported Mugabe in spite of his Marxist beliefs. Official spokesmen made a number of statements which were factually wrong. For instance President Carter himself, on 7 January, said that the Rhodesian Constitution had been drafted by the whites without black participation, blithely ignoring the fact that it was the result of long and often difficult negotiations between Smith and three African leaders. The United States Administration was concerned with its own internal negro pressures and its relationships with the rest of black Africa and was, apparently, prepared to twist the truth in furtherance of this aim.

The Senate, on the other hand, saw the issue in quite different terms. A majority of Senators believed that power had indeed been transferred to the Africans and that Muzorewa did represent a majority of his people. A resolution was adopted in the Senate on 16 May calling on the President to recognise the Rhodesian Government and drop sanctions not more than ten days after Muzorewa was installed as Prime Minister (this in fact meant 10 June).

A struggle ensued between the President and the Senate with the President using every procedural device to avoid having to take any action. The labyrinthine complexity of the relationship between President and Congress was such that he was successful in doing so.

The Commonwealth was as a body inexorably opposed to Muzorewa. On 18 May, under the energetic instigation of Ramphal, its clever, ebullient but, in this matter, wildly biased Secretary General, it produced a consensus of the High Commissioners in London condemning the elections. This, entirely predictable, ploy had added impact because the three major white non-British members of the organisation – Australia, New Zealand and Canada – were parties to it.

This chorus of total rejection of what had been achieved in Rhodesia was supplemented even by NATO when the Ministers of that body at a meeting on 1 July warned Carrington of the dire implications of recognising Muzorewa. The OAU and the United Nations, too, added to the cacophony.

It is, perhaps, interesting to examine why there was this near unanimity of condemnation. One thing is certain: it was certainly not a reasoned reaction to the actual situation on the ground in Rhodesia. Whatever the terms of the Rhodesian Constitution had been, it would certainly have been condemned. Even if the Rhodesian Government had been operating under precisely the same Constitution as that agreed later at Lancaster House, the opposition would have been equally strident and near-universal. The Constitution was of importance only in so far as it furnished ammunition for an attack which would certainly have taken place anyway. If one particular part of the Constitution had not been available to be used for this purpose, others would have been found. The real reason for condemnation was that neither Nkomo nor Mugabe were involved, and they were the protégés of Kaunda and Nyerere respectively. In fact these two latter men had been almost entirely unsuccessful in directing the economies of their own countries. Kaunda had some excuse since the Rhodesian affair had undoubtedly added greatly to his difficulties, but the performance of Zambia's agricultural sector had been bad primarily because of his attempts to socialise it, not because of sanctions. Tanzania was in an appalling economic mess due to chronic mismanagement and the disastrous effects of so-called African Socialism. But these two men did have a status in anglophone Africa which gave them considerable authority. It had been pressure from these two above all which had eventually brought about the joining together of those two arch rivals, Nkomo and Mugabe, in the Patriotic Front. Machel from Mozambique and, to a lesser extent, Seretse Khama from Botswana had also been involved, but their pressures had not been decisive. Kaunda and Nyerere had had many quarrels, over Biafra for instance, but in the final stages of the Rhodesian drama they were agreed that the Patriotic Front, and not the Muzorewa regime, did represent the people of

Rhodesia.

The left wing establishment in Britain and (of less import-ance) the United States saw Kaunda and Nyerere as heroic figures. To them, these two men represented the humane, civi-lised, incorruptible face of Africa, men of stature and dignity who had taken over from their corrupt colonialist predecessors and forged truly African nations. Kenyatta in Kenya, although far more successful in economic terms, had not con-formed to their image. He had been an unabashed capitalist as were his successors. The African Socialism as practised by Nyerere and, to a lesser extent, by Kaunda was far more in tune with left wing philosophy. Amin was a disaster, not to be mentioned in polite society. As for Banda of Malawi – a country of comparative economic success – he was an Uncle Tom figure of ridicule.

This general view of affairs in anglophone Africa came to have a currency which extended far beyond the extreme left of politics. As the white Rhodesians continued with their intran-sigent attitudes, it gradually extended its range until those who questioned its validity were to be found mainly on the extreme right of the political spectrum. The absurdities of apartheid in South Africa, too, had the effect of shifting middle ground opinion towards those African leaders who refused to have any dealings with that country. The complexities of the Southern African problem came to be submerged in a polarisa-tion of attitudes. On the one side stood Smith, the archetypal bad white man and his stooges including Muzorewa: on the other were Kaunda and Nyerere, Nkomo and Mugabe, repres-entatives of the great and good. To the ever widening circle of their admirers, Kaunda and Nyerere were known by their Christian names (Kenneth and Julius) – that ultimate, and rather patronising, mark of acceptance in British circles, what-ever their political hue.

Kaunda and Nyerere did indeed have considerable virtues and attainments. They had by and large maintained national unity and peace in their own countries. They were not racia-lists and had set their faces steadfastly against black victimisa-tion of the whites remaining in their country. It was true that they had silenced all political opposition, using methods which would not have been accepted in Britain, but there was nothing exceptional or, indeed, particularly terrible about this: the Westminster pattern of democracy was, and is, clearly unsuitable for Africa. They were not cruel despots in the sense that Amin and Bokassa were. Although certainly addicted to the exercise of power and unwilling to cede it without a considerable struggle, they were trying, albeit almost totally ineffectually, to create ordered and prosperous societies in their respective countries. They saw the Rhodesian problem as the touchstone of British intentions towards Africa as a whole, believing that Britain could have settled the whole affair with comparative ease if the will to do so had existed. Furthermore, Smith, who had been built up in African eyes as a kind of ogre, remained a member of the Rhodesian cabinet. It seemed impossible that he was not still directing affairs from behind the scenes, and they probably did genuinely believe that Muzorewa was a stooge, although there was no question of any objective enquiry by them into the facts of the situation.

But they also had an interest in the end product. Kaunda had supported Nkomo throughout and Nyerere had, at an early stage, adopted Mugabe as his nominee. The Chinese had been Mugabe's principal supporters and Nyerere had had a close relationship with them. Mugabe was based in Mozambique, Tanzania's neighbour. It was clearly to the advantage of both Kaunda and Nyerere in the context of pan-African politics that their particular protégé either achieved power in Rhodesia or, at least, played an important role in the new Government. If the Muzorewa administration succeeded in establishing itself internationally, Kaunda and Nyerere would have been seen to have failed. They would certainly have lost stature and influence in Africa as a whole.

It was the steadfast refusal of Kaunda and Nyerere to accept the Muzorewa Government which ensured that international opinion would, too, reject it. The ripples spread outwards from these two men via the OAU and the Commonwealth to the United Nations and thereafter, by force of appeal to national interest, to the vast majority of international opinion. There was no discernible advantage for a country like Germany, for instance, in standing out against the common view. To do so would be to court opposition and perhaps even attract trade sanctions in pursuit of nothing related even vaguely to the interests of Germany.

To put it another way if, by some miracle, Kaunda and

Nyerere had supported Muzorewa, the international community would almost certainly have followed suit.

The future of Rhodesia, therefore, was decided not by those who lived in that country and not by any objective view of events there but by outside forces and pressures with very little relevance to the actual situation on the ground.

This is an inevitable consequence of the internationalisation of any national problem. The interests of others rather than those actually involved will be the deciding factor. The greater the degree of internationalisation the less likely it is that these interests will coincide. It may well be true that in this case the long-term interests of Rhodesia were indeed served by non-recognition of Muzorewa but, if so, this was mainly because recognition would not have stopped the war and this in its turn was largely due to Kaunda's and Nyerere's attitudes.

Muzorewa tried desperately to retrieve the situation by visiting Washington on 10 July and London three days later. He saw Carter and Mrs Thatcher, but was unable to obtain any definite assurances of recognition. Mrs Thatcher had given him some hope when she said in Australia on 1 July that she doubted very much whether sanctions would get through Parliament when they came up for renewal in November. This statement caused considerable alarm in Commonwealth circles. It is not clear if it was an unguarded remark in answer to a question or whether it was designed to put the Commonwealth Prime Ministers on notice that they should not try to push Britain too far at the forthcoming Conference in Lusaka. Some additional comfort for Muzorewa also came on 15 July when Kibaki, the Kenyan Finance Minister said that the reality of Muzorewa as Prime Minister must be accepted. But these were straws to be clutched at, not straws in the wind.

CHAPTER SEVEN

Lancaster House and the Elections, 1979–80

The Commonwealth Prime Ministers' Conference opened in Lusaka on 1 August 1979. There had been some concern for the Queen's safety since ZIPRA was operating in strength within Zambia and the Rhodesian security forces were attacking ZIPRA bases in that country. But Nkomo and Muzorewa both gave assurances that the Conference would not be interfered with. Ironically, the red carpet provided for the Queen's arrival was specially flown in from South Africa as were many items essential for a gathering of this size, including even squash balls! The Queen, dignified and serene, brought an air of effortless authority and unprejudiced concern to the opening proceedings, reminding those present of the traditional virtues of the founder nation of the organisation of which they were part.

In the event, what was expected to lead to a major confrontation between Britain and the rest of the Commonwealth ended on a note of sweetness and light. Having taken the decision not to recognise the Muzorewa Government, the main British aim was to keep affairs firmly in British hands and not to be encumbered by any commitments to outside participation either in the Conference which the British Government hoped to convene or in the subsequent proceedings. In return for this, Britain was prepared to agree that the Constitution should be changed and that it should be comparable to other ex-Colonial Constitutions it had granted. In fact, these two concessions had already been made!

Nigeria saw fit to announce on the opening day of the Conference that she had nationalised BP's assets. This was an inept and immature attempt at pressure which had no effect whatever except, perhaps marginally, to strengthen the British determination not to concede more than was absolutely necessary. Nigeria went on to demand that the election should be conducted under UN supervision.

After considerable backstage negotiation, in which Mr Fraser, the Prime Minister of Australia, with an eye to his domestic constituency, played a leading, unhelpful, and devious role, complete agreement was reached. British responsibility was clearly affirmed. All parties to the conflict would be involved in a settlement which would include a democratic Constitution with safeguards for minorities. There would be fair and free elections supervised by Britain. Hostilities and sanctions would come to an end. The Commonwealth role was confined to producing observers.

Much credit for the success of the Conference was due to Mrs Thatcher. She managed to convince her fellow Prime Ministers of her sincerity. Had she failed to do so, it is quite possible that they would not have trusted Britain either to run the subsequent Conference or to supervise the elections. In spite of the obvious fact that the Conservative Party was inherently far more sympathetic to the white Rhodesians than was the Labour Party, the Conservative Party had the advantage that it had stuck to its word at the time of the Pearce Commission and had not been involved in the tortuous gyrations over NIBMAR as had Wilson's Labour administration. Indeed, it is probably true to say that the Afro/Asian elements of the Commonwealth found the Conservative Government easier to deal with than the previous Labour administration in spite of the fact that the Conservatives were basically less sympathetic to their aspirations.

The agreement was immediately attacked both by Muzorewa and Mugabe. Muzorewa categorised it as an insult. Decisions on his country's future had been taken without any representatives of Rhodesia being present. He had been elected Prime Minister in an election which had been called free and fair by Mrs Thatcher's own Commission. But now he was being told to start the whole process again. He certainly had a point.

Mugabe, for his part, said on 7 August that the Constitutional arrangements would have to ensure acceptance of the guerilla forces as the national army of Rhodesia. The Security

Forces would have to be disbanded and the Smith/Muzorewa regime would have to come to an immediate end. There was, of course, nothing to that effect in the Commonwealth Prime Ministers' communiqué and Mugabe's remarks were virtually repudiated by Nyerere and Kaunda on the following day.

Although the agreement led to a general feeling of euphoria in many circles in Britain including most of the media, which had excellent material in photographs of Mrs Thatcher dancing with Kaunda, a sizeable section of the Conservative Party was greatly alarmed at what it saw as a sell-out. These feelings were expressed with characteristic vigour by Julian Amery, the leading figure on the right of the Conservative Party.

The next problem for Carrington was to persuade all sides to attend a round-table conference to be chaired by Britain. He was in a strong position. Nkomo and Mugabe were to a very large extent dependent on Kaunda and Nyerere who had signed the Commonwealth communiqué calling for a Conference. It was, therefore, virtually impossible for the Patriotic Front to set any preconditions other than those in the communiqué, and these were almost non-existent. Muzorewa, for his part, knew perfectly well that his country could not carry on as it was. South Africa would certainly not countenance continued intransigence and the guerilla war showed no sign whatever of diminishing.

Muzorewa, on 8 August, was the first to agree in principle to attend talks, even before the actual announcement of the venue (Lancaster House) and the date (10 September) was made. It was at this stage that the British tactics first became apparent. They let it be known that if the Patriotic Front did not attend the Conference, Britain would carry on with Muzorewa alone. The logic was impeccable. Britain had agreed to give the opportunity to all parties to the conflict to take part in a Conference held in order to frame a new Constitution followed by the holding of fresh elections. Britain had not agreed to give a veto to any one party. If the Patriotic Front opted out, that was their affair, but they could not hold Britain to ransom.

Agreement having been reached in Lusaka, Carrington lost no time in setting the wheels in motion. Draft constitutional proposals were published on 14 August. They had two main

166

features which were not present in the existing Rhodesian Constitution. First, there was to be no white blocking mechanism against constitutional amendments and, secondly, the Prime Minister was to be able to make senior civil service appointments himself with the proviso only that he should consult the appropriate Commission. These amendments went a long way to meeting much of the criticism of the previous Constitution.

On 20 August the Patriotic Front announced that it, too, would attend the Conference. It tried to cloak its climb down with a continuing refusal to accept the authority of Britain and it still demanded United Nations involvement, but it was clear that Carrington had won the first round.

Carrington's tactics during the Conference which opened on 10 September as scheduled, were masterly. He decided to take the issues one by one, getting agreement on each before proceeding to the next stage. He would announce his proposal, wait for the inevitable storm from the Patriotic Front, persuade Muzorewa to agree to it and then give the Patriotic Front a deadline, hinting, or indeed at the later stages actually announcing that he would go ahead with Muzorewa if the Patriotic Front did not agree too. At each stage there was an agonising display of brinkmanship while the Patriotic Front thundered and roared defiance. But, in spite of the deadlines not being kept on every occasion, the Patriotic Front always in the end agreed. There were two reasons for this. First, they really did believe that Carrington would go ahead wihout them. He managed to convince them of his firmness of purpose. Without that, there would not have been the slightest chance of success. A lesser, vacillating, Foreign Secretary or a dithering Prime Minister in the background would have been fatal: any sign of weakness would have led to escalating demands which would certainly have put Muzorewa in an impossible position. And, secondly, Kaunda and Machel both wanted agreement badly. Their economies were in a parlous state and a continuation of the war would have compounded their already very considerable difficulties.

Of course, if these tactics were to succeed, it was vital that Muzorewa was prepared to agree to the Carrington proposals at every stage, and to do so without very much delay. He had great problems. Ian Smith was in his delegation as were other whites including David Smith (the Finance Minister), Cronje (a deputy minister), and Anderson (the Minister of Justice), together with Sithole and Ndiweni. Ian Smith was in a strange mood. He had not been able to play any active role in the new Government. As Minister without Portfolio he had sat in a small office with virtually no power and very little to do, although he was being cast by the Nationalists in the role of the real power behind the scenes. But at Lancaster House he saw himself as the last hope of the whites, defending their interests to the bitter end. On his arrival in Britain he was lionised by many people to whom he was a great hero and this added to his belief that he alone stood between Rhodesia and chaos. But he must have realised that the Rhodesian Government had very few options open to it. If they walked out of the Conference, Britain would go ahead with the Patriotic Front and the repercussions of that would have been too dreadful to contemplate. His role was, therefore, clearly to be one of persuading the Muzorewa delegation to block every concession for as long as possible without actually going so far as to walk out. In this he did not have the support of David Smith who believed Carrington when he argued that once he changed his proposals in any fundamental way during the course of the Conference, there would be no end to it and the result would be confusion. In fact, during the whole of the negotiations, Carrington, except for some very minor amendments, did not vary his proposals at all. He made up his mind and stuck to it.

There were two further considerations which added to Muzorewa's difficulties. Senator Helms, the powerful right wing figure in the Senate, who was leading the pressures in the United States for the dropping of sanctions, sent over to England two emissaries who informed the Muzorewa delegation that the United States would drop sanctions soon, come what may. Clearly, if this was true, it would greatly weaken Carrington's leverage on Muzorewa.

More important was the fact that the Conservative Party Conference was to take place at the beginning of October. Smith was told that the Conservative Party would force the British Government to drop sanctions and to recognise the Muzorewa Government whether or not the Lancaster House Conference was successful. If this was true, the pressures which Carrington was bringing to bear on Muzorewa were largely bluff. David Smith, who played a vitally important role at this stage, was persuaded that there was no substance to this claim. The arguments were overwhelming. First, Conservative Party Conference resolutions had no binding application on Government policy. Second, it was most unlikely that the Conservative Party, in the first flush of victory, would repudiate its own leadership. Third, the Conservative Party Conference would take place before the end of the Lancaster House meeting and the Government would undoubtedly argue that to attempt to prejudge the issue in the middle of delicate negotiations would be highly irresponsible: this argument would have a strong effect on delegates' minds. And, lastly, the party bosses, past masters at the art of avoiding confrontation, would certainly see to it that the resolution which was actually debated was not susceptible to any radical interpretation. As regards sanctions, upon which a vote had to be taken in November,[31] if necessary the Government would accept a back-bench revolt and rely on Labour support to obtain renewal rather than prejudice its entire international position.

Ian Smith gradually became an isolated figure with little impact on events.

Carrington's initial objective was to get agreement that the Constitution would be dealt with first before discussions were held on how it should be implemented. The second hurdle would probably be more difficult to surmount than the first, but if the first could be cleared the Conference would attain a momentum which, it was hoped, would carry it forward. On the opening day, Carrington announced that this was how he intended to conduct the Conference, giving no grounds whatever for any suspicion that he might change his mind. After an initial display of intransigence by the Patriotic Front, who demanded separate Constitutions for the transitional period and for the situation after majority rule had been achieved, the arrangement was agreed to by both sides.

Attention now turned to the Constitution itself. The British proposals provided for the retention of separate voting rolls for black and white but reduced white representation from the existing 28 to 20 seats out of 100. There was to be no blocking mechanism. On 16 September Nkomo agreed in principle to specially reserved seats for the whites, but two days later the Patriotic Front put forward a plan for the transitional period

169

envisaging a Government consisting of four representatives from the Patriotic Front and four from Britain together with a United Nations force to supervise the elections. On 21 September, after a vote of eleven to one, the Muzorewa delegation accepted the Carrington proposals. The sole dissentient was Ian Smith who argued that the white blocking mechanism should be retained. On 24 September the Patriotic Front gave way on the twenty white seats and on 25 September talks began on the details of the Constitution.

Muzorewa had been in an extremely difficult position. He was the leader of a delegation the members of which had many different aims. He and his black colleagues were not concerned with the blocking mechanism except in so far as its retention would keep whites with them. But, if the whites had been united in opposition, he would have had either to carry on without them, with all the consequent appalling repercussions of that in Rhodesia, or to abandon the whole enterprise. It was, therefore, essential that the white members of the delegation split from Ian Smith – and this they did. In a speech on 25 September, Muzorewa explained his actions by saying that if he had not accepted the terms, sanctions would have remained and international recognition would not have been forthcoming.

On 3 October Carrington published the detailed Constitution. The Patriotic Front had been demanding an executive Head of State combining the jobs of President and Prime Minister. This had obvious dangers in terms of possible abuse of power and Carrington would have nothing of it. There was to be a constitutional Head of State and a separate executive Prime Minister. A further contentious item related to the protection of the rights of white farmers against arbitrary expropriation, one of the very real worries of the whites. This protection appeared in the Bill of Rights which was itself fully entrenched against any amendment for ten years. This was a clever device designed to allay white fears arising out of the abolition of the blocking mechanism.

The Patriotic Front rejected the Constitution on 8 October and put forward an alternative which would have been totally unacceptable to Muzorewa. On 15 October, in an article in the *Guardian*, Dr Claire Palley, who had been adviser to Nkomo at the Geneva Conference and who had been much quoted by the media, also rejected the Constitution as unworkable. Muzorewa accepted the Constitution but the Patriotic Front remained adamant. Carrington announced that he would go ahead with Muzorewa, if necessary without the Patriotic Front, in discussions on the transitional arrangements. His proposals were made public on 17 October. This announcement was followed the next day by Patriotic Front agreement to the Constitution.

The pattern was continuing – proposals tabled by Carrington, agreement by Muzorewa, objection and all kinds of threats by the Patriotic Front, Carrington announcing that he would go ahead with Muzorewa alone, Patriotic Front agreement. It was an elegant and highly successful scenario.

It was the next stage – the transitional arrangements – which were to cause Muzorewa the maximum difficulty and heartache. The British plan involved Muzorewa abdicating power, the dissolving of Parliament and the arrival in Rhodesia of a British Governor to take overall charge of affairs. This was to be followed quickly (in about two months) by an election supervised by Britain. Here was the real crunch for Muzorewa. He had an agonising choice. He did have a number of assurances. The guerillas would not be free to roam the country during the election campaign but they would be confined to assembly areas: the police would continue to function and the Rhodesian Security Forces would not be disbanded. All this was in direct contrast to the Patriotic Front demands. But – and this was the cruel reality – he would have to cede power in spite of the fact that he had been elected by a majority of his people. He could not be sure of the outcome of any election: he was indeed being asked to put his head on the block. He argued with all the force he could muster that he was being unfairly treated. But Carrington was rigid. Either Muzorewa accepted the proposals or Britain would turn her back on him. There were siren voices telling him not to trust Britain and that she would rat on him once he had ceded power. It was even said that the Governor would introduce direct rule from Britain for an indefinite period. Muzorewa was a religious man and he prayed for guidance for long hours alone on his knees. Although he is often portrayed as weak, there was little doubt that he would carry a majority of his delegation with him whatever conclusion he came to. The decision was his and his alone, and on it depended many lives. Had he rejected the proposals the war would have continued indefinitely almost certainly ending in chaotic bloodshed and confusion. He decided to agree; the decision was ratified by his delegation and announced on 27 October.

The introduction of a British Governor not only made certain that the whole transitional period would be under British control but it also avoided any possible difficulty over the lifting of sanctions and recognition. Once the Governor was *in situ* there could be no question of a continuation of sanctions whatever United Nations resolutions there might be. Clearly, Britain could not impose sanctions against herself. Nor could she fail to recognise her own Governor.

The Patriotic Front tried, in vain, to rally the Commonwealth against the British plan at a meeting of the Commonwealth Southern African Committee. Nyerere, who had in fact been extremely helpful at Lusaka, now tried to bring pressure to bear on Carrington to accept a longer period of direct rule before the elections were held. He also called for a Commonwealth force to supervise the elections. Carrington would not agree to either of these proposals.

The next few days were to test Carrington's resolve to the full. There was considerable doubt as to whether the Patriotic Front would agree to the proposals or whether it would walk out. On 7 November Ian Gilmore, who answered for Carrington in the House of Commons, introduced an Enabling Bill to allow the Government to provide for the Governor's arrival in Rhodesia and to grant the Independence Constitution. This was enacted on 8 November. It was clear that the Government was indeed determined to go ahead with Muzorewa if the Patriotic Front did not agree. This was brinkmanship of a very high order and Carrington was not at all certain what the outcome would be. In the event the great gamble came off and the Patriotic Front agreed on 15 November. There was an audible sigh of relief in much of the world, perhaps particularly in Zambia, since Muzorewa had banned the sale of any more maize to that country on 5 November, and starvation was very close.

Having surmounted this major hurdle there were, however, still many considerable difficulties. On 16 November the British tabled their proposals for the cease-fire. The Governor

172

would be in control of all the armed forces in Rhodesia including the Rhodesian Security Forces, the Auxiliaries and the guerillas. There would be a Joint Commission to supervise the cease-fire. The Security Forces and the guerillas would be kept separate and there would be a British Monitoring Force to supervise them. The Patriotic Front would have no role in policing the election and its forces would be concentrated in a number of assembly areas. Normal policing of the country would be carried out by the existing police with the assistance of the Security Forces if necessary. Zambia, Mozambique and Botswana would be asked to co-operate in stopping cross-border military activities. It was hoped that the cease-fire would come into operation in the first week of December and that the guerillas would be in their assembly areas within seven to ten days after that.

The Patriotic Front was aghast at these proposals. It seemed to them that they were being asked to remain in assembly areas which would be easy targets if the arrangements broke down, while the Security Forces, the police and the Auxiliaries were to be allowed to roam the rest of the countryside at will. They protested and Carrington did make some minor concessions. He agreed that the Security Forces would be monitored down to company level. He also said that the Cease-fire Commission would remain in being until the new Government was formed after the election and that the Monitoring Force would remain until independence.

Muzorewa agreed to the cease-fire proposals on 26 November. The Patriotic Front did not agree. By 3 December Carrington was in near despair and said so in public, adding that he intended to go ahead with Muzorewa if the Patriotic Front did not accept his proposals soon. The Patriotic Front agreed two days later.

But the negotiations were still not finished. There remained the military details of how the cease-fire was to be operated. The talks on this final item were soon bogged down in argument about the status and dispositions of the two rival armies. Lieutenant General Peter Walls, the chairman of the Rhodesian Joint Operation Committee, who was emerging as a powerful political figure in his own right, had been in London for some time and his agreement was vital at this stage. Indeed Walls, together with Ken Flower, the head of the Rhodesian

173

security services, and Air Vice Marshal Hawkins, the Rhodesian Representative in South Africa, had formed a highly influential and very responsible group within the Rhodesian delegation throughout the latter stages of the proceedings. The negotiations which had originally been scheduled to last from three weeks to a month were now in their thirteenth week. Tempers were short. The guerillas were flooding over the border into Rhodesia, especially from Mozambique, and, hoping to disrupt this flow, the Rhodesians mounted yet another attack on guerilla bases in Zambia and Mozambique.

The question now arose as to whether Lord Soames, who had been appointed Governor on 6 December, should go to Rhodesia before the final agreement was signed. There were those, including the Labour Opposition, who argued that it would be wrong and highly dangerous for him to take over in Rhodesia before the necessary signatures actually appeared on the document. But Carrington wished to keep up the momentum of events and to emphasise that even if the Patriotic Front did not sign, it was the British intention to go ahead come what might. Soames went on 12 December and British sanctions were lifted on the same day. Muzorewa accepted the details of the cease-fire on 13 December and the Patriotic Front finally agreed four days later, having secured one additional assembly area at Gwelo. The advance party of the Monitoring Force arrived in Salisbury on 20 December and the agreement was finally signed by all parties on 21 December.

The negotiations had been a triumph for Carrington. He had hardly deviated at all from his original plan. With immense patience and diplomatic skill, allied to a total firmness of resolve, he had succeeded when all had failed before him. Wilson, Douglas-Home, Vorster, Kaunda, Kissinger, Callaghan, Crosland and so on – they had in the end all failed. It is of course true that at no stage before Lancaster House had the conditions for agreement been so favourable. Kaunda and Machel both needed a settlement badly (indeed at one stage Machel is believed to have told Mugabe that if agreement was not reached he had a comfortable villa available to him for his retirement). Carrington had only two delegations to deal with and no direct outside involvement. But the latter point was largely due to the British achievement at Lusaka. And, in any event, success was by no means pre-ordained: if Carrington had put a foot wrong the outcome could easily have been a total disaster. He, rightly, received world-wide acclaim for his brilliant achievement.[32]

There now remained the extremely difficult pre-election period over which Soames was to preside.

The choice of Governor had been difficult. The first requirement was that the incumbent must be a man of considerable political stature and experience. He would have to deal with a vast range of issues, internal and external. Problems would crowd in on him minute by minute. Decisions would be called for, many of which could, if wrong, well throw the whole enterprise into jeopardy. Clearly, it would be a great advantage if he could be a member of the British cabinet, privy to the general feelings of that body and armed with the authority which cabinet status gives. He should also, if possible, have some experience of Africa but he should not be too closely personally identified with either side of the main argument. He should be as acceptable as possible to both sides.

Although not in the cabinet, Lord Harlech was clearly a possibility, but he had been a member of the Pearce Commission in 1972 and, although a Conservative, was identified in white Rhodesian minds as a 'wet liberal'. The possibilities were narrowed down to Whitelaw and Soames. Soames had great diplomatic experience and he was chosen.

Through no fault of his own Soames was to suffer initially from his lack of knowledge of Rhodesia and its people. His experience lay largely in Europe. He had been an EEC Commissioner and the British Ambassador in Paris. Rhodesian Europeans were very different to those who walked the corridors of power in Brussels or Paris. He found it difficult to understand them and they him. Neither could he establish much of a rapport, until very late in the day, with many of the Africans. He had not been present at Lancaster House and had not been privy to the atmosphere of the negotiations and this was just as important as was the written agreement.

Soames' style of relaxed accessibility and much personal charm, to which his wife Mary – the daughter of Winston Churchill – added so much, was misunderstood by some white Rhodesians who were used to more formal meetings. The Africans, and particularly Muzorewa, were shy of him, and he did not know how to deal with them. Plunged head first into the

175

final stages of a long and highly complex saga and the focus of all the almost paranoic suspicions of black and white alike, without having any actual power himself, he did indeed have a near-impossible task. He had two basic options. He could either try to impose his considerable personality on events from the start or he could sit back, do very little, but hope to nudge affairs in the right direction. Once he had failed to take a firm line in the early stages, it would be impossible to do so later. But he needed time to find his feet and to be able to evaluate the strength of arguments put to him and the reliability of those who put those arguments. It would have been extremely difficult for him to take strong action immediately on arrival into a situation about which he knew so little. The result of all this was that, certainly in the early stages, he did very little indeed. His contacts with the leading whites were, on the whole, unhappy – at one stage he did not even meet Walls for about six weeks. He also failed to establish any kind of rapport with Muzorewa or Mugabe (until much later).

The main problem was that large numbers of Mugabe's army (ZANLA) did not in fact enter the assembly areas scheduled for them. By the terms of the agreement they should have all been in the assembly areas by 4 January. Much to the Security Forces' fury, the drawbridge was not pulled up on that day and an additional short period was allowed. This was an entirely reasonable decision, but it nevertheless caused much anger. By the end of 5 January there were about 16,000 people in assembly areas (12,000 ZANLA and 4000 ZIPRA). But in fact many of those from ZANLA consisted of Mujibas (young camp followers). Large numbers of hard core guerillas remained outside the camps and continued to intimidate. Such was the scale of this intimidation that Muzorewa's supporters could not go into many areas at all in order to electioneer. If they did so they were murdered. There was no doubt about this fact. It was reported in the *Guardian* on 9 February that the eight British election supervisors had told Soames that in five out of the eight electoral districts free and fair conditions did not yet exist. They went on to say that the worst areas, where many guerillas had ignored the cease-fire instructions, were dominated by ZANLA. It was reported in the *Daily Telegraph* of 6 February that Soames himself told the election council on 5 February – 'Almost daily there are reports of attacks on party officials and their houses, of intimidatory statements at the meetings of certain parties, of meetings not being allowed to be held in certain areas and of attacks on members of the public which show every sign of being politically motivated.'

By far the greatest number of cease-fire violations accepted by the Cease-fire Commission, which included a ZANLA representative, were perpetrated by ZANLA.

Attempts to maintain the unity of the Patriotic Front during the election had failed: ZAPU and ZANU were to campaign separately. Cunning as ever, Nkomo had pre-empted Mugabe by registering his party (ZAPU) as the Patriotic Front. Mugabe had to be content with the designation 'ZANU (PF)'.

Soames' dilemma was acute. In his closing speech at the Lancaster House Conference, Carrington had said the following – 'Having committed themselves to campaigning peacefully and to comply with the cease-fire agreement, no party or group could expect to take part in the elections if it continued the war or systematically to break the cease-fire and practise widespread intimidation.'

In spite of its clumsy grammar, this statement had not been lightly made. Every word had been carefully chosen and indeed bargained over by the Muzorewa delegation which had insisted on a statement of this nature before it would sign the final agreement. The implications were clear. If ZANLA continued to intimidate on a large scale, Mugabe's party (ZANU [PF]) should be banned from the election. And in spite of Soames' remarks there was absolutely no sign of any diminution of the very considerable ZANLA intimidation.[33]

But what would be the result if ZANU (PF) was banned? Externally, of course, there would have been a volcano of criticism. The Commonwealth, the United Nations, the OAU and even the EEC, to say nothing of the Labour Party in Britain and even a few left wing Conservatives, would have erupted in fury. They would all have said that it had been the British intention from the start to see that Mugabe did not win the election. Whatever evidence of ZANLA intimidation had been produced, it would have been lost in a storm of selfrighteous indignation. Britain would have been isolated. If the election had been held without Mugabe, very few, if any, countries would have recognised the new Government.

177

The internal implications would have been even more serious. ZANLA would probably have run riot. They might well have killed the British – and perhaps Australian, New Zealand, Kenyan and Fijian – monitors before anyone could have saved them and set forth on an orgy of rampaging murder. The Security Forces would certainly have retaliated. ZIPRA would probably have joined in and the situation within Rhodesia might well have become totally chaotic with no chance whatsoever of proper elections being held. This was recognised by the Rhodesian Joint Operations Command which, when it came to the point, advised against the outright banning of ZANU (PF).

On the other hand, Muzorewa had only conceded power on the clear understanding that Britain would see to it that the elections would be free and fair and that his party would have a chance of winning equal to that of the other contestants. How could that be the case if his supporters could not even enter large areas of the country, let alone campaign in them?

There were, also, other complicating factors. The Auxiliaries, who were loyal to Muzorewa, were being accused of intimidation by Mugabe and much of the media. There was some truth in this, and the UANC Youth Wing was also responsible for some attempted assassinations, but their activities were on a minor scale when compared to the massive and continuing ZANLA intimidation over a high proportion of the Shona areas. The murders of those who would not co-operate with ZANLA continued. But, on top of that, the very presence of a ZANLA guerilla in a village was enough to terrorise the inhabitants. Many villages had been the object of appalling atrocities. In one case in the North-East for instance, the whole village had been forced to watch while the headman had his eyes gouged out prior to disembowelment and a slow death. After death, the villagers were forced to continue watching while the dogs ate the remains. With that as the background, it is small wonder that the very presence of one of those guerillas who had perpetrated this horror was enough to terrify the whole community.

During the election, Rhodesia was descended upon by the world press. Many journalists came to the country with almost no knowledge of the background, and in many cases there was a failure to understand even the bare essentials of the situ-

178

ation. If, for instance, a journalist, fresh from England, had visited the village mentioned above he would probably go away and blithely report an atmosphere of calm and peace. Furthermore, because of the sheer terror the guerillas had occasioned, tribesmen would not inform against them. On the other hand, the Auxiliaries, although undoubtedly guilty of some intimidation, did not operate on that kind of scale. Tribesmen were prepared to inform on them. The result was that the media, in any case psychologically attuned to contradicting statements by any establishment – and the establishment in Rhodesia was, this time rightly, emphasising the extent of ZANLA intimidation – in general reported that intimidation was being practised at least equally by both sides and if anything the Auxiliaries were worse. A BBC Panorama broadcast just before the election was a particularly blatant example of biased reporting. The Auxiliaries were slated but little was said about the immeasureably worse ZANLA intimidation. A general climate of opinion was created in which both sides were, quite wrongly, thought to be as bad as each other.

On the whole the Rhodesian Security Forces were kept under control and there were very few incidents of violations of the cease-fire or bad behaviour by the Rhodesian army. This was greatly to the credit of Walls who had forged a disciplined and effective force. The police, too, were restrained in their activities, although at one stage they stupidly arrested Garfield Todd, who was released as soon as the low level decision reached higher authority. There was, however, one black spot on an otherwise clean sheet. The Selous Scouts, an elite body of mixed white and black soldiers trained to operate in small groups, were accused of numerous attempts to create incidents which looked as if they were the responsibility of ZANLA. There was some evidence that this was the case when the body of a member of the Selous Scouts was found in suspicious circumstances after an explosion. Bombs were left outside churches with clumsily written notes tying responsibility to ZANLA. The printing press of the Roman Catholic newspaper *Moto* – a very pro-Mugabe journal – was blown up and there was an attempt on Mugabe's life. There was no actual proof that the Selous Scouts were responsible for any of these incidents (or, if there was, it was suppressed) but the general view was formed, in the author's opinion rightly, that at least

179

in some cases that organisation was indeed involved. This made Soames' job vastly more difficult.

Soames had another highly delicate problem. There was no doubt that it had been agreed at Lancaster House that the South African Forces would leave Rhodesia during the election period. Most did leave, but some were left in the Beitbridge area. Protestations to the effect that their sole purpose was to guard the all-important bridge between South Africa and Rhodesia cut very little ice. As long as they remained in Rhodesia, Britain was clearly in the wrong, and this made it all the more difficult to take firm action on other, far more important, issues. They eventually left on 30 January.

It was announced on 28 December that the elections for the eighty African seats would be on the three days 27, 28 and 29 February (the white election was to be on 14 February). Mugabe's tactics were clear. He knew that many of his troops were not in the assembly areas: indeed there were explicit orders from the ZANLA High Command to the effect that large numbers were to remain at large and to dominate their areas. But he would try to cloak this total breach of the letter and the spirit of the Lancaster House agreement by a sustained and vehement attack on the Governor. This process began on 2 January when he attacked Soames on the grounds that the Security Forces were being allowed to operate over the whole country and were intimidating. On 8 January he said that he would dishonour the cease-fire unless the South Africans left Rhodesia and the Auxiliaries ceased to operate. He went on in the same vein throughout the pre-election period.

On 15 January it was announced by Government House that a considerable number of those in the assembly areas were not guerillas, that many were still outside the camps and that a large number had infiltrated across the border after the cease-fire. Soames clearly had to take some action. On 5 February he announced possible steps, short of outright banning, to be taken against political parties which continued to intimidate: these were restrictions on meetings, suspension from the campaign of candidates personally guilty of intimidation and disqualification of a party from the election altogether in certain areas. Limited action was taken on these lines. Enos Nkala (ZANU [PF]), subsequently to become Finance Minister, was banned from campaigning and on 14 February ZANU (PF) was forbidden to hold meetings in the Triangle and Hippo Valley areas. But these actions had very little effect. Indeed ZANU (PF) supporters derided the Governor's authority.

Nkomo was also highly incensed at the ZANLA actions. His supporters, too, could not go into ZANLA areas and on 5 February, Nkomo openly blamed ZANLA for murdering one of his candidates.

Muzorewa was indeed in a very difficult position. He did have some very obvious advantages. His UANC party organisation still remained more or less intact. The experience of fighting the 1979 election should have been a great help to him. The whole of the Government machine – civil service, army and police clearly wished for a Muzorewa victory. But he had two crippling disabilities. First, he had already had a period of power as Prime Minister, but the promises of peace and prosperity which he had inevitably made during the previous election campaign had not been achieved. In fact this was not his fault. He had only been in power since the end of May 1979 and for much of his period of office had been in Britain at the Lancaster House Conference. Muzorewa argued that one of the reasons for this lack of achievement lay in the refusal of the British Conservative Government to keep its promise to recognise his Government and drop sanctions. But that cut little ice.

The second and, in fact, clinching issue which led to Muzorewa's defeat was the general belief that if he won there was every possibility that the war would continue. Whatever promises were extracted from Mugabe and Nkomo to abide by the result of the election, the mass of the people simply did not believe that the Patriotic Front would accept a Muzorewa victory. The expectation was that it would revert to the bush and begin the war again. On the other hand, if the Patriotic Front – and in particular Mugabe – won, the war would certainly come to an end: there could be no question of Muzorewa continuing the fighting. There was a possibility of a white coup, but that was not a significant factor in the equation as far as most Africans were concerned. By voting for Mugabe, therefore, the Africans would ensure that the war would be stopped: by voting for Muzorewa there was every chance that the war would continue. No amount of protestations by Muzorewa and his supporters could persuade the mass of the popu-

181

lation to the contrary.

Muzorewa campaigned valiantly, working himself to the bone and often exposing himself to high risk. He returned to Salisbury first of the three leaders but his reception was muted: in African terms he had a small rally to celebrate his arrival – only 50,000 people turned out for him, whereas Nkomo had 100,000 and Mugabe, who returned on 27 January, had some 200,000 – a massive and highly significant event. Muzorewa had difficulties with money, too, and there were allegations to the effect that not all the money raised for his party was in fact used for the purposes for which it was given. Although Muzorewa was personally blameless, these allegations were not without foundation.

In theory, the campaign was about which party would be the best to rule Zimbabwe and there were indeed great ideological differences. Mugabe's party was avowedly Marxist. The document of Appendix 4 produced during the election campaign, gives the full flavour of the fact. It is true that the ZANU (PF) Manifesto played down this aspect and indeed on his return Mugabe called upon the whites to remain in the country if he won. During the campaign, too, he was studiously moderate in all his references to the whites and to his conduct of the economy after victory. But his final objective of a Socialist State was not in doubt and he never denied that this was indeed his eventual aim. Muzorewa, on the other hand, was convinced of the virtues of the mixed economy and used Mugabe's Marxism to the full. There could have been much appeal to the black electorate in this, since state (as opposed to tribal) ownership of property is wholly alien to African custom and tradition. However, all this fell on deaf ears. It was the end of the war which was the prime requirement in the minds of the Africans and, in comparison to this, the niceties of economic theory were of no interest whatsoever.

Nkomo was, as ever, a pragmatist. His economic policies were apt to follow whatever wind was blowing at the time. He had a secure base in the Ndebele part of the country but little appeal elsewhere. His national appeal had gone beyond recall.

There was a further factor which confused the issue. All the reports from the Rhodesian authorities were to the effect that the result would be a 'hung' election in which no party would receive a majority of seats, necessitating some kind of coalition. Muzorewa and Mugabe were each expected to obtain something between 25 and 35 seats with Nkomo getting perhaps 15 and Sithole and Chikerema, who had left the UANC and started his own party, perhaps one or two each. Twenty white seats had already been won (in the white election on 14 February) by the Rhodesian Front. But, under the Constitution, the whites could not form a coalition with any but the largest African party in order to produce a majority in Parliament. If, for instance, Mugabe had 33 and Muzorewa 31 seats, the whites could not join Muzorewa in a coalition with their 20 seats so as to produce an overall majority of 51 out of 100. But if two African parties were involved, even if one of the African parties only had one seat, then that was acceptable. For instance, if Muzorewa had 31 seats and Sithole had one seat, then the 20 whites could join the other two parties to form a Government. The permutations of this situation were almost limitless.

The white objective was to keep Mugabe out of power. Clearly, therefore, it was to their advantage to try to bring about a coalition not involving Mugabe and to press for talks between the other parties before the election took place. Ian Smith had already stated that Nkomo was the best bet for the whites: he thought nothing of Muzorewa. There were other whites who disagreed with him and believed that Muzorewa should be supported and helped. Nkomo kept his own counsel, refusing to be drawn. Muzorewa became ever more bitter. There were talks at a low level between supporters of Muzorewa and Nkomo, but no commitment was made on either side and Nkomo kept his options entirely open.

Mugabe insisted throughout the election campaign that it was the British intention to keep him out of power at all costs. It was of course true that the British would have liked to have had a non-Marxist Government in Rhodesia. For a Conservative Government in effect to be responsible for overthrowing a moderate pro-Western black Prime Minister, a devotee of the mixed economy, to be replaced by the avowedly pro-Marxist Mugabe was hardly the ideal solution. But this was a comparatively minor consideration when compared to the prize of a peaceful transfer of power and the granting of independence to a Government ruled by a party which had been chosen by the people of Rhodesia in an election which was recognised internationally to have been free and fair. For Britain to fix the election in Muzorewa's favour, as Mugabe never ceased to insinuate, would not only have been out of character but in the long run a total disaster. As far as Britain was concerned, the first requirement was to see that the election was as free and fair as possible and accepted as such: if the result was a defeat for Mugabe, so much the better.

Towards the end of the campaign, Muzorewa began to feel that the election was slipping away from him. As he saw it, Soames would take no effective action to stop the intimidation which Muzorewa believed was ruining his chances. He became extremely bitter. In spite of all the British promises he was not being given a fair chance to win this truly vital election. The appeals he made to South Africa fell on deaf ears. The South Africans were powerless to help, short of the use of force, and they were certainly not prepared to take any form of military action on his behalf: the result of such action would in the long run have been devastating both to Rhodesia and to their own country and they knew it. Muzorewa began to think in terms of having the election postponed.

The Monitoring Force, largely British, but with Australian, Fijian, Kenyan and New Zealand detachments, carried out its job with great efficiency and much heroism. Determined not to be sucked into any continuing military obligation, Mrs Thatcher had originally jibbed at producing any British soldiers at all and then, when it became clear that some military establishment was necessary in order to monitor the cease-fire, she had tried to keep the numbers to a minimum and to cut back on the arms and equipment they took with them. Eventually she gave way and reasonable numbers were agreed, together with enough arms and equipment for self-defence.

The difficulties which the Monitoring Force faced were immense. Those with the Rhodesian Security Forces had a comparatively simple job, although there were obvious pitfalls if great tact was not used. But those attached to the Patriotic Front – both ZANLA and ZIPRA – had very great problems. As far as the British were concerned few, if any, of them had been to Africa before. They came straight from Britain, Northern Ireland or Germany and, shortly after arrival, found themselves sitting at a table in the bush of Central Africa, waiting for the Patriotic Front guerilla to walk towards them, perhaps two or three hundred strong, waving their sub-machine guns around and looking very fierce. They had no idea whether or not they would be immediately murdered in cold blood. It only required one young (or old) soldier to lose his nerve and fire a shot, or indeed to run away, and the result would certainly be the slaughter of the whole party. It is a vast tribute to the discipline and determination of the British army that in no case did any soldier lose his nerve at the crucial moment. Leadership at a low level was at a premium and there was no doubt that the training the army had had in Northern Ireland stood it in good stead.

Then, having surmounted the first hurdle, small groups of soldiers had to live with the guerillas in the assembly areas for some ten weeks. They had to undertake all kinds of tasks for which they were not trained. Medical orderlies in effect became doctors, in some cases delivering babies and under-taking minor operations at the point of a gun. At no stage were any of these soldiers certain that they would not be murdered. As a result of their experiences in Zambia and Mozambique, both ZIPRA and ZANLA were terrified of aircraft and when-ever one was seen the tensions were greatly heightened. It was not at all certain what would happen in the ZANLA camps if Mugabe was defeated at the election: it was very possible that the guerillas would set off on a rampage, murdering the moni-tors before they left. Indeed in one assembly area the guerillas announced their intention of marching on Salisbury if Mugabe was defeated.

On top of all this there were great logistic problems in supplying and looking after small bodies of troops spread around the country, and above all of feeding and trying to find amusements and pastimes for the guerillas themselves.

Relations with the Rhodesian Security Forces, too, were inherently difficult. The Monitoring Force was almost entirely dependent on local assistance for supplies and transport. But it was supposed to be checking on the Rhodesians who were nominally under the control of the Governor, who in his turn had no power to exercise that control. The Security Forces were trying to kill those guerillas who were not in the camps while those who were in the camps had the monitors virtually as hostages. It was indeed a confused situation. Major General Acland and his staff did well to avoid disaster. But the princi-

185

pal accolade must go to the British soldier, adaptable as ever, able to strike up an instant friendly relationship with anyone and imbued with that inexhaustible sense of humour which brings a sense of proportion to every difficulty and danger.

Although their numbers were far smaller, the contingents from the other Commonwealth countries also did extremely well – particularly the Australians and New Zealanders who, being white, were also viewed by the guerillas with extreme suspicion.

The white Rhodesians were in a near-impossible situation. They had made a massive effort in the running of the 1979 elections. Virtually every able-bodied man had been called up, and the economic life of the country had been greatly disrupted. Now they were asked to do the same again – this time with the very real possibility that their efforts would result in eventual expulsion from the land they loved. There can hardly be a more ironic situation. Without the full co-operation of the mass of the white population it would certainly be impossible to run the election at all. It is indeed surprising that they were prepared to take part in it.

Whatever happened subsequently and whatever the eventual outcome of the Mugabe regime may be, the fact was that the mass of the whites thought at that time – and had ample reason to think so (see Appendix 4) – that ZANU (PF) was determined to set up a Marxist regime which would inevitably lead to a white exodus. There was much talk of a white coup if Mugabe won. Indeed this action was certainly contemplated in high circles. But at no stage was there an official plan, sanctioned by the Joint Operations Committee, for a coup, even on a contingency basis. However, preparations for some such eventuality were undoubtedly made at a lower level and, certainly, plans were made to deal with the guerillas if they tried to take the law into their own hands.

The consequences of a coup would of course have been catastrophic. Civil war of the most bloody kind imaginable would undoubtedly have broken out. Many of the Monitoring Force would probably have been killed. There would have been cause for military intervention by Britain and, if this had been resisted, some kind of United Nations action would undoubtedly have been taken. The South Africans might well have felt obliged to intervene. The powder keg would have blown up.

186

The white position would have become totally impossible and there would certainly have been a mass white exodus, leaving the country in a state of total chaos.

As the election approached, the tension rose. Continued efforts were made in many quarters to forge some kind of alliance between Nkomo and Muzorewa. The South Africans, who had been reluctant to support Nkomo in any way because they thought of him as a rigid Communist, reluctantly came to the conclusion that a coalition on these lines would be the best solution in the circumstances. Machel was asked by the white Rhodesians what his reactions would be to this arrangement and whether he would continue to support the guerilla war from Mozambique by ZANLA if this happened. His reply was equivocal, but not wholly discouraging. Reports from the security services and the army continued to show that Mugabe could not possibly obtain an overall majority of seats. The question arose as to what Soames' proper course would be if there was a 'hung' result. Mugabe argued that if his party had the most seats, he should be asked to form a Government: only if he failed to do so should the Governor call in the leader of the second largest party and so on. This was resisted by Soames who said he would call in all political leaders and tell them to go away and see who could secure a majority of seats. This was a key issue, as if Mugabe alone had been asked to form a Government, he would undoubtedly ask Nkomo to join him, and Nkomo would find it difficult to refuse. It would be easier for Nkomo to form a coalition with Muzorewa if all leaders were called in immediately the results were declared. It was clear that the first few days after a 'hung' election would be highly dangerous. It was not known what the reaction of ZANLA would be. Would the ZANLA guerillas leave their assembly areas and march on Salisbury? How would ZIPRA react? There was a whole range of imponderables.

Throughout the election campaign Soames had wished to establish good personal relations with Mugabe, as with the other leaders, but had been unable to do so. However, at their last meeting before the election, the two men really got on terms with each other for the first time. They both put the past behind them and the atmosphere was extremely friendly. Mugabe was probably scenting victory and clearly hoped for a smooth transfer of power. He was a man of high intelligence

and, unlike either Nkomo or Muzorewa, was able to talk to
Soames as an intellectual equal. He was also aware of his own
limitations in experience of government and, even more so,
those of his principal supporters. He wanted help and Soames
was only too ready to give it. This was underlined when, after
the election, Mugabe actually asked Soames to stay on for six
months. This meeting, therefore, set the pattern for what, subsequently, was going to be a very close relationship of great importance. It was to the great credit of Soames that, in spite of
all the vicious attacks which Mugabe had made on him during
the course of the election campaign, he was prepared and able
to get on terms of near intimacy with Mugabe at the crucial
moment. He was a big enough man to do so and this was a
vital element in what was to be an almost miraculous transformation of the situation. Whatever the arguments might
have been about Soames' lack of firmness in the earlier stages
and his ignorance of conditions in Rhodesia, in the end he certainly steered the country with poise and assurance through
what might have been a most traumatic period.

As the election became imminent, worries about the
outcome among those opposed to Mugabe grew. Muzorewa
had concluded that he was not going to win, and that there
could be a landslide against him. Ian Smith, also, was highly
apprehensive about a possible Mugabe victory, as were
Sithole and Ndiweni. They jointly decided, as leaders of the
Zimbabwe/Rhodesia Government which had ceded power on
the understanding that the election would be free and fair
(David Smith refused to have anything to do with the proceedings), to go to the Governor and *demand* (not ask, *demand*) that
the election should be postponed on the grounds that the conditions for a free and fair election did not exist. They must
have realised that Soames would be most unlikely to accede to
their request, and that in that event the situation would
become extremely difficult. The positions of Walls and Ken
Flower, the very powerful head of the security services, were
crucial and they were summoned to attend a meeting. When
Walls and Flower came into the room there was an embarrassed silence and then Muzorewa asked Ian Smith to speak
for them all (an ironic twist indeed). When the proposal was
put, however, Walls and Flower refused to go along with it.
The fact was that actual power lay in Walls', and to a lesser

extent Flower's, hands and the proposal was quickly dropped.

It is indeed astonishing that any such move could have been contemplated – a reflection of the depth of despair which was felt by Muzorewa and many of the whites. As Muzorewa saw it, Britain had manoeuvred him out of the position of power which he had obtained through free and fair elections on the promise that the 1980 election would also be free and fair. But Mugabe's party had been allowed to practise intimidation on a massive scale without let or hindrance, thus breaking Carrington's specific promise in his statement at the end of the Lancaster House Conference.

On 25 February Nyerere made the astonishing statement that Tanzania would not recognise the results of the election if the Patriotic Front failed to win. He went on to say – 'The results that are going to be announced by the Governor Soames are rigged results.' It is difficult to think of any remark which could more clearly have revealed the totally biased attitude of this leader of African Nationalist opinion. He had, perforce, to eat his words when the results in terms of seats were announced – Mugabe 57, Nkomo 20, Muzorewa 3. Mugabe had a clear majority of seats – 57 out of 100 (this latter figure including the 20 white seats).

Although he had refused to take part in demanding postponement of the election before it began, Walls had become increasingly bitter about the way the election had developed and what he saw as the total lack of firm action by Soames. When the election actually started, and reports about the likely result began to reach him, he realised that the optimistic reports he had been receiving were wrong and that Mugabe was probably going to win a landslide victory. He believed this to be due to the massive ZANLA intimidation which had taken place. While he was in London at the Lancaster House Conference, Mrs Thatcher had said that he could have access to her at any time if Walls thought this to be vital. He therefore sent her a message asking her to cancel the election results and to rule through a Council of Ministers. He did this without consulting his colleagues on the Joint Operations Committee, who did not support him when he told them of his action the following day. Any action by Britain on these lines was, of course, out of the question and Walls received the inevitable refusal through Sir Anthony Duff.

189

In retrospect it is clear that Mugabe's victory was inevitable. The scale of this, however, was due to the African tendency to jump on a band wagon. The *Daily Telegraph* made a good point when it said that in Africa an election represents not so much a choice as a prediction. Once the pendulum started swinging towards Mugabe, it was certain that he would have a considerable majority. There was a great deal of intimidation, a vast proportion of which was committed by Mugabe's supporters, but Mugabe would have won anyway. For whatever reasons, Muzorewa had failed to bring about peace, and a vote for Mugabe in most Africans' minds meant peace. Muzorewa, contrary to the views of much of the media, mounted a valiant campaign. But he had no real hope from the start. The actual election process was scrupulously fairly conducted, and the 500 British policemen who appeared at the polling stations helped to bring about an atmosphere of calm. The hand-over of power to Mugabe was achieved without the bloodshed which might well have resulted if the direction of affairs had faltered at the end. If Soames had been able to prevent massive ZANU (PF) intimidation, then Muzorewa's party might have been able to improve on their situation, but they would still have lost.

CHAPTER EIGHT

White and Black Attitudes

The end result of the fourteen or so years of Unilateral Independence was the advent to power of Mugabe – a Marxist. The extent to which his regime will in fact turn to Socialism must be a matter of conjecture. And, indeed, there must be doubt as to whether his Government can survive. These points will be covered in the next chapter. But what of the white, and black, attitudes which brought about this state of affairs?

To take the whites first – it is easy to criticise and to indulge in smug superficial generalities. The fact is that the attitudes of the whites sprang not from original sin, or virtue, but from the environment in which they lived, some of them for four or more generations.

The white community was, of course, diverse. Farmers, businessmen, civil servants, professional men, technicians, artisans – white Rhodesia produced the whole gamut of occupations except for manual labour. The whites provided the brains, the innovators, the leaders in every field, certainly until very recently. The whites directed: the blacks carried out their orders. There were some exceptions, and the visitor was proudly shown houses in which black businessmen lived in comparative affluence. But the very fact that these had to be pointed out demonstrated the truth: the whites dominated Rhodesia in virtually every sphere.

Within these categories, also, there was of course great diversity, notably between those who had arrived recently and those whose families had settled in the country up to ninety years ago. Those with a long Rhodesian ancestry felt themselves to be superior to recent arrivals (in fact the most intransigent whites were often those who had arrived most recently).

There was also the inevitable disdain felt by those who lived in the country for the town dwellers – and vice versa. But, by and large, white Rhodesians were remarkably homogeneous. They faced similar problems, they or their forbears had all taken a conscious decision to quit their homes and to start a new life in a new and challenging environment, and on the whole they had been highly successful.

The first and essential point to grasp is that up to 1980 the white Rhodesian life-style had been virtually frozen since 1945. Unlike in Britain, the middle classes had not had to change their whole way of life. Black servants continued to cater for their domestic needs. The artisans who had arrived in the country since 1945 had, similarly, been able to afford black servants and in many cases a swimming pool.

Many of the images of white Rhodesian life were of a Britain long since gone. Sunday Mattins at the Anglican Cathedral in Salisbury, the men and women in their Sunday best with the special glow of the insider which typified the Church of England in a bygone era, and hardly a black face to be seen, is one example. Boys in blazers and straw hats, their hair short; girls in uniform, round-hatted, gawky but demure, walking through the streets of Salisbury is another. No drop-outs, no teenage rebels, no drug problems, the straightforward drinking of the rugby team or of the farmers in for a binge from the country. There were of course many exceptions to all these images, but by and large Rhodesia had not yet approached the very real problems which loss of Empire, comparative affluence and mass communication have brought to Britain.

There were a number of reasons for this. The country was physically very far away from Europe. It had a totally alien environment to the North and a tight-lipped enclosed puritanical society to the South. The pioneering days were only just receding into the past. Challenges and opportunities existed in large measure. Boredom, if it was there at all, was self-created – not a function of the environment – needing a special kind of person to overcome it without rebellion of one kind or another. Fortunes could still be made very quickly indeed. A carpenter emigrating aged twenty-one to Salisbury with his tools as his only asset apart from his own skills, was the proud owner of a furniture factory employing 200 people in the space of ten years or so. A well-known leading European, who emigrated after the 1939–45 war with nothing save his Scottish acumen and capacity for hard work, eventually farmed enough land to employ fifteen European managers. The old-fashioned virtues were admired, the old-fashioned vices tolerated.

Then there was the sense of isolation, a superior kind of isolation – not the friendless beleaguerment of a race at bay but, as they saw it, the proud knowledge of achievement. It was the whites who had created their country. It was the whites who, by their drive and questing spirit, had turned the scrub into rolling acres of fertile farming land. Many of those still farming had started by pitching their tent in the bush, hiring some labour on borrowed money, ploughing a few acres, digging out a dam for water, planting their first crop and gradually working upwards from there. The affluence in which they eventually lived belied long years of toil and worry – in particular during the hard time of the depression in the 1930s. It was the whites who had developed the mines, inspired and directed the building of the roads, the railways and the erection of the towering office blocks. It was the whites who had conserved the wild life in glorious game parks, brought the rule of law, had largely formed the incorruptible civil service and police, and had forged the whole structure of Rhodesian life in the Western image. In their view they were not rapacious foreigners, skimming the cream off someone else's milk; they had made Rhodesia into what it was and they were proud of it. They were not British people living in Rhodesia; they were Rhodesians, born and bred. To them, accusations that they had only achieved all this by oppressing the blacks was absurd. They were certain that Rhodesia had higher standards of education, medical care, rural development, African housing and so on than any other African country to the North. They were secure in the belief that they had nothing to be ashamed of – very much the opposite.

Unlike the settlers in Kenya – the nearest equivalent of the white Rhodesian community in British Africa – the white Rhodesians did not send their children back to Britain to be educated, When they emigrated, they cut their roots with Britain to a degree unknown in Kenya and the other British colonies in Africa. But, in another sense, the opposite was true. They remained obsessed with Britain and their British heritage. They re-created Britain in the Rhodesian towns and, as far as they could, in the countryside. Balmoral Drive, Windsor Crescent – the streets were, many of them, given names in order to perpetuate what was eventually to be a mirage – a continuation of the British way of life in wholly alien surroundings. However, to a large extent they lacked the cross-fertilisation with developments in Britain which would, inevitably have diluted this obsession with a way of life which had passed into history. Their attitudes became frozen, their values remained constant in a changing world.

The deep-seated reluctance to change felt by the vast majority of whites in Rhodesia was fuelled by what they heard of the impact of change in that country. London had become shabby, British youth was long in hair but short in morals, the English disease was apparently now endemic and what they believed to be the debilitating Welfare State was all-pervading. To them, the British loss of self-confidence and apparent lack of personal endeavour was a function, not of a complex amalgam of historical causes, but of a conscious change in attitudes which they were determined to resist.

One of the results of all this was that they were unable to come to terms with African Nationalism. The greater the force of the wind of change to the North – and the refugees from the Congo had a deep impact – the greater their resistance to acceptance of the inevitability of a hand-over of power: until a late stage they refused even to contemplate such a development and were not prepared to begin the process by making a real effort to train the Africans for the responsibilities they would eventually have to undertake.

There were indeed a number of white liberals. These were mainly businessmen who feared a holocaust if African Nationalism was rejected out of hand, but there were also a number of intellectuals from the universities and elsewhere, together with some church men and women – particularly from the Catholic Church – and even a few farmers, who felt themselves in profound disagreement with the prevailing white consensus. A series of political parties was formed in order to rally liberal opinion and to attempt to challenge the Rhodesian Front in elections. But, in the event, they never made any significant impact. The fact was that, although there were more 'liberals' in Rhodesia than is often supposed, they were utterly untypical of the bulk of the white

Rhodesian community.

There were, of course, analogies with the South African situation which were seized upon by the enemies of the white community in Rhodesia, but the resemblance was largely superficial. The attitudes of the whites in both countries had overtones of paternalism, but the white Rhodesians were never prone to the sometimes vicious bitterness which was, and is, one of the saddest features of race relations in South Africa.

A further factor in the equation was that the extreme rigours of apartheid in South Africa originated from the whites of Boer origin. Although there were many Rhodesians from this background, particularly in the farming areas, they did not really shape the prevailing ethic which remained predominantly British. Indeed some of them had come to Rhodesia in the first place because they preferred the more easy-going atmosphere in Rhodesia to that in their own country.

There was, indeed, a vast difference between the general ambience of race relations in Rhodesia and that in South Africa. It was to be seen in the look on the faces of the blacks, in the way the police walked the streets, in the many social contacts between black and white which existed even in the most difficult days, in the sight of a queue in the shops with whites taking their place behind the blacks, in the whole fabric of life. Such was the contrast, that many whites of all political persuasions actively disliked going to South Africa, resenting not only the big-brother attitude of some South Africans, but also the general attitude of the whites towards their black compatriots. Moving across the frontier one felt an immediate and striking change in race relations even at the height of the war in Rhodesia. Indeed many whites, faced with the decision as to what to do if life becomes impossible for them in Zimbabwe are now showing extreme reluctance to moving to South Africa because of their distaste for what they feel to be a generally unhappy atmosphere there.

But, nevertheless, the white Rhodesians did see themselves as a separate and superior segment of society in Rhodesia. The farmers and their white farm managers totally dominated their black labour force. The whites in the armed services, the civil service and the police, while they did belatedly try to bring about some African advancement, were in total control of their respective organisations. The white businessmen,

195

while many of them professing an absence of colour consciousness, in fact ran their businesses with whites in all the positions
of real responsibility. Until very recently black graduates from
Salisbury and other universities, did not find it at all easy to
scale the ladder of advancement. The few who succeeded were
used as examples of white tolerance. The reason for all this was
not, however, based entirely on a conscious decision concerning the continuation of white dominance. There was also a
genuine fear of the onset of inefficiency, nepotism and corruption – endemic to a greater or lesser degree in almost all
African countries to the North.

There were, of course, some Africans who adopted European standards, but to the extent that they did so they were untypical of the mass of the population. The fact was that the
African and European cultures and ethics were fundamentally
different. Both had their virtues: both had their vices. Because
of their very different tribal traditions, it is dangerous to
generalise about the Africans in Rhodesia, let alone in the
whole continent. There was, nevertheless, a wide and recog-
nisable gulf between the African and European approach to
life which could be identified. By and large the Europeans saw
efficiency as a self-evident virtue and the individual as responsible for his own actions. The Africans were not so concerned
with individual responsibility and did not view efficiency as an
end in itself. They were far more closely identified with their
families and tribes than were the Europeans. They saw responsibility more as a joint than a personal matter. Many of them
expected a man in a position of power to use his position in
order to further the interests of his family and tribe, and to this
end they were tolerant of corruption and nepotism. There was
little, if any, social stigma in being caught out in corruption –
however exalted the offender might have been. Most Africans
did not 'lay waste their powers' by 'getting and spending', they
had little sense of urgency, and time had no meaning for many
of them. The European and African cultures were different in
the way that provision was made for the future. The Europeans tried to build up some kind of secure economic base.
Traditionally the Africans provided for their old age by raising
large families of children (a practice which now, too often,
leads to poverty, not prosperity). Although many Africans
would make considerable sacrifices to help pay for their chil-

196

dren's education, in general they took little thought for the morrow. This had many advantages. They laughed easily and were tolerant to a fault. Unless in the presence of actual or imminent disaster, on the whole, they had happier natures than the Europeans, too often beset by care in the complicated structure of life they had created for themselves. (However, as medical science reduces mortality and education widens horizons, Western ideas of efficiency, with all they imply for changes to the African way of life, are essential if mass starvation is to be averted and aspirations are to be satisfied.)

A further divisive element has lain in the fact that the general standard of education of the two races was of a different order altogether. The education in European schools was of a very high standard indeed, in many ways superior to the best schools in Britain. African education, even before the onset of the war forced the closure of many rural schools, was designed on totally different and vastly inferior lines. It was indeed possible for some Africans to attain professional qualifications both at Salisbury and at other foreign universities – notably South African – but they were the exceptions. The veneer of European culture had indeed tinged the edges of a proportion of the African community, but the roots were not yet deep. Even the most educated Africans in some cases still felt the presence of a spirit world determining events beyond their individual control as rational beings. However, 'chance' played no part in African tribal culture. For instance, if a man was ill this was thought to be the result either of an affront to the ancestral spirits, who had to be mollified in some way, or of a curse by some malevolent person. A witch doctor had to be approached to discover the cause and a remedy found (often at considerable expense).

In view of all this, it is not surprising that Europeans, secure in their Western traditions and, on the whole, contemptuous of the African way of life which they saw, rightly or wrongly, as vastly inferior to their own, were chary of entrusting real responsibility to Africans in almost every field. If there was something to be done which required a continuing and unsupervised exercise of responsibility, they found a fellow European to do it. And the fact that Africans were not given the opportunities of political and economic power led to a debilitating acceptance of a second-class status. The European was

197

in the end responsible and, therefore, acceptance of responsibility became alien to the African way of life.

The catchword, much used by Smith and others, was 'standards'. The whites were loth – indeed they refused – to 'lower their standards' of administration, probity and general efficiency and they thought, probably rightly, that to give Africans a chance would immediately lead to just that. One heard stories, perhaps many of them apocryphal, of instances when an African seemed to have all the qualifications for a senior post and was given it, only to discover later that he had been fiddling the books in some way – probably in order to have enough money to satisfy his many relations who flocked round him to get a share of the spoils.

There were, however, a number of other factors at work on white minds, particularly since UDI. The media in Rhodesia was largely controlled by the Government. The radio and television, particularly, constantly emphasised and vastly exaggerated the state of comparative chaos which characterised black Africa. It was virtually impossible for white Rhodesians to travel in these countries and an impression of barbaric anarchy was created in many white minds, only too ready to absorb such tales as justifying the stand they had made. The truth was that race relations in, for instance, Kenya and Zambia were extremely good until the Zambian situation deteriorated just before the Lancaster House Conference. But if a visitor pointed this out, he was simply not believed.

As a whole, the white Rhodesian community was ready to accept without question the simplistic interpretation of affairs to the North in terms of a Communist atheist advance against the ramparts of Christendom along the Zambezi. And, in the terms of reference which they gave themselves, there was more than a grain of truth in this interpretation. The Russians, and at times the Chinese, did have a hold in many African countries either directly or through the Russian puppets, the Cubans and East Germans. Mozambique and Angola did eventually fall to regimes which held Communist beliefs. The guerillas who committed appalling atrocities within Rhodesia were armed, trained and to a certain extent directed by the Communists. There was a tidy, if horrifying, pattern, clear and easy to understand, which motivated a proud and tough people to a stand of heroic proportions – a successful resistance

198

to the pressures of virtually the whole world, less South Africa and in the initial stages Portugal, over a period of no less than fourteen years.

There would have been no question of this if the racial conflict within Rhodesia had been anything like that depicted by those who compared Rhodesia to South Africa. A mere 250,000 – and later even fewer – whites out of a population of some six million could not possibly have succeeded in this resistance if the blacks in their country had been uniformly sullen, oppressed slaves of an arrogant white aristocracy. The South Africans are worried now about their future and the proportion of whites to blacks in that country is in the order of 1 to 4 as against the Rhodesian 1 to 25 or more.

The white sense of superior isolation was intensified because of their hearty dislike and distrust of post-war Britain and its successive Governments. In all colonial territories with settler communities, a deep distrust of the colonial power existed among those whites who lived in the country. This was partly because the settlers were convinced that the administrators who came from Britain, and who almost certainly intended to return there, did not really understand the country or the problems which they faced. This dislike was even more marked in the case of the Colonial Office in London where the overall decisions were taken by people who, it was thought, had sometimes not even visited the territories in question (in fact this was very rarely the case). Furthermore, the aims of the two sides – the settlers and the Colonial Government – were fundamentally different. The settlers were trying to make a good life for themselves and their families: the Colonial Government was trying to 'bring the natives on' so that they would eventually achieve self-government and at the same time to protect them from unreasonable exploitation by the settlers. On top of this was the inevitable inferiority complex of the 'colonial', who often felt himself to be rough and unsophisticated when compared to the apparently suave, wordly-wise but effete long- or short-term visitor from Britain.

Rhodesia, being self-governing, was of course in a different situation. It produced its own administrators, its own Government. But Britain retained the ultimate responsibility and suspicions of British intentions ran deep, particularly as those who took the decisions in London had – as the white

Rhodesians saw it – absolutely no knowledge of conditions in Rhodesia. There were, of course, British Governors but, again, these (until the advent of Sir Humphrey Gibbs) were transitory birds of passage without, the white Rhodesians believed, any real commitment to the country.

These deep suspicions of Britain became vastly more intensified in the period up to and after UDI. The white community in Rhodesia saw Britain as a predatory ignoramus, intent on sacrificing everything they had achieved in the interest of appeasing their enemies. Many of them, certainly the majority, believed that Britain had gone back on her word consistently, from what they saw as Butler's perfidy in his dealings with Winston Field at the Victoria Falls Conference through the whole period up to Lancaster House when the final betrayal took place. Every twist in the story seemed to give more credence to their belief. And this at a time when it seemed to them that Britain was herself losing ground in every field, economic, moral and social.

With all this as a background to their thinking, it is small wonder that the white community became more and more intransigent and that many of them saw every concession to black advancement as a further step on the road to ruin. Most found it difficult to understand why the British, their own 'kith and kin', should have turned against them and be actively conspiring to bring about disaster.

The final irony seemed to come with Britain's reaction to the guerilla war. Beset on all sides, less the comparatively short South African frontier, by groups of murderous terrorists and straining every muscle, physical, moral and economic, to hold their own, the white Rhodesians were appalled by the British Government's apparent indifference to their agony. Indeed, it often seemed to them that Britain was actually conniving with, if not helping, their mortal enemies, trained and armed by Communists of one kind or another. The fact that the vast majority of those murdered, often in the most ghastly circumstances, were black seemed to be totally ignored by a Britain mouthing platitudes about an end to violence, but refusing even the most modest help to those who were fighting for their lives. Indeed what help was given went to the countries which succoured their enemies – Tanzania, Mozambique, Zambia and, to a lesser extent Botswana (although that

Government's attitude was understood if not condoned). The equivocal attitude of the British and World Council of Churches who channelled medical aid to the 'freedom fighters', added fuel to the fire.

It is, therefore, not surprising that the white community was not open to rational argument by Britain or anyone else as to how they should run their country or as to the long-term advantages of ceding power. The fact that they did, in the end, decide to do so arose out of necessity, certainly not as a result of an change of mind on the principles involved.

The war, also, had other profound effects on white attitudes. The call-up gradually affected more and more people for longer and longer periods of their lives. Eventually nearly every able-bodied man was on active duty for many months of the year. This made the whole conduct of the economy in every field – business, farming, mining and general administration – extremely difficult. Wives had to take over the direction of farms while their husbands were away, carrying guns and ready to protect their own lives and those of their families for much of the year. There were many stories of extreme heroism by men, women and even children in isolated farms. Businesses, factories and mines had to cope as best they could with the disappearance of white staff at frequent intervals. Quite apart from the direct costs of maintaining the armed services and police at such a high level, the drain of the war effort on the economy was very considerable. Many whites left the country. But the structure of white society did not collapse. On the surface, life continued as it had always done and the casual visitor probably noticed little difference. Sudden death became a constant companion to many white Rhodesians, viewed as a necessary part of the scene, talked about as an inevitable consequence of existence in their country, tragic to close relatives but not seen with the horror which similar incidents evoke in countries long at peace. It is one of the constant wonders of the human condition that humanity seems to be able to adapt itself to almost anything.

But the sense of heroic isolation, of a joint struggle against overwhelming odds, which was one of the consequences of the war, binding the whites together as a cohesive whole, had other more unfortunate effects. Much of the white youth of Rhodesia was coarsened by its experiences. While in the army

201

the young whites led very exciting lives, often operating deep in Zambia and Mozambique. Groups of young men, taut, supremely fit, well-trained, experienced and mature beyond their years, were sent off in helicopters to attack and kill collections of guerillas once located inside or outside Rhodesia by small bodies of Selous or Greys Scouts trained to exist for long periods in the bush. Others operated in more conventional ways from company bases throughout the country. Success was measured by the number of 'kills' achieved. It often happened that innocent people were 'caught in crossfire'. When tribesmen were suspected of growing crops for the 'Terrs', as the phrase went, these were destroyed. Villages were sometimes burnt. What happened in the bush, far from prying eyes, would, if known, certainly have horrified much of the white Rhodesian establishment, let alone public opinion in Britain. The contrast between the atmosphere in Salisbury or other towns, whence many of these youths came, and the fierce, immediate and fleeting brush with death was vast and, in many ways, overwhelming. The 'Terrs' degenerated to 'Gooks', barely human in the minds of some of those whose objective it was to slaughter as many as possible. And the further step of attacking all blacks found in the bush, whether guerillas or not, was only too easy. The parallel with Vietnam in the later stages of that tragedy was close – the difference being that in Rhodesia the young soldiers were, as they saw it, fighting for the very existence of their country whereas this was not the case in Vietnam.

Many of the parents of these young men were shocked by the realisation of what the attitudes of their children had become; but there was absolutely nothing they could do about it. They, too, were involved in the general struggle and, short of emigrating, they had no control over the situation. It also became extremely difficult for those white Rhodesians who were not regular soldiers to settle down to ordinary life when they returned from reservist duty. Not only was there the contrast in their daily life from war to peace, or comparative peace, but, unless they were officers, in the army they were trained to take, not to give, orders. A young white Rhodesian in his normal life was expected to take responsibility, to make decisions, to give orders: many reservists found the return to civilian life a difficult transition. And, as is always the result of violent conflict, the general effect of the war was to sharpen the edge of intolerance, particularly among the white youth.

In spite of all this, however, the whites as a whole still retained an overall regard for and tolerance of their black compatriots – and not only 'as long as they know their place'. The paternalistic approach was indeed deep-rooted, but there was more to it than that. The sea-change which occurred when the whites eventually accepted the inevitable move to 'majority rule' would not have happened with such comparative ease had it not been for the generally good race relations which, paradoxically, typified that part of Africa in which the deepest passions had been aroused.

And what of the black attitudes? The first point to make is that whereas the whites were, on the whole, remarkably homogeneous, the blacks were not. There was the vast gulf between those who had been educated in the Western sense and those whose education barely existed, if at all. Many other differences of background also existed: there were those in the Tribal Trust Lands who lived on what is now known as the 'subsistence economy' (a much misused phrase, often in fact denoting contentment not want); there were those working for European farmers – although a surprisingly high proportion of these people came from Malawi or, to a lesser extent, Mozambique; there were those who worked in the towns or in the mines; and there were the domestic servants. Each of these groups lived very different lives, with different pressures and often different ambitions. Most of those living outside the Tribal Trust Lands did indeed have their homes there to which they returned occasionally; but contact with the European way of life eroded acceptance of the rigid shibboleths of tribal tradition, many of which were in fact based on commonsense, without any positive replacement. And then, perhaps most important, there were deep tribal differences, leading to apparently endless conflict. Europeans who pour scorn on the dire results of tribal rivalry should consider what evils are attributable to tribal differences in their own continent over the last five hundred or so years. It is only now that there are some signs in Europe that the greater good of the whole is beginning to take precedence over the claims of narrow national advantage – and even that may well prove to have been an illusory and temporary advance in the long run. Zimbabwean leaders are well aware of the dangers and are attempting to wean their people away from what they know as 'tribalism', but suspicions of the Shona run deep among the Ndebele and vice versa. The disease – if it can be called so – is chronic and not susceptible to easy cure. The Shona, too, are deeply divided on tribal lines with many sub-tribes each with their own traditions and often jealous of each other. The positive features of the African culture leading to a deep regard for their own families and tribes result in a lack of sympathy or, indeed in many cases, to a total absence of compassion for anyone of another tribe. Shared responsibility within a tribe or family leads to an absence of individual responsibility for anything which may happen to a member of another tribe. A universal sense of nationhood has yet to be created in Zimbabwe, and it certainly did not exist among the majority of the people in Rhodesia during its troubled years.

But, nevertheless, there was among the Africans a general feeling of frustration and a desire for black majority rule. To the educated Africans, the situation was intolerable in the years leading up to independence. The precise form of discrimination varied according to which Government was in power and the extent to which the whites felt themselves threatened at any particular moment. But throughout the last few decades of white rule the almost total lack of opportunities for advancement and the indignities of segregation would have turned almost any educated black person into a revolutionary frame of mind. Further down the economic and social scale the affront to dignity was indeed less – and many tribesmen in the Tribal Trust Lands probably thought little about it. But even in the most uneducated circles there was undoubtedly some resentment at many of the laws and practices imposed by the whites, who themselves were often surprisingly ignorant of the likely impact of their decisions, however benevolent, on the African tradition. The Land Husbandry Act, for instance, which was supposed to improve African agriculture, was widely resented because it led to tribes having to move away from their ancestral lands, to the slaughter of cattle which to the tribesmen represented virtually their only worldly asset, and to a complete reversal of the traditional qualifications for those who were entitled to work the land. The motives were impeccable; efficiency would have been greatly improved if the

Act had been enforced. But efficiency was not the criterion in African minds, and the measure was eventually more or less abandoned, but not before much resentment had been aroused.

The pass laws, too, caused great feelings of injustice. It is true that, certainly in the later stages, these laws, which heavily circumscribed the Africans' right to live in European areas were honoured more in the breach than in the observance, but they did exist and the police could, and sometimes did, carry out raids in the towns in an attempt to enforce what the Africans saw as a wholly unjust measure directed against them – not the Europeans.

There was, therefore, a general feeling of discontent, varying greatly in depth and urgency, which was present in African minds throughout the country under the later stages of white rule. It was greatly enhanced by the more repressive and stupid measures enacted by the Rhodesian Front Government and, of course, it was grist to the mill of the Nationalist elite, who were able to blame every man or heaven made difficulty on white rule. A ready scapegoat for every failing, personal or group, was poised and ready for exploitation.

The struggle, when it came, was between two elites – virtually the entire white population on one side and the bulk of the educated Africans on the other. In spite of the general feelings of unease and latent discontent among the Africans, for long periods the mass of the population did not wish to take part. The Nationalist movement did not arise as a result of a spontaneous eruption by an enslaved and suffering people throwing up leaders who articulated and gave concrete expression to their feelings. It spread downwards from the top, gaining enormous impetus from the events to the North, and picking up adherents among those who were genuinely dissatisfied for a variety of reasons and who were often promised instant prosperity under black rule. It was, too, above all, succoured by the chilling power of the guerilla with his gun.

At no stage were 'the masses' in a state of insurrection. They had their grievances but they did not feel so strongly about these that they were prepared to turn to violence in order to achieve 'freedom'. This was no 'peasants' revolt'. The urban Africans, who daily saw the contrast between European and African living standards, were easier meat for the Nationalists than were those who lived in the Tribal Trust Lands. But even they were by no means in a revolutionary mood at any stage and the almost total lack of guerilla activity in the towns confirmed this. As has already been pointed out, a high proportion of Africans working on European farms were alien anyway, but the indigenous Africans in this situation were on the whole unaffected by revolutionary fervour. They may have given help to the guerillas voluntarily or, more often, at the point of a gun: they did not, by and large, initiate violent action themselves.

If an atmosphere of general revolution had existed it would have been totally impossible for the whites to sustain the loyalty of the armed services and police, which were largely composed of Afrcans, to say nothing of the Department of Internal Affairs, the Civil Service and the whole infrastructure of Government which were totally reliant on African support.

The insurrection came about because the African elite managed to get hold of the young unemployed of whom there were very many and to persuade them of the advantages of a change of regime. As the campaign developed and the violence increased so the numbers of the unemployed multiplied: success led to further success. Those that joined the guerillas were given a cause to fight for, an ideology (Marxism) to study and embrace, an attainable – indeed an apparently noble – objective which they thought would bring about prosperity and freedom. Those who doubted were often forced across the border at gun-point and made to undergo training in one Communist, or near-Communist, country or another with the rest. But, in spite of the white Rhodesian claims to the contrary, unwilling recruits were the exception rather than the rule. It would have been impossible to sustain the guerilla warfare for long if the bulk of the guerillas had not themselves been fully behind its objectives whatever their essential motivation might have been. The young guerillas were undoubtedly brainwashed with Marxist ideology and had to undergo the mind-deadening tedium of conventional Communist indoctrination, but they were given a glimpse of a possible future for themselves which contrasted strongly with the turgid half-truths and paternalistic condescensions of the Rhodesian Front Government. They were, too, given a gun; and this became for them their symbol of manhood, their badge of freedom. Having been given this agent of death, they used it, freely, sometimes against the whites but in the vast majority of cases against any black who was suspected of helping the Security Forces or the police. Indeed there were many cases of murder without any particular cause, and as the ghastly rhythm of death began to increase its tempo, so their callousness increased until little remained between many of them and total barbarism.

And so, on both sides of the battle, those taking part were coarsened and scarred by what they did. The scale of guerilla atrocity was vastly more horrifying, but the whites and their black subordinates were certainly far from being knights in shining armour. They, of course, had the advantages of greatly superior equipment, discipline and communications. But the guerillas had the numbers and the support of the bulk of world opinion. Both sides had clearly defined and apparently noble aims. The whites were fighting for their homes, their families, for what they believed to be justice and Christendom – against the forces of evil. The blacks were fighting for freedom, for the right to equality and justice; they were fighting against what they believed to be racial oppression. The resulting violence degraded both the participants and distorted their objectives. The whites were wrong, not necessarily in moral terms – for who can make definitive judgements of this kind about people who genuinely believed themselves to be right in what they did? They were wrong because, in the long run, they had no hope of winning. The black insurrection was imposed by an elite, sustained and even directed by forces outside Zimbabwe; it was not a genuine mass movement springing from a universal sense of despair. But it was no less valid as a result of this. There was indeed much that was intolerable in Rhodesia and the efforts to alleviate, and indeed to eliminate, the palpable injustices of the situation with the advent of the Muzorewa Government were too late. The pendulum had begun to swing and in the climate of international opinion which existed, nothing could have prevented it from reaching at least as far as Mugabe. The question now is whether he will be able to arrest its passage further towards an ultimate chaos.

But why was all this violence necessary? Could the politicians have secured a more gradual transition without all the agony and disruption of civil war?

One has to differentiate here between lasting solutions and cosmetic palliatives, apparently of the utmost urgency at the time but failing to satisfy the aspirations of the African elite and to measure up to the demands, however unfair these might have been, of international opinion. Many people will argue that if only the Rhodesian Front Government had made more concessions earlier – whether on HMS *Tiger* or HMS *Fearless*, at the time of the Douglas-Home negotiations, or at the many other opportunities listed in this book since that time – the violence could have been averted or shortened and a solution found. 'Too little and too late' is the cry. The author does not take this view. The problem was not concerned with constitutional niceties, with the number of seats in Parliament, with blocking mechanisms and the rest. It was concerned with attitudes. Were the whites, or were they not, prepared to concede real power to the blacks? This was the essential question to be answered and peace could not come until the reply was 'Yes'. The unpalatable fact is that it took the guerilla war, with all its prolonged agony, to change the white attitudes. And, even then, without Lord Carrington's enormous diplomatic skills, the situation could have continued for a considerable period before deepening chaos would have led to total white surrender under even worse terms, and in a vastly worse atmosphere, than that eventually achieved.

Throughout the whole period, the British role was subsidiary, whatever is said to the contrary by many white Rhodesians searching for a scapegoat. From the time when the Charter was granted in 1899 until UDI, Britain did have constitutional powers to influence affairs within Rhodesia which she exercised to a varying degree throughout the story. But she had no direct control over the country. It can be argued that this was her fault and that Rhodesia should have been treated as a normal Crown Colony, ruled from Whitehall. But, as explained in Chapter One, in the circumstances of the time this was never a realistic option. Given that situation, Britain could only try to edge Rhodesia towards a solution. To the extent that Britain did exert an influence, this was directed towards improving the social, economic and political position of the Africans. If she had opted out, the African situation would have been worse and this would have led to worse violence. The white Rhodesian claim that if Rhodesia had been left alone she would have sorted out her own difficulties, is simply not true. Sooner or later the Africans would have erupted and, without Britain to hold the ring at a Conference between the two sides, the end result would have been chaos. It was embarrassing for Britain to be saddled with responsibility for a situation over which she had scant control but, that being so, she did not create the difficulties which arose from the inevitable conflict between white and black within Rhodesia. Britain, no doubt, made many mistakes, but these were not the cause of the essential problem. International opinion on the whole played an unhelpful role, fanning the flames of violence and intransigence on both sides. But white Rhodesia could not be isolated from the rest of the world, try as it did to achieve that impossible goal.

The crucial turning-point came in the 1962 election when the whites threw out Whitehead and the blacks (in retrospect, inevitably) refused to take part in the constitutional process. If Whitehead had been more of a leader, he might have succeeded in being returned to power and in abolishing the Land Apportionment Act, but it must be doubtful if, with policies of that kind, any Prime Minister could have survived in the long run. The ousting of Winston Field and his replacement by Ian Smith was a second decisive moment. If Winston Field had fought his corner with greater resilience he might have remained in office and perhaps averted UDI, although there must be grave doubt about this. If Smith had had more vision he might, with the personal authority he achieved in the later stages, have been able to persuade the whites to accept black rule at an earlier stage. But he did not have this vision, and the whites did accept him as leader. They knew precisely what he was doing and they had every opportunity to make judgements as to the way things were going: indeed Smith hardly moved at all without either an election or a referendum.

The conclusion must be that the whites by their intransigence – understandable and indeed inevitable in the circumstances, but nevertheless intransigence – brought about a situation where those African Nationalists who believed that violence was the only way forward were able to persuade or cajole enough of their compatriots into their way of thinking so that, with outside help, a successful civil war, with all its terror and agony, could be mounted. If the blacks had been more united, the story might have been different and much bloodshed might have been averted but, again, they were rent by differences due to historical and social causes over which they had little individual control.

The transformation of Rhodesia into Zimbabwe was, therefore, both a triumph and a tragedy. It was a triumph for violence and tragic for the reason that violence was necessary. In the circumstances Rhodesia could not have become Zimbabwe without it – certainly not in a time scale acceptable to African opinion – and the eventual transformation was inevitable from the moment that the pioneers raised their flag at Salisbury. To say this is not to condone the violence: it is to recognise the inevitability of it. There was, indeed, a tragic inevitability about every succeeding twist to the story. At every stage, circumstances seemed to lead, inexorably, to the next step on the road to disaster. And, perhaps most important in this context, both sides thought they were right – and, in their own terms, they were.

If a great leader, black or white, had appeared on the scene, able to transcend local prejudice and literally to force moderation on both sides by sheer power of personality, then the drama could perhaps have taken a different course. But men of this stature are rare indeed: they appear by chance not design. There were none inside Rhodesia.

CHAPTER NINE

Epilogue

The problems which Mugabe faced on his advent to power were formidable indeed. First and foremost there was the necessity of a smooth transition without a complete breakdown of law and order. There were also very real dangers of a total economic collapse. In order to avert these twin disasters, the one dependent on the other, it was vital to persuade the bulk of the whites in the armed services, the police, the civil service and indeed in the whole capitalist structure of society, to remain at their posts and to serve the new Government with tolerable loyalty, if not devotion. The results of an immediate white abdication of responsibility in the Congo, Mozambique and Angola were only too apparent. Mugabe had realised the implications of all this some time before his victory (but not, according to his speeches at the time, as long ago as the Geneva Conference) and had been making conciliatory noises. But the whites had not been convinced and at the election he was still regarded by many as the arch demon. In order to retain a measure of white confidence and to have the benefit of the advice of one who had very considerable experience of Government, he asked Soames to stay on for six months. Soames did remain until the independence celebrations which did not take place until two months after the election. But the request for a six-month period was refused. This was a difficult decision. A postponement of independence to allow Soames to remain as Governor for six months would have led to all sorts of problems, internal and external, and Britain had been saddled with responsibility without power for long enough in all conscience. On the other hand Mugabe needed all the help he could get. Soames could have added stability and given

211

wise advice to the new regime for a longer period than he in fact did, and the establishment of a stable and viable Zimbabwe looking towards the West for help was certainly a prime British, and indeed Western, interest. It did seem a pity that Britain was not able to accede fully to Mugabe's request. But, without knowing all the considerations which led to the decision, including the precise form in which the request was put, it would be arrogant to make a definitive judgement.

In any event, it was of high importance to Mugabe to achieve and retain a measure of white confidence. Conciliatory speeches were one thing; action was another. Clearly there could be no question of nationalisation, either of the intricate and highly efficient industrial and commercial structure built up over the years or of the white farms. But white confidence did not only depend on that. The positions of Lieutenant General Walls, the Chief of Police (Peter Allum), the Head of the Security Services and, to a lesser extent, the permanent secretaries in the civil service were all of prime importance. In spite of all the pressures on him, Mugabe showed remarkable powers of leadership and decision. He asked them all to stay on. They agreed to do so – and this undoubtedly had a considerable impact on white confidence.

There can rarely have been a similar situation in world history; a successful revolutionary leader confirmed in power many of the leaders of the whole structure against which he had been fighting – men who had themselves for many years been striving every muscle to destroy him and all he stood for. It is true, of course, that it was the custom for the Governments of newly independent British ex-colonial countries to take over the existing administrative machine. But in virtually all other transitions to indpendence in British colonial history the indigenous leaders were already *in situ* when independence came. Normally they actually held the position of Prime Minister or the equivalent, and there was a planned evolution from one constitutional position to the other. In Zimbabwe, although there was of course a transitional period between the election and independence, this was only of nominal duration and those who had actively been trying to kill their opponents only a short time before were faced with the necessity of working closely with them either as subordinates or superiors. One of the permanent secretaries, for instance, was given a

Minister who only a few months previously had been leading one of the guerilla groups inside Rhodesia.

The acquiescence of Walls was crucial. He had played a vital part at Lancaster House, particularly when it came to the issue of the military arrangements for the cease-fire. Although in theory he had no official status as a delegate at Lancaster House, if he had refused to accept the cease-fire proposals the Conference might well have collapsed. He had very considerable influence on the whites and his resignation at that time would, at the least, have led to great confusion. His acceptance of the proposals had led some of the more diehard white elements to write him off as a traitor to their cause. But, nevertheless, he was still seen by the majority as a guarantee against chaos. Mugabe owed a great deal to Walls when he agreed to remain as Chairman of the Joint High Command (he was never in fact Commander of the armed forces, and this was one of the reasons which led to his susbequent resignation).

Important as the retention of a measure of white confidence was to Mugabe there were, however, other problems of similar, or even greater, magnitude. In the formation of his cabinet he had to balance a whole range of conflicting imperatives. Partly as a further concession to white feeling but, perhaps, primarily in order to use at least some of the white experience and knowledge built up over the years, he gave the portfolios of Commerce to David Smith and Agriculture to Denis Norman, the Chairman of the white Farmers' Union. Both of these men had acquired a reputation among the blacks for moderation and good sense. But the very fact that he was relying, heavily, on a continuance in office of much of the white establishment added emphasis to one of the most difficult problems with which he was faced. Revolutionary leaders, particularly those who actively participate in the fighting, do not necessarily make good politicians in office. Indeed it is probably true to say that the professions of arms and politics are inherently incompatible: the certainties and the need for radical decision of the one are incompatible with the inevitable requirements of compromise of the other. When they took over their satellite empire in Europe, for instance, the Russians solved this problem quite simply: they exterminated or immobilised in one way or another the old-guard Communists who had borne the burden of the day in the revolutionary phase.

213

But there was no question of Mugabe following their example even if he had wished to. Claims to the spoils of office by those who had personally taken part in the fighting, had to be balanced against the ambitions both of those who had spent the last few years politicizing outside Rhodesia and of those who had not been personally involved at all but who had been educating themselves either at universities or in positions of sometimes high responsibility in the United Nations and elsewhere. There were also conflicts to resolve between those who believed in an immediate move to Socialism and those whose approach, like that of Mugabe himself, was pragmatic and gradualist.

On top of all this there was the grave problem of what to do with the Patriotic Front led by Nkomo, which by that time mainly represented the Ndebele vote. This party was extremely touchy, ready to seize and exploit any question of undiluted Shona domination. And, within the Shona majority, there were a host of rival tribal claims all to be balanced and if possible reconciled.

Mugabe's competence as a leader was tested to the full, not least because he had to come to a decision very quickly. In the event, with the help of Soames and his staff, he contrived a brilliant solution, giving the post of Minister of Home Affairs – albeit reduced in scope – to Nkomo together with three other ministerial posts to members of the Patriotic Front and contriving a balance of the other demands upon him which more or less satisfied the majority of the supplicants. Nkomo had been offered the post of President but turned it down on the grounds that he would not be fobbed off with a sinecure. The Reverend Canaan Banana, an old campaigner, became President.

However, as a result of the many necessary compromises which were made, the resulting Ministers varied greatly in competence. Some of them were of far higher intellectual calibre than their white predecessors and quickly grasped the essentials of their new jobs. Others were less successful. A further complication was that the Central Committee of Mugabe's party – ZANU (PF) – insisted on scrutinising and deciding upon all important issues before they were discussed in cabinet. This caused much delay and indecision, and was resented by the Patriotic Front members of the cabinet. Some

214

Ministers, notably Edgar Tekere, of whom more anon, made some very stupid speeches totally at variance with official Government policy and Mugabe had to spend much of his time dealing with the many protests which arose. The easy rhetoric of the revolutionary was not suited to the responsibilities of office: the public is apt to take ministerial pronouncements seriously. Mugabe's difficulties in this matter were particularly acute because many of the remarks made by his wild men were often not directed against the whites or the West or some such target which could be relied upon not to react with too much virulence, but against the Ndebele. This was really playing with fire. The dangers of civil war were acute. Not very long previously ZANU and ZAPU forces had been fighting each other within Rhodesia, they had opposed each other in the election and age-old rivalries were far from slumbering. The two guerilla armies were still intact and a sufficiently powerful spark could well lead to a conflagration. Local elections were scheduled which, too, had the effect of sharpening existing divisions. A number of people were indeed killed and it was only due to the extreme exertions of Mugabe and Nkomo, both of whom fully realised the dangers, that widespread bloodshed was averted.

But perhaps the most serious problem concerned the guerilla armies themselves. The theory was that a crash programme of integration of the three forces concerned – the existing Security Forces, ZIPRA (Nkomo's army) and ZANLA (Mugabe's army) – would take place. But for long periods nothing very much happened. The blame for this was variously apportioned, depending on who was speaking. The whites were blamed for dragging their feet (in particular, the Rhodesia Light Infantry – an entirely white force – refused to be integrated). Walls seemed to be unable to implement any viable and immediate action. Both ZIPRA and ZANLA were said to be unwilling to lose their identities – and at least in ZIPRA's case this was almost certainly true. Whatever the reason may have been – and as is so often the case there were probably a whole series of inter-related causes – large numbers of guerillas remained in their assembly areas, receiving rations and pay (there were great difficulties in this due to the absence of any reliable nominal rolls) but having very little to do. They would not surrender their arms: as has already been said, a weapon represented to a guerilla his only, and much prized, security. They had looked forward to, and indeed had been told to expect, a promised land of purpose and prosperity when the war was won. They had received virtually nothing. Before independence they had been existing in a twilight world where might was right. Murder, rape and arson had been commonplace; indeed, as far as they were concerned, these were part of the struggle for independence. Now they were expected to obey the rule of law – often enforced by their erstwhile enemies – and to sit patiently awaiting they knew not what for apparently indefinite periods. It is indeed not surprising that many incidents of violence did take place. And to the extent that this happened, white and middle-class African confidence was eroded. Such was the demoralisation that, for instance, in September a ZIPRA battalion near Bulawayo mutinied when there was a muddle over pay, their officers taking refuge in police stations and elsewere: Nkomo eventually had to appear in person to persuade them to desist. A far more serious conflict occurred in February 1981 when fighting between ZIPRA and ZANLA broke out in the Bulawayo area. Mugabe had demoted Nkomo from his position as Minister of Home Affairs and had taken other action which was seen by the Ndebele as confirming their worst fears about Shona determination to dominate the country. At the cost of 300 dead, Mugabe re-established his authority mainly by the use of the white officered Rhodesian African Rifles and the Air Force. After much agonising, Nkomo remained in the Government.

Apart from the urgent problem of keeping the whole structure of Government intact in the immediate aftermath of indepedece there were, of course, many other longer-term problems which had to be tackled.

It was clearly essential to bring in immediate measures leading to further Africanisation of the civil service and police. There was a very difficult balance to be maintained here between the very understandable desire of the Africans to take what they saw as their rightful place in the running of their country, and the fact that very few Africans had the requisite training or experience to merit high positions. There was also the question as to whether the Europeans whose jobs were to be taken over by Africans, should be retired or, perhaps, moved sideways.

On the whole, these problems were tackled with great realism by the Government: if anything the policy tended towards caution. Heads of Department were given a percentage African staffing ratio to achieve within a reasonable period of perhaps three years and left to get on with it.

The major long-term problem, however, concerned the economy. The war had ravaged the countryside. A high proportion of rural schools and clinics had been destroyed. Agriculture in many rural areas had almost come to a standstill. Large-scale irrigation schemes had been suspended. Becuase dipping had been prevented, many cattle had died: indeed many had been slaughtered. The birthrate was very high indeed (about 3.7 per cent growth a year leading to the doubling of the population in about nineteen years). How could all these young people be employed?

During the guerilla war, ZANU (PF) had produced an economic blueprint to be put into effect when it gained power, but this proved to be totally impossible to implement: without any access to the actual state of affairs inside Rhodesia in any detail this was inevitable. A new ministry of economic planning was set up under Bernard Chidzero, who returned to Zimbabwe from his post as Director of the Commodities Division of UNCTAD. But producing a relevant and viable development plan is a lengthy process and, in the meantime, there was no clear sense of direction. The economic difficulties were compounded because a number of African Ministers delighted in the opportunites they had for international travel to attend lengthy, and almost entirely pointless, conferences arranged by agencies of the United Nations and others. Not only did this denude the Ministries of their leaders who should have been immersed in the many problems with which they were faced, but on these jaunts they had to be provided with senior civil servants, thus adding even more to the enormous load which those who remained had to carry. International conferences which spend their time arguing about the finer points of a communiqué expressing general goodwill are a luxury which even the most sophisticated country can ill afford. They can be a near disaster for a new nation like Zimbabwe.

Then there was the whole question of aid. There was, and is, a very real danger that Zimbabwe, like other third world

217

countries, could rely on others to provide the wherewithal for economic growth, or indeed economic survival, thus diluting the essential national effort which is vital for any country if it is to prosper. Clearly, Zimbabwe needed considerable assistance if it was to repair the ravages of war. But the mentality of holding out the begging bowl is a dangerous virus, difficult to eradicate. Some aid began to flow – notably from Britain and the United States, and this was greatly increased (to nearly £900 million) after a donors' conference in March 1981. However, white Rhodesia prospered without any aid at all. There is no reason why black Zimbabwe should not, in the long run, do the same if properly administered.

In spite of all these difficulties, however, Zimbabwe did have a number of great advantages. It had vast national resources including a breadth of agricultural produce which must be almost unique for a country its size. It could produce tobacco, wheat, barley, oats, cotton, rice, soya beans, groundnuts, maize, tea, sugar, sorghum, almost every fruit and vegetable in common use, a large range of timber, fish, beef and so on. Even rubber was (1980) being tried as an experiment. On top of all this, Zimababwe possessed a wide range of minerals, all of them in the process of production: the only notable absentee was oil and a significant proportion of Zimbabwean oil was being produced from sugar. It also had a highly developed and efficient infrastructure of roads, railways, electricity, water resources and the rest. It had an effective civil service. Its industry, largely as a result of sanctions, was diversified and efficient. And, perhaps most important, it had a highly intelligent leader who had learnt from the mistakes of other nations like Mozambique, which had tried radical and, in the event, disastrous solutions to the problems of the transfer of power from white into black hands. Indeed some Rhodesian Front leaders were heard to say that the whole white effort over fourteen years had been worth it if only to allow Mugabe to learn at first hand the appalling consequences of the initially rigid Socialist and narrow black Nationalist regimes in Mozambique and elsewhere.

On independence, Mugabe had to decide quickly upon his international posture. The guerilla effort had been almost entirely reliant on Communist arms and training. His partner in the coalition, Nkomo, had depended on the Russians and their satellites. In the early stages of the war he had relied on the Chinese, and the Russian arms, with which ZANLA were later largely equipped, had come through the OAU. He was himself a Marxist (albeit pragmatic in his approach) and many of his supporters had been heavily indoctrinated with the turgid irrelevances of Communist doctrine as taught to the masses. But he was taking over a highly successful capitalist economy, totally orientated towards Western culture and assumptions. In spite of what he had believed to be their bias against him, the British had presided over his accession to power and had not tried to avert it by sleight of hand. Indeed he had achieved a remarkable rapport with that prototype of British Conservative tradition – Soames. He had a personal dislike of the Russians and, above all, of the East Germans, who had tried to bludgeon him into dropping the Chinese connection (the Chinese, by contrast, had not attempted to attach strings to their aid). The South Africans were, as always, heavy-handed in their handling of the new situation. They accepted the Selous Scouts, almost to a man, in South Africa. They tried to entice the key whites away from Zimbabwe and generally behaved in a thoroughly hostile manner. But he was dependent on South Africa for much of his trade and to give succour to South African 'freedom fighters' must clearly be courting South African military action.

There was the lure of international acclaim, of strutting the African, indeed the world, scene in the role of conqueror instead of getting down to the massive practical problems with which he was faced. Many African leaders, notably Nkrumah, had succumbed, in the end fatally, to the heady wine of international statesmanship – if that is the right word for it. To his credit, Mugabe did not fall into this trap. He did attend an OAU Conference in Sierra Leone; he went to North Korea and the United States and he attended Tito's funeral. But, by and large, he remained in Zimbabwe.

In the event, Mugabe steered a canny path through the labyrinth of East/West rivalries. He expelled the South African Diplomatic Mission, but he kept his trade links with that country and refused to allow South African and Namibian 'freedom fighters' to use his territory as a base. He resisted the heavy Russian overtures of friendship – totally ignoring the Russian mission to the independence celebrations. He kept the

219

vital avenues to the West open while making enough anti-Western speeches to keep his more extreme supporters happy. The burden of the day to day, let alone month to month, responsibilities must have been immense. But he survived.

A number of whites had left Zimbabwe before independence and some more departed at that time. But most remained in the country waiting to see which way things would go. The strict currency control regulations which had been imposed were retained and this made it extremely difficult for anyone who had a stake in the country, whether in the form of a house or a farm or whatever, to leave. Furthermore – and this cannot be over-emphasised – the whites were, in the main, natives of the country. They were not expatriates. They did not wish to leave their homes unless conditions became utterly impossible. In fact, certainly in the initial stages, the European lifestyle was not greatly affected by the transfer of power. Most of them still lived a comfortable and rewarding life. In the event, in spite of incidents of lawlessness which received full treatment in the media – particularly abroad – there seemed to be no need for panic. Even in the minor, but highly emotive, matter of the changing of street names and the removal of statues and monuments redolent of the colonial era, the Government was cautious. Jameson Avenue, the principal Salisbury thorough-fare, was renamed Samora Machel Avenue and one statue of Rhodes was removed, but these were the only early conces-sions to the very natural Nationalist feeling that the whites should in this way be made to realise that a new country had been born (a number of other changes were made after). Much white resentment was caused by the new style of the broad-casts on radio and television, which seemed to revel in the use of the word 'comrade' at every opportunity and which, in their external coverage, dwelt almost exclusively on events in Com-munist countries. It was indeed these broadcasts which, more than anything else, brought home to the whites the changed, and to them alarming, situation. The extreme bias of the pre-vious broadcasts under Rhodesian Front control was replaced by an equally distorted and partisan view. But most of the whites gradually learnt to live with these broadcasts (largely by not listening to them) and propaganda, however slanted, does not by itself damage a way of life.

The long-term problem lay with the young whites. Many

sons of farmers remained, hoping to be able to inherit their properties but, on the whole, the future for the young whites leaving school in Zimbabwe did not appear to be bright and most of them looked elsewhere. In the long term, therefore, it seems that the white population will greatly diminish.

In the early autumn of 1980, two events occurred which were to test the maturity of the new regime. Tekere, the Secretary General of ZANU (PF) and Minister for Manpower Planning and Development, was accused of murdering a white farmer and Walls, who had resigned as Chairman of the Joint High Command and was on terminal leave, gave an interview for the BBC in which he revealed that he had asked Mrs Thatcher to declare the election null and void. He also spoke about the possibility of civil war, attacked President Banana for being involved in politics and ascribed Mugabe's electoral victory to intimidation. These remarks was clearly directed against the Mugabe Government and liable to cause much trouble – particularly since Walls was still in theory a serving officer. They raised questions about the loyalty of the entire white establishment to the new Government, and Mugabe clearly had to react in some way.

Tekere was perhaps the most radical of Mugabe's Ministers. He had made a number of most unwise speeches in public and was beginning to form a rival power base for himself in opposition to Mugabe. He had some support in the guerilla camps and among the more extreme Nationalists. At first he refused to submit to arrest and the whole structure of law and order was instantly in question. Mugabe realised, immediately, the very grave implications of this. He insisted that the law must take its course and that Tekere must submit to arrest. After a short period of high drama, when it was not clear whether or not Tekere would submit, the arrest did take place. Tekere was then, however, granted bail. But his trial was certain to raise issues of the greatest delicacy. If it appeared that Tekere had evaded the due processes of the law in some way, the whites would conclude that law and order had broken down. It he was dealt with severely, there was a danger that his supporters would run amok. When, in December, he was acquitted on the vote of the two assessors – one black and one coloured – against the view of the white judge, white morale took a severe blow and the more radical elements

221

in ZANU (PF) received a great boost. However, with great skill, Mugabe managed to oust Tekere from the Cabinet after the storm had abated.

As far as Walls was concerned, the difficulties were not on the same scale. The whites had little sympathy for him and he was generally considered to have acted most unwisely. But Mugabe did have the opportunity to take action against a prominent white to balance any possible measures against Tekere. Walls, who had gone abroad, was forbidden to re-enter Zimbabwe. This was wildly unfair – Walls had Zimbabwean citizenship – but in the circumstances it might well have been the best course of action.

But the real problem in Zimbabwe remains, as it always has been, one of human relations. In spite of their tribal and social differences, can the Africans live with each other in peace? Even with the potentially unifying force of a common enemy during the years of struggle, the African elite had spent much of their time squabbling and fighting each other. Now that they have power, after the initial euphoria of victory has worn off, the temptation to continue in this mould is great. The tendency to look for scapegoats when expectations are not fulfilled is universal and not confined to Africa. In Zimbabwe possible scapegoats abound – the whites, other tribes, the West and so on. The governing elite in Zimababwe wish to create a modern state, to wrench their African compatriots out of centuries of tradition and tribal custom into an entirely new way of life. They must succeed in this if they are to avert mass starvation. They have a formidable task. The real problem they have is psychological, not economic or political. It is a mistake to imagine that they can be helped in this by others, whether from the East or from the West. Only they can tackle and achieve it. It is possible that Mugabe himself may be displaced – and this would indeed, in the circumstances, be a disaster. A further long-term difficulty concerns the continuance of the multi-party system. The idea of a loyal opposition is alien to African tradition and it may well be that a change to the single party concept is essential if national unity is to be achieved. But how to bring this about without tearing up the Constitution and causing a major crisis of confidence? Above all can Zimbabwe avert continuing and escalating conflict between the Shona and the Ndebele? Can these two, very different, peoples achieve peaceful co-existence?

Apart from the problems within the black community, there is the question of the future relationship between black and white. Many whites will leave. But if the rapidly growing population is to be fed and if there is not to be massive unemployment, a measure of white expertise and drive is essential in Zimbabwe for a very considerable period. The whites who do remain, for their part, will have to accept a certain lowering of standards. They will, as one leading white figure put it, have to emigrate from Rhodesia to Zimbabwe and accept the reality of black power. The blacks will have to take real responsibility and not search for white scapegoats for their own failings. They will have to accept white advice in many fields and not squander their inheritance in irrelevances. They will have to turn the other cheek, and not replace one form of racism by another.

All this is a lot to ask, of both communities. But the prize is there, for the taking. Zimbabwe could become a centre of prosperity and racial co-operation with an enormous impact on the future of the whole of Southern Africa. If black and white can live together in harmony in Zimbabwe and create a successful state under black leadership, why should South Africa not eventually learn from Zimbabwe's success? On the other hand, if Zimbabwe disintegrates into chaos and squalor and if the whites all leave, it will be difficult to blame the white South Africans for fighting to the last kopje to avoid the same fate.

At the time of writing the future of Zimbabwe is obscure. Almost anything could happen and, in any event, clear cut answers to the questions posed above will not emerge for some time. Many of the problems are far from being solved. One can but hope that Zimbabwe will rise, phoenix like, from the violence and antagonisms of the past and that a new country will be created in which its citizens, of whatever tribe or colour, can live in freedom and peace.

APPENDIX 1

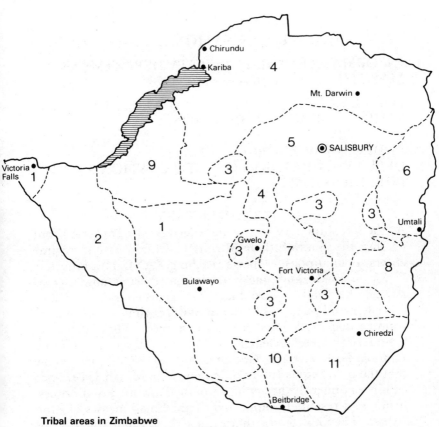

Tribal areas in Zimbabwe

NDEBELE ORIENTATED TRIBES		SHONA ORIENTATED TRIBES		OTHERS	
Tribe	*Percentage*	*Tribe*	*Percentage*	*Tribe*	*Percentage*
1 Ndebele	14%	3 Rozwi	9%	9 Tonga	2%
2 Kalanga	5%	4 Korekore	12%	10 Venda	1%
		5 Zezuru	18%	11 Shangaan	1%
		6 Manyika	13%		
		7 Karanga	22%		
		8 Ndau	3%		

APPENDIX 2

ZANU Death List

ZIMBABWE AFRICAN NATIONAL UNION (ZANU)

INFORMATION AND PUBLICITY DEPARTMENT.
MAPUTO   13th November, 1978.

FOR BLACK ZIMBABWEAN TRAITORS, THIS IS A
TIME OF CRISIS AND DECISION.
        BY
EDDISON J.M. ZVOBGO.
DEPUTY SECRETARY FOR INFORMATION AND
PUBLICITY, ZANU.

A COMMENTARY

As the Revolutionary war being waged by the Patriotic Front
against the Smith-Sithole-Muzorewa-Chirau fascist regime
enters its final phase, reports reaching ZANU Headquarters
in Maputo, Mozambique indicate that there is now a crisis
among the Zimbabwean black bourgeoisie, traitors, fellow
travellers and puppets of the Ian Smith regime, opportunistic
running-dogs and other capitalist vultures. These black reactionary and feudal elements in Salisbury, Bulawayo, Gwelo,
Umtali, Fort Victoria, Gatooma and Que-Que, now know
that the treacherous Internal Settlement of March 3, 1978 has
collapsed under the heavy blows of the Patriotic Front Forces,
firmly and resolutely supported by the broad masses of Zimbabwe. They now know that the Patriotic Front will soon be
ruling Zimbabwe and are woundering [*sic*] what may be in
store for them.

These enemies of Zimbabwe know that by supporting the
Internal Settlement of Ian Smith, Abel Muzorewa, Ndabaningi Sithole and Jeremiah Chirau, they have participated in
the massive programs of torture, murder, massacre and terror

perpetrated by the iniquitous regime on the Zimbabweans in Zimbabwe and on Zimbabwean refugees in Mozambique, Zambia and Botswana. They know that each day they wake up to new programs of committing fresh crimes. Yet they continue to stick by the regime.

There criminals know that white settlers who have committed these crimes will flee Zimbabwe on judgement day. Already many thousands of them have left the country. Where will black collaborators and traitors go?

Of course there are some African traitors whose complicity by participation in the racist regime places them in a class of their own. Among these:-

Traitor   Abel Tondekai Muzorewa
Traitor   Ndabaningi Sithole
Traitor   Ernst [sic] Leanard Bulle
Traitor   Aaron Zenzo Mgutshini
Traitor   Elliot Mdutshwa Gabellah
Traitor   Joel Mandaza
Traitor   John Kadzviti
Traitor   James Robert Chikerema
Traitor   Gibson Mubayiwa Magaramombe
Traitor   Chief Kayisa Ndiweni
Traitor   Francis John Zindoga
Traitor   Jeremiah Singareta Chirau

have, by accepting Cabinet positions, declared war on our people. They have joined the enemy. Many of them, notably Bishop Muzorewa and Ndabaningi Sithole are already preparing to flee to the United States. Others preparing to flee Zimbabwe include James Chikerema, George Nyandoro, Enoch Dumbujena. Elliot Gebellah, Ernest Bulle and capitalist criminal professor Samkange. However, there are many others who followed Muzorewa, Sithole and Chirau into the Internal Settlement, who have nowhere to go to who have no money to live on for the rest of their lives abroad. They wish to live in a liberated Zimbabwe despite their having sold the seven (7) million Zimbabweans.

The Patriotic Front wants to give these Zimbabweans the *first and last* opportunity to withdraw from their criminal collaboration with the Ian Smith racist regime. If they comply with this warning, all will be forgiven. If they persist, they will be doomed as their principals.

This warning is being addressed to the following Zimbabweans:-

1. *Puppet Mazaiwana*, who calls himself Secretary General of Muzorewa's gang.

2. *Olivier Muchena*, a foolish and naive Zimbabwean woman, who calls herself director for Women in the puppet Muzorewa gang. Olivier Muchena's activities are offensive to all Patriotic Front forces.

3. *Dr. Mundawarara*, founder member of ZANU in 1963 was until recent years, a staunch patriot. During 1965, 1966 and 1967, he acted as underground treasurer, receiving large sums of money from Comrade Chitepo, our late Chairman, for the purpose of financing the armed struggle in Zimbabwe. He played an important role in the preparation of the Battle of Sinoia in 1966. However, Dr. Mundawarara now calls himself Treasurer General of Muzorewa's criminal gang. In that capacity, the former supporter pf ZANLA, now finances the criminal programs directed at the destruction of ZANLA.

4. *Opportunist Lovemore Mbanga*, who calls himself Organizing Secretary of Muzorewa's criminal gang. This young Zimbabwean has had a long career of dividing and selling-out the Zimbabwean people. At one time, he boor-licked [*sic*] for his uncle Dr. Chavhunduka and promoted various criminal programs against Zimbabweans, encouraged by another of his uncles, Detective Sergeant Magamha of the fascist C.I.D.

5. *Puppet Bernard Basera*, who calls himself Secretary for Welfare in Muzorewa's criminal syndicate but who in fact is Secretary for the Inflicion of tortures and misery on the Zimbabwean masses.

6. *Opportunist puppet Leanard Nyemba.* founder member of ZANU and one of staunchest supporters during the 1960's. Nyemba calls himself First Vice President of Ndabaningi Sithole's criminal syndicate, ZIPA forces know that Nyemba calls traitor Ndabaningi Sihtole "father-in

law" merely because the criminal gave him money with which to pay his lobola.

7. *Puppet Ruth Mupisaunga*, who calls herself assistant to Oliver Muchena in criminal Muzorewa's so-called Department of Women. Ruth married to Etherton Mupisaunga is so ambitious that she is prepared to disregard the safety and welbeing [*sic*] of her husband and family, by persisting in the treac[*sic*]erous alliance of Muzorewa and Ian Smith.

8. Black puppet members of the illegal puppet parliament:-
   – Ronal Sadomba   (Harare)
   – Joel Mahlangu   (Mpopoma)
   – Joseph Bheka   (Pakati)
   – John Maposa   (Insulamini)
   – Patrick Bwanya   (Zambezi)
   – Micah Bhebe   (Ntshonalanga)
   – Lot Dewa   (Mabvazuva)
   – Austine Mabika   (Highveld)
   – Elijah Nyandoro   (Mabvazuva)
   – Peter Nkomo   (Kariba)
   – Zephania Bafana   (Tuli)
   – Thomas Zawaira   (Kunyasi)
   – W.B. Chimpaks   (Nemakonde)
   – N.A. Gadanzara   (Manica)
   – J.A. Hungwe   (Lowveld)
   – B.P. Mbouisa   (Pioneer)

To these money-monging [*sic*] scoundrels we say, *"You have collaborated with the enemy long enough. It is time to resign and align yourselves with the masses"*.

9. *Puppet John Hungwe*, former inspector of schools, now puppet supporter of the feudal Chief Chirau and member of the dummy.

10. *Puppet Ishmael Adam*, a puppet of Indian decent, who calls him-self Secretary for Finance in the Muzorewa criminal gang. In this capacity, he assists Dr. Mundawarara in financing the terrorist programs of puppet Muzorewa thereby assisting and abbetting the murders massacre and genocide of Ian Smith regime.

11. *Puppet Mukarati*, who calls himself Organising Secretary

(Mashona-land North) for the criminal Muzorewa clique.

12. *Puppet Mrs Mhembere*, who calls herself Organising Secretary (Mashonaland South) for the Muzorewa criminal clique.

13. *Puppet Chifamba*, who calls himself Organiser, (Mashonaland South) for the Muzorewa criminal clique.

14. *Criminal David Mukome*, reputed public enemy No. 1 and close ally of puppet Muzorewa.

15. *Criminal Mutasa*, who recruits bandits for military training in Iran for Muzorewa puppet clique. The bandits he recruits and train are known to be terrorising the masses in Zimbabwe.

16. *Criminal Kesiwe Malindi*; who in the early 1960's served ten (10) years for acts of arson on the Salvation Army School near Goromonzi but became a staunch member of ZANU in prison. Kesiwa Malindi is puppet ally of Chief criminal puppet Ndabaningi Sithole who has helped to train a handful of bandits in Uganda at the invitation of Amin's Bandit and Criminal regime. On his return to Zimbabwe, criminal Kesiwa Malindi has worked closely with Detective inspector Robinson of Smith's C.I.D. in setting up a military training program for the training of terrorists at a Camp provided by the Smith regime. Kesiwa Malindi is known to have murdered an innocent Zimbabwean who opposed and denounced his criminal mercenary programs.

17. *Criminal Muzanenhamo*, Chief Security Officer for puppet Muzorewa.

18. *Puppet and criminal James Dzvova*, who now calls himself Publicity Secretary of Ndabaningi Sithole criminal clique, following the reported recent disappearance of criminal puppet Masangomayi. James Dzvova's record and connections with London Capitalists and criminal is well known to ZANU and ZANLA.

19. *Baffon [sic] and puppet Aaron Mutiti*, who calls himself the legal Adviser to the Muzorewa criminal clique. Like criminal and puppet Gabellah, Aaron Mutiti also calls

himself 'doctor' although any Zimbabwean dog is more educated and certainly wiser. This puppet suppossedly advises Muzorewa that murders and massacres committed by the regime are lawful.

20. *Puppet Dingindhlela Sithole*, and Tobias Chizengeni son and son-in-law respectively of criminal Chief puppet Ndabaningi Sithole. These young goons have participated in numerous acts of terrorism on the Zimbabwean civilian population in an attempt to gain support through banditry for thier father's criminal campaigns against the Zimabwe People's War for National Liberation.

21. *Criminal puppet Solomon Nenguwo*, who calls himself Special Assistant to the puppet and criminal Bishop Muzorewa.

22. *Criminal puppet Elton Razemba*, who has just returned to Zimbabwe after a stint as representative of the regime, on behalf of puppet Bishop Muzorewa, at the United Nations. His new role is not yet known but it is believed that he will act as adviser to puppet criminal Abel Muzorewa.

23. *Puppet traitor Z.T. Chigumira*, a Bulawayo businessman. He blindly supports Criminal Ndabaningi Sithole in his criminal activities.

24. *Puppet traitor Noel Mukono*, who calls himself Secretary for Foreign Affairs in Ndabaningi Sithole's criminal syndicate. For many years he supported ZANLA but now seeks to destroy it.

25. *Puppet traitor A.G. Rumano*, who calls himself Information Assistant to traitor Ndabaningi Sithole.

26. *Puppet traitor Dr. J.M. Gopo*, who calls himself Secretary for Education in Traitor Ndabaningi Sithole's criminal syndicate.

27. *Puppet traitor Dr. E. Chitate*, who calls himself Secretary for Health in Ndabaningi Sithole's criminal syndicate. In the 60s, this so-called Dr, Chitate murdered a woman in the process of perfoming a criminal abortion.

28. *Puppet traitor Musomi*, who regards himself as legal Adviser

to feudal traitor Chief Jeremiah Chirau.

29. *Puppet traitor Chirenda,* who calls himself National Chairman in traitor Feudal Chief Jeremiah Chirau's Criminal Syndicate.

30. *Puppet traitor Badza,* who calls himself Political Research Officer in traitor feudal Chief Chirau's criminal syndicate.

31. To the list we have just made must be included all members of the Police Force and armed forces of the regime. They too, should realise that they will have to live in a liberated Zimbabwe. Their continued adherrence to the racist regime and their willingness to continue to be used as tools in terrorising murdering and massacrering [*sic*] their own people is not one way of making sure they will continue to live in Zimbabwe after liberation.

The above is the Patriotic Front's first list. A second list is under preparation and will be broadcast at the end of December as a Special Christmas Bulletin.

Everyone whose name has been read-out tonight must now listen carefully.

(a) Your name and address will be widely circulated among all ZANLA forces throughout Zimbabwe with immediate effect.

(b) For those who belong to the leadership of the political gangs led by puppet criminals Muzorewa, Sithole and Chirau, you have 30 days from tonight i.e. you have until midnight, 13th December 1978 to resign and sever all ties with puppet political party as well as with your puppet, criminal political leadership. You should also sever all connections with the racist Ian Smith regime.

(c) For those of you who are black puppet members of the illegal parliament *and* those of you who are members of the puppet Internal settlement Cabinet whose names have been read-out tonight, you have until midnight the 15th of December 1978 to resign your seats in the dummy parliament or Cabinet and from your political criminal clique and to sever all ties, permanently and publicly with the Internal Settlement regime.

(d) For those of you in the criminal police and criminal armed forces, you must resign or abscond with immediate effect, i.e. as from tonight, the 13th November, 1978.

(e) All those persons named tonight who belong to the Muzorewa, Sithole and Chirau criminal gangs who choose to comply and who resign are required to announce, publicly, their resignation. Our forces will immediately remove your name from the danger list. You and your family will then be protected by ZANLA forces and you will be safe.

(f) Any person whose name has been announced tonight who does not resign as required during the required period automatically becomes a priority military target. You are liable to be arrested or shot in sight, There is no hiding place in Zimbabwe. The hand of revolution is long, very long indeed. Let those with ears to hear, now hear. So it has been written, so let it be done.

PAMBERI NE ZANU!
PAMBERI NA COMRADE PRESIDENT ROBERT
MUGABE!

EDDISON J.M. ZVOBGO
(DEPUTY SECRETARY FOR INFORMATION
AND PUBLICITY)

APPENDIX 3

Conclusions of the Boyd Report (April 1979)

(a)   Although not specified in our terms of reference our investigations were throughout coloured by the phrase – 'free and fair' – which has become common currency in this matter.

(b)   In our view the elections were 'fair' in the sense that the electoral machinery was fairly conducted and above serious reproach. In arriving at this conclusion we have applied the strictest Western European criteria.

(c)   The question whether the election was 'free' is more complex. There is no doubt that the people who actually voted were free to choose which party they wished to support. It is true that in conditions of war, and with the other pressures which we have described, it would have been impossible to hold a fully free election in the sense that everyone qualified to vote could either do so or abstain precisely as he or she wished. However, in our opinion, neither individually nor in conjunction did these pressures amount to such curtailment of freedom or imposition of direction as to invalidate the election. On the contrary the people expressed their own view, in numbers which demonstrate a significant judgement on the constitutional basis of the election itself. They also exercised their right clearly to choose the party which they wished to lead the next Government.

(d)   Finally we note that neither Patriotic Front party proffered candidates for election. Despite this we think that the result represented the wish of the majority of the electorate of the country however calculated.

APPENDIX 4

ZANU's Party Line and Policy

ZIMBABWE AFRICAN NATIONAL UNION (ZANU)
POLITICAL EDUCATION
ZANU'S PARTY LINE AND POLICY

The Zimbabwe African National Union was found [*sic*] after realising that there was no other method that could be employed to gain genuine independence for the Zimbabweans besides the method of direct confrontation. The Party's general principles of Armed Struggle until final victory is well defined and is well known by international imperialists and by the reactionary Salisbury-Pretoria Axis more than anyone else.

ZANU does not underrate the power and military potential of the international imperialists fighting against the people of Zimbabwe but it sincerely believes that by meticulously adhering to the Party Line of armed struggle it will grow from strength to strength and together with the unswervering determination and sacrifice of the heroic masses of Zimbabwe. ZANU will smash the advance defences of imperialism, settlerism and colonialism, and usher in the new era of political freedom in Zimbabwe.

IDEOLOGY
In ideology ZANU is guided by the Marxist-Leninist Principle. ZANU aims to achieve a socialist revolution. While we are still executing the general line of armed struggle against the enemy, it is not possible to effect a socialist revolution. We need to unite with all forces in Zimbabwe that oppose the

235

settler regime. These include businessmen, Trade Unions, Women's Organisations, students, peasants and intellectuals, despite their ideological beliefs. But ZANU must make sure that it remains the vanguard of the National Democratic Revolution against the enemy. This revolution is democratic in the sense that Zimbabwean nationals, peasants, workers, national bourgeoisie, etc want the democratic freedom to choose their own representative and voice their own opinions without fear. This cannot be done under the Smith regime, so we must unite with all these nationals.

But after the settler regime has been swept off there will be other nationals who thought [sic] had been opposing the settler government, would like to step into the shoes of the outgoing capitalists, exploit even more the peasants and workers.

It is here that ZANU, the vanguard of the revolution will intervene by instituting measures that will put all means of production under public ownership. All practices that involve exploitation of man by man will be uprooted so the wealth of Zimbabwe which is an inheritance of all the Zimbabwean nationals will equally be distributed. This then will be the socialist revolution which will be received with displeasure and even resistance by some African national bourgeoisie, teamed up with a hoist [sic] of other reactionaries. It is therefore extremely important to understand the Party's ideology and Policy in order to be able to defend the gains of our revolution.

POLITICS

Politically, ZANU will not deviate from its stated principle of armed struggle until it has crushed the settler regime and has seized political power. After the political power domination of foreigners in Zimbabwe with their imperialist and capitalist tentacles have been removed, ZANU intends to build a free country, its people possessing the democratic freedom to choose the leaders who will be answerable to them and who will work whole heartedly for them. This is independence and reconstruction of our beloved country.

ECONOMY

Economically ZANU aims to create a self-supporting socialist economy. All the means of production and exchange will be publicly owned by the people of Zimbabwe and will benefit the whole nation. The present wealth grabbing instinct of the west will be abolished. Economic co-operation will be established and strengthened with the socialist world so as to bring capitalist U.S.A., Britain, West Germany, etc to ultimate doom. When these capitalist countries cannot exploit our wealth and the wealth of other countries, then they will ultimately have economic chaos which will result in the expulsion of the money grabbing capitalists by the workers and peasants in a violent revolution.

LAND

ZANU holds the view that all the wealth of Zimbabwe belongs to the people. This wealth can be defined as all the minerals, land water and all the flora and fauna. This wealth belongs to the people of Zimbabwe in perpetuity. The people's government shall hold the land and shall be the administrator and trustee for the present and the future generations. Consequently, there cannot be any private ownership of the natural wealth as it belongs to the people as a whole. The people's government shall hold the land as administrators and trustees for the present and future generations. Landlord estates and state will have no place in the socialist Zimbabwe since all will have been returned to the people and the capitalists associated with their propriatorship [*sic*] will have been expelled.

EDUCATION

ZANU will introduce compulsory education to all school eligible groups. It will also introduce adult education and open up technical schools and vocational centres. Certain education standards which hitherto had been opened only to exclusive social strata which reek with wealth, will then be opened to everybody This will open new prospects to students of our beloved country. Theoretical education received at schools, technical schools and university will be made to conform with practice and will be drafted to serve the broad masses. Workers and peasants will be provided with elementary education to help them to improve their skills and opportunities and to erase illiteracy.

CULTURE

The imperialists have diluted our rich cultural heritage by way of films, literature, mass media, schools and church and doctrinaire. These have plunged our people into a morasm [*sic*] of emotional confusion.

Most of the people are now at cross-roads. They believe the western culture is right and that ours is wrong and uncivilised. This is the process that has taken years of instance cultural agression [*sic*] and which has resulted in the loss of our cultural heritage. In an independent Zimbabwe, strenous efforts will be made to restore the nation to its noble sell [*sic*] once more. People will be assisted in building a new Zimbabwe culture derived from the best of what our heritage and history have offered to us. Zimbabwe will also take from foreign culture that which is good transfare [*sic*] it with the indegeous [*sic*] culture, and then develop it to meet the moods on the socialist state. Our country will need mental decolonisation just as much as it needs political and economic independence.

LABOUR AND WELFARE
Workers will be organised into workers co-operations which will be our direct or indirectly the factories for which they work. All discriminatory laws will be abolished

FOREIGN POLICY
ZANU will follow a policy of progressive non-alignment when it forms a government in Zimbabwe, but the government will follow two cardinal points:
  a. To fight against imperialism,
  b. To unite with all progressive forces throughout the world.
Because the progressive forces throughout the world are engaged in a titanic global conflict with capitalists and imperialists, ZANU is obliged to throw its whole weight on the side of the progressive forces of the world over. The enemies ZANU is fighting now consist of the local settler tyrants and the transnational imperialists. When the local tyrants are crushed ZANU will feel obliged to give aid to countries still under colonial and capitalists' oppression, as an international duty of the socialist state. Internationally, ZANU will see to it that it cultivates individual initiative and agricultural experts will have to come from the people of Zi, babwe [*sic*], and not from expatriates. Popular initiative must be in keeping with socialist reconstruction and programmes.

238

ZANU FLAG

The flag of our heroic nation consists of four colours, BLACK is in the middle because it represents the heroic people of Zimbabwe, the masses who are bearing the full brant [*sic*] of the enemy's reprisal or unprovoked attacks.

The next colour is RED, represents the precious blood that is being shed by our galant [*sic*] people in their struggle for independence and peace. YELLOW, which is next in line represents the natural resources i.e. all that is obtained in the form of minerals. GREEN is for life and crops of Zimbabwe the natural vegitation [*sic*] of our country.

CO/skm
7/1/80

NOTES

1. Nkomo is actually a Kalanga, a tribe absorbed in the Ndebele tradition on their arrival. But he married an Ndebele Abe zansi lady.
2. A further factor in this contrast was that ZIPRA, under Russian influence, was geared more to conventional warfare whereas ZANLA was influenced by the Chinese guerilla tactical doctrine.
3. The concept of the granting of a Charter was, of course, not a new idea. It had been used before in the early years of the acquisition of Empire. It was resuscitated in late Victorian times in East Africa, North Borneo and elsewhere. As far as the British South Africa Company was concerned, although it had wide powers, in theory its operations depended on the acquisition of concessions (all powers of Government and administration had to be obtained from Lobengula) and, by the terms of the Charter, it was bound to respect the customs and laws of those who came under its jurisdiction. It also had to furnish to the Imperial Government annual accounts and an annual report. Furthermore the Colonial Secretary did have a power of veto over most of its activities. In practice, however, in the early stages little control was exercised over the Company, and indeed in 1891 the senior Imperial official – the High Commissioner for South Africa – was instructed not to interfere with the Company's activities.
4. The Berlin West Africa Conference of 1884–5 laid down the rules of the game.
5. To give some idea of the scale – Zimbabwe (Southern Rhodesia) is 1½ times the size of Britain, and about the size of Spain. Zambia (Northern Rhodesia) is about twice the size of Zimbabwe.
6. Executive matters remained the responsibility of the Administrator acting on the advice of an Executive Council consisting of the Administrator, the Resident Commissioner and four Company Representatives.
7. One of the myths believed by many white Rhodesians has been that the settlers bore the sole financial burden of the transition to Responsible Government. The fact is that as the result of a highly complex series of court cases and negotiations the British taxpayer had to provide £1,750,000 in compensation to the Company as part of the settlement (the Rhodesian Government had to pay £2,300,000).

8. Southern Rhodesia was invited as an observer to the Commonwealth Prime Ministers' Conference of 1935. From 1948 on she was invited as a full participant to most of the Conferences. The Federal Prime Minister was invariably asked to attend.

9. Southern Rhodesia had a 'Legislative Assembly'; Northern Rhodesia and Nyasaland had 'Legislative Councils'.

10. Mr Dingle Foot, QC, visited Dr Banda in prison in Gwelo, Southern Rhodesia in January 1960. The conversations were bugged and are reproduced in Sir Roy Welensky's *Welensky's 4000 Days* (pages 175–8). Dingle Foot apparently said that he had seen Monckton who had told him that he was not going to be restricted by the terms of reference.

11. Lord Home, *The Way the Wind Blows*, Collins 1976, p. 133.

12. This title was in common use in British Colonial Territories when a Governor was absent.

13. The two statements were as follows:-

    11th November "It is our view, ... I believe that the Governor had made the statement in Rhodesia, that it is the duty of public servants to carry on with their jobs, to help maintain law and order, certainly the judges and the police, at this critical time but they must themselves be the judges of any possible action which they might be asked to take which would be illegal in itself or illegal in the sense of furthering the rebellious act."

    12th November. "I think the House would agree that it is the duty of public servants to remain at their posts and especially to maintain public services and public order."

    The first statement was highly equivocal and, if taken literally, would have put public servants in an impossible situation. In practice it was taken to mean (as did the second statement) that all public servants should continue to function in their existing jobs. (This policy was changed after the declaration of a Republic in 1970.)

14. This resolution enabled Britain to institute a naval blockade of the port of Beira in Mozambique in order to prevent, if necessary by the use of force, tankers discharging oil into the pipeline which ran from Beira to Umtali in Rhodesia. At considerable cost, Britain maintained a naval patrol for many years under both Labour and Conservative Governments. It was successful in preventing oil for Rhodesia reaching Beira but it had virtually no effect on the flow of oil to Rhodesia which entered that country from South Africa. The resolution was however a precedent for later mandatory resolutions on sanctions.

15. President Kaunda of Zambia had asked for British troops to protect the installations at Kariba upon which Zambia depended for power. This had been refused but a Squadron of RAF Javelins, together with some RAF Regiment supporting troops, had been sent in early December to the airfields at Lusaka and Ndola. Wilson had said, however, on 1st December, that if Smith used his power over the Kariba dam (the generating station was on the Southern Rhodesian side) to destroy the Rhodesian economy – and thereby seriously damage the British

economy which depended on Zambia for copper – "we cannot stand idly by".

16. Wilson always insisted that the abbreviation should be NIBMR – in order to avoid the implication that the word 'African' appeared between 'Majority' and 'Rule', thus opening him to attacks on grounds of *black* racialism. But 'NIBMAR' remained in common currency.

17. The very tight timetable with which Smith was confronted was also probably a mistake – although it could be argued that Smith's capacity for procrastination was limitless and unless he was faced by a deadline no clear answer would be forthcoming (the lack of a deadline after the later talks on HMS *Fearless* did not lead to a solution either).

18. Maudling used precisely the same words on 17th June 1968 after the Security Council had imposed a mandatory requirement on all members of the United Nations to cease all trade with Rhodesia.

19. It has been argued that the Conservative Party should have dissociated itself from the five principles during its time in opposition. But to do so would have caused immense dissension within the party. Furthermore a bilateral agreement between the British and Rhodesian Governments without giving the Africans any chance to give their verdict on it (thus ignoring the fifth principle) would certainly not have solved the problems.

20. The terms of reference of the Pearce Commission were:- "To satisfy themselves that the proposals for a settlement as set out in Annex 3 to Comd Paper 4835 have been fully and properly explained to the population of Rhodesia; to ascertain by direct contact with all sections of the population whether the people of Rhodesia as a whole regard those proposals as acceptable as a basis for independence; and to report to the Foreign and Commonwealth Secretary accordingly."

21. The Pearce Report stated that "the proposals were acceptable to the great majority of Europeans but were not acceptable to the majority of Africans. Therefore the people of Rhodesia as a whole did not regard the proposals as acceptable as a basis for independence."

22. A high proportion of those nations, whose representatives at the United Nations and other assemblies of one kind and another were making high-flown speeches about the Rhodesia situation, were in fact breaking sanctions themselves. France, Japan, Germany, Switzerland and many other countries were all taking full advantage of Rhodesia's market and its production of minerals and agricultural produce. Their goods were flooding into the country and/or they were buying Rhodesian exports. Whatever Britain might have done – and the Bingham Report later made a number of accusations about oil – this was as nothing compared to the blatant wholesale circumvention of sanctions by very many, including a number of African, countries. A series of reports of concrete examples of sanctions breaking were made by Britain to the United Nations Committee which was supposed to deal with these matters, but very little was done. Indeed virtually no countries, apart from the United States, the United Kingdom and Denmark prosecuted their nationals for breaking sanctions.

23. The Catholic Commission for Justice and Peace was eventually to

become almost wholly devoted to the revolutionary cause and its Marxist leaders – a strange development.

24. The Labour Government did, later, have official representation at Salisbury from June to November 1977.

25. However, in the latter part of 1978, Callaghan made an ill-advised offer to send troops to help Kaunda.

26. There had been some cross-border raids before September 1978, e.g. January and March 1978.

27. For instance in 1973 there was no African officer in either the police or the armed services. There was not one African District Commissioner and no African trainee being groomed for that post.

28. The principle of proportional representation had been suggested by the British during their previous negotiations with Smith as a method whereby elections could be held quickly.

29. The Mission was given the task of observing the election in Zimbabwe/Rhodesia and reporting to Mrs Thatcher on the circumstances in which they were held. Its leader was Lord Boyd, a man with great experience of Africa. He had been Minister of State in the Colonial Office (1951–52) and Secretary of State for the Colonies (1954–59). He also had considerable experience of Government in other capacities. The other members were: Lord Colville of Culross, QC, who had been Minister of State at the Home Office (1972–74); Lord Elton, who had been an opposition whip in the House of Lords and was to become a Minister at the Northern Ireland Office after the 1979 election; Sir Charles Johnston, a very prominent member of the National Union of the Conservative Party and Chairman of its Executive Committee; and the author. John Drinkwater, QC, who was a Boundary Commissioner, produced a separate and independent report.

30. The conclusions are set out at Appendix 3. John Drinkwater's report was, broadly, similar.

31. It turned out that, for technical reasons, many sanctions could be retained whichever way Parliament voted – although, strangely, this point had not been made in the many previous debates on this issue.

32. It is interesting that Mugabe himself admitted the effect of the change of responsibility from Owen to Carrington in a speech he made on 27th August 1980 in reply to President Carter's speech welcoming him to the United States. Mugabe said – "I remember those days when, with Andy Young and Don McHenry here and later with Cyrus Vance in Dar-es-Salaam, we battled to reach agreement to get a compromise between the British side and our side. It was not possible at the time to conclude the discussion *because there wasn't in Britain the presence of an authority which would have effected a decision in Salisbury* but you did your best." (author's italics)

33. It was a tragedy that General Tongogara, the military commander of ZANLA, was killed in Mozambique, apparently in a car accident, before Mugabe returned to Rhodesia. Tongogara had been one of the most reasonable elements in Mugabe's delegation during the Lancaster House Conference. He was capable of understanding and reacting with common sense to the complicated political and military issues involved.

243

His successor, Rex Nhongo, was not of the same calibre. The precise circumstances of Tongogara's death are obscure and it has been said that he was in fact murdered – clearly a possibility in the atmosphere of tribal and political dissention within ZANU (PF) at the time. But on the whole it seems more likely that his death was indeed accidental.

BIBLIOGRAPHY

Blake, Robert, *A History of Rhodesia,* Eyre Methuen, 1977.

Butler, Lord, *The Art of the Possible,* Hamish Hamilton, 1971.

Cary and Mitchell, Robert and Diana, *African Nationalist Leaders in Rhodesia,* Who's Who, Books of Rhodesia Publishing Co, 1977.

Conservative Research Department, *Rhodesia. Notes on Current Politics,* No. 24 (31 Dec 1965), No. 3 (15 Feb 1967), No. 16 (7 Oct 1968).

Davidson, Slovo and Wilkinson, *Southern Africa. The New Politics of Revolution,* Pelican, 1976

Denoon, Donald, *Southern Africa Since 1800,* Longman, 1972.

Fisher, Nigel, *Iain Macleod,* André Deutsch, 1973.

Good, Robert, *UDI: The International Politics of the Rhodesian Rebellion,* Faber and Faber, 1973.

Greenfield, J.M., *Testimony of a Rhodesian Federal,* Books of Rhodesia, 1978.

Hanna, A.J., *The Story of the Rhodesias and Nyasaland,* Faber, 1960.

Home, Lord, *The Way the Wind Blows,* Collins, 1976.

Kaunda, Kenneth, *Kaunda on Violence,* Collins, 1980.

Kissinger, Henry, *The Kissinger Study on Southern Africa,* Spokesman Books, 1975.

Lake, Anthony, *The 'Tar Baby' Option,* Columbia University Press, 1973.

Linden, Ian, *The Catholic Church and the Struggle for Unity in Zimbabwe,* Longman, 1980.

Macmillan, Harold, *At the End of the Day 1961–1963,* Macmillan, 1973.

Mason, Philip, *The Birth of a Dilemma: The Conquest and Settlement of Rhodesia,* Oxford University Press, 1958.

Meredith, Martin, *The Past is another Country, Rhodesia 1890–1979,* André Deutsch, 1979.

Mitchell, Diana, *African Nationalist Leaders in Zimbabwe, Who's Who 1980,* Mitchell, 1980.

245

Moorcraft, Paul, *A Short Thousand Years*, Galaxie Press, 1979.

Murray, D. J., *The Governmental System in Southern Rhodesia*, Clarendon Press, 1970.

Nyangoni and Nyandoro, *Zimbabwe Independence Movements – Select Documents*, Rex Collings, 1979.

Palley, Dr Claire, *The Constitutional History and Law of Southern Rhodesia 1888–1965*, Oxford University Press, 1966.

Palley, Dr Claire, *Zimbabwe Rhodesia. Should the present government be recognised?* Minority Rights Group, 1979.

Palmer, Robin, *Land and Racial Discrimination in Rhodesia*, Heinemann, 1977.

Ransford, Oliver, *The Rulers of Rhodesia*, Murray, 1968.

Rhodes – Livingstone Institute, *Seven Tribes of Central Africa*, Oxford University Press, 1951.

Rifkind, M.L., *Land Apportionment in Perspective*, 1972.

Samkange, Stanlake, *Origins of Rhodesia*, Heinemann Educational Books, 1968.

Sithole, M., *Ethnicity and Factionalism in Zimbabwe Nationalist Politics 1957–79*, Center for Inter-racial Studies, University of Rhodesia, 1979.

Sithole, M., *Zimbabwe Struggle within the Struggle*, Ruzeko Publishers, 1979.

Summers and Pagden, *The Warriors*, Books of Africa, 1970.

Thompson, Leonard, *African Societies in Southern Africa*, Heinemann Educational Books, 1969.

Weinrich, A.K.H., *Black and White Elites in Rural Rhodesia*, Manchester University Press, 1973.

Weinrich, A.K.H., *Chiefs and Councils in Rhodesia*, Heinemann Educational Books, 1971.

Welensky, Sir Roy., *Welensky's 4000 Days*, Collins, 1964.

Wilkinson, Anthony, *Insurgency in Rhodesia 1957–1973*, International Institute for Strategic Studies, 1973.

Wilson, Harold, *The Labour Government 1964–1970*, Weidenfeld and Nicolson and Michael Joseph, 1971.

Windrich, Elaine, *The Rhodesian Problem. A Documentary Record 1923–1973*, Routledge and Kegan Paul, 1975.

Windrich, Elaine, *Britain and the Politics of Rhodesian Independence*, Croom Helm, 1978.

Young, Kenneth, *Rhodesia and Independence*, Eyre and Spottiswoode, 1967.

Index

Acland, Major-General Sir John, 185

Adams, Sir Philip, 97

African National Council, The (ANC), 100, 104, 110, 111, 113, 114, 117

Allum, Peter, 212

Alport, Lord, 77

Amery, Julian, MP, 166

Amin, Idi, 161, 162

Anderson, Mr, 168

Anderson, Major-General, 48

Angola, 111, 112, 120, 121, 122, 198, 211

Auxiliaries, The, 141, 173, 179, 180

Banana, The Rev. Canaan, 214, 221

Banda, Dr Hastings, 29, 34, 45, 161

Beadle, Sir Hugh, 51

Beira Blockade, The, 241

Bevin, Ernest, 56

Bledisloe, Lord, 26

Bokassa, President, 162

Botswana, 123, 173, 200

Bottomley, Arthur, 45, 49, 57, 66, 74

Bowden, Herbert, 74

Boyd, The Viscount of Merton, 152, 156, 242

Bretton Woods Agreement, 21

British Council of Churches, 100, 201

Brown, George, 62, 90, 91

Butler Rab (Lord Butler), 41, 43, 200

Byrd Amendment, The, 120, 131

Callaghan, James, 126, 134, 174

Carrington, Lord, 91, 138, 149, 150, 153, 155, 158, 160, 177, 189, 208; & The Lancaster House Conference, 166–174

Carter, President, 130, 131, 159, 163

Carver, Field-Marshal Lord, 132, 139

Catholic Commission for Justice and Peace, 242

Central Africa Council, 26

Charter, The, 8, 9, 16, 17, 18

Chidzero, Bernard, 217

Chihota, Lovemore, 108

Chikerema, James, 33, 34, 108, 183

Chirau, Chief, 136, 137, 141, 152

Chitepo, Herbert, 108, 113, 114, 116, 126

Chitnis, Lord, 152

Churchill, Sir Winston, 39, 175

City Youth League, The, 33

Coghlan, Sir Charles, 17, 22, 23, 24

Colonial Office, 17, 19, 22, 26, 29, 30, 63, 64

Colville, Lord, of Culross, QC, 243

Commonwealth, The, 48, 62, 79, 150, 158, 159, 162, 165, 166, 186

Commonwealth Prime Ministers' Conference, 25, at Lagos, Jan. 1966, 62; London, Sept. 1966, 73, 80; Singapore, Jan. 1971, 93; Lusaka, Aug. 1979, 154, 155, 164

Commonwealth Relations Office (CRO), 62, 63, 64, 127

Company, the British South Africa,

247

119, 133, 138, 140, 174; & détente, 112–114, 122; & Kissinger, 125, 126; & reactions to internal settlement, 160–3; & Lancaster House, 166, 167
Kent, HMS, 78
Kenya, 163, 193, 198
Kenyatta, Jomo, 161
Khama, Seretse, 113, 160
Kibaki, Mr, 163
Kissinger, Henry, 120–6, 130, 133, 134, 146, 174
Kleynhause, Mr, 108
Kruger, 7

Labour Party (British), 24, 40, 54, 57, 60, 67, 69, 76, 97, 99, 101, 130, 151, 165
Labour Party (Rhodesian), 22, 25
Lancaster House Conference, 142, 160, 166–174, 175, 177, 180, 189, 198, 200, 213
Land Apportionment Act, 15, 23, 24, 36–8, 79, 209
Land Husbandry Act, 204
Land Tenure Act, 79, 123, 133, 139
Lardner-Burke, Desmond, 45
Law and Order Maintenance Act 1960, 34
Leahy, John, 87, 88
Liberal Party (British), 54, 97
Lippert, 12
Lloyd, Selwyn, 71, 91
Lobengula, 5–9, 12, 22
Longden, Sir Gilbert, 68
Low, Stephen, 132, 139
Luce, Richard, 84
Luce, Sir William, 84

MacDonald, Ramsay, 24
Machel, President Samora, 118, 138, 160, 167, 174, 187, 220
Macleod, Ian, 33
Macmillan, Sir Harold, 33, 34, 41, 43, 56
Malawi (Nyasaland), 47, 161, 203
Mansfield, Philips, 97
Matabeleland, 12, 22, 23
Matopos hills, 13

Maudling, Reginald, 58, 76
Menzies, Sir Robert, 47
Milton, 14
Moffat, H.U., 23, 24
Moffat, John, 7
Moffat, Robert, 6
Monckton, Lord, 34
Monitoring Force, 173, 174, 184, 186
Montgomery, Field-Marshal Lord, 56
Morris Carter, Sir William, 23
Moyo, Jason, 108
Mozambique, 11, 108, 109, 111, 116, 117, 119, 121–3, 140, 141, 160, 162, 173, 174, 185, 187, 198, 200, 202, 203, 211, 218
MPLA, 120
Mugabe, Robert, 5, 43, 127, 133, 138–141, 157, 159, 160–2, 191, 207; & single minded approach, 113, 115; & character, 117, 118; & ZANU, 123, 125; & Geneva Conference, 126; & Internal Settlement, 143, 144, 153; & Lancaster House, 165, 166, 174; & the 1980 election, 176–186, 187–190; & post-Independence, 211, 212–16, 218, 219, 221, 222
Mutasa, Dr, 46, 80
Muzorewa, Bishop Abel, 5, 14, 22, 100, 113, 114, 117, 123, 125, 134, 207; & talks with Smith, 104, 110, 111, 133; & Geneva Conference, 126; & Internal Settlement, 136, 138, 140, 141, 143, 152, 153; & Government, 158–163; & Lancaster House, 164, 166–8, 170–4; & 1980 election, 175–178, 181–4, 187–190
Mwene we Mutapa, The Empire of, 4
Mzilikazi, 4, 5

National Democratic Party (NDP), 34. 118
Ndebele Tribe, 4, 5, 9, 11, 12, 13, 15, 22, 117, 118, 125, 143, 152, 182, 204, 214, 222

249